BRITAIN SINCE THE SEVENTIES

Politics and Society in the Consumer Age

JEREMY BLACK

REAKTION BOOKS

For Ron Fritze, a good friend

Published by Reaktion Books Ltd
79 Farringdon Road
London EC1M 3JU, UK

www.reaktionbooks.co.uk

First published 2004

Printed and bound in Great Britain
by Biddles Ltd, Guildford and King's Lynn

British Library Cataloguing in Publication Data

Black, Jeremy
    Britain since the seventies : politics and society in the consumer age.
    – (Contemporary worlds)
    1. Popular culture – Great Britain – History – 20th century
    2. Great Britain – Civilization – 1945- 3. Great Britain – History –
    Elizabeth II, 1952- 4. Great Britain – Social conditions – 1945-
    5. Great Britain – Social life and customs – 1945- 6. Great Britain –
    Politics and government – 1945- 7. Great Britain – Economic
    conditions – 20th century
    I. Title
    941'.085

ISBN 1 86189 201 2

CONTEMPORARY WORLDS explores the present and recent past. Books in the series take a distinctive theme, geo-political entity or cultural group and explore their developments over a period ranging usually over the last fifty years. The impact of current events and developments are accounted for by rapid but clear interpretation in order to unveil the cultural, political, religious and technological forces that are reshaping today's worlds.

SERIES EDITOR
Jeremy Black

In the same series

Sky Wars: A History of Military Aerospace Power
David Gates

Contents

Preface:

The Strange Death of Tory Britain

This title captures a major theme of recent years, and also the unpredictability and volatility of this period. In the 1980s, when Margaret Thatcher was at the height of her power, winning re-election with large majorities in 1983 and 1987, it seemed to most commentators that the Conservatives were the natural party of government, that the Labour Party had been wrecked by Thatcher (and by its own weaknesses and divisions), and that these changes were being made permanent by a process of socio-economic transformation including widespread privatization in the economy and the sale of council housing. Yet, although the Conservatives, now under John Major, won re-election in 1992, against the predictions of many polls and commentators, and held on to office until defeated by Labour in 1997, it was already apparent that this 'strange death' had occurred.

That was one of the original subjects of this book. It accorded with my sense that it was necessary not to look at developments through the focus of government policy making, but, rather, to emphasize the limitations of government. It is easy to list a litany of failures that suggest that British politicians and government had lost the capacity to identify problems correctly and to devise appropriate solutions: BSE, the Millennium Dome, foot-and-mouth disease or the debacles of policies over transport generally, and the rail system in particular, as well as over asylum seekers in the early 2000s, or the chaos over 'A' level examination marking in 2002; while the wobbles of London's

Millennium Bridge in 2000 indicated a failure to plan likely usage regarding the engineering of public works. The way in which a small group of protestors was able to bring fuel distribution to a stop in September 2000 also epitomized the weakness of government.

Weakness is not, however, the same as inconsequence. To suggest that major changes occurred, in, for example, the environment or demographics, without government policy playing a major role would be to ignore subjects such as planning permission and public health issues. Thus, it would be wrong to write the history of these years with government only having a walk-on role towards the close. Indeed, education and the NHS (National Health Service) exemplified a compulsive 'tinkering' mentality in which both Conservatives and Labour sacrificed stability for action. However, although the activities of government punctuate the text, they do not set its direction. Instead, it is social, cultural and environmental trends that attract particular attention.

It is also necessary to present British history in a wider context. This history has particular characteristics, but Britain is not on a separate planet. Thus, many of the pressures and shifts discussed in this book also affected other countries, and, in order to understand developments in Britain, it is useful to consider how responses there differed. In particular, the environmental pressures seen in Britain were part of a wider process, a point made by referring to global warming. Many of the social shifts were also more common, at least to the Western world. These included a greater prominence for women, higher rates of divorce, longer lifespans and secularization. In the global context, the political focus tends to be on left versus right, the chronology of which varies by state, although there was a general rightward move in the 1980s and a leftward one in the mid-1990s. At a deeper level, however, there were important similarities between countries arising from greater individualism, the breakdown of class-based politics and a reluctance to engage in war at the cost of heavy casualties. The first was also important both to economic activity, much of which was driven by the individual consumer, and to the vexed question of identities, which became more fluid and contentious.

Writing this book in the space allotted necessarily involves choices of what to include. There is no point pretending some Olympian detachment or Delphic omniscience. The choices made, for example the thematic approach, and the determined attempt to avoid a political 'spine', are personal. They reflect my views as a historian faced with the difficult tasks of trying to cover such a large subject, and of writing about a world on the cusp from experience to memory, that both writer and reader have experienced in person. I hope my decisions on what to include and how best to cover the subject prove as stimulating for the readers as they have done for the writer, and that they can be seen as individual (as all history is), but not eccentric.

It is important for the reader to be aware that what is here, how it is treated and organized, and what is omitted reflects a process of choice. The past is viewed very differently by commentators, and these differences should lead us to more searching questions about what is discussed and about the process of writing history. This is most apparent and valuable when discussing the recent past. Reading any work of history that deals with this period necessarily throws light on both subject and process. This book will work if it makes you think – not only about what is written here, but also about what you have experienced. If you disagree, think why. Look around and consider the significance of the changes you see. The historian is not a magician able to unlock the past, but a guide who stimulates you to see with your own eyes. Readers should consider how *they* would organize the book and approach writing about the subject as an active part of considering the topic. This point is stressed because it is my conviction that books should not talk down to the readers or treat them as a passive body that is there to be entertained. I work on the basis that readers are intelligent people like me who do not wish to be restricted to the comforting pattern of a conventional narrative.

I have benefited from the large number of people willing to discuss this topic with me. This includes colleagues, politicians, family and friends. I owe particular observations to Kenneth Baker, Melvyn Bragg, Oliver Letwin, David Lidington, Peter Luff, Chris Patten, Robert Runcie, Chris Smith, Margaret Thatcher and Harry Woolf. I am most grateful to Roger Burt, Bill Gibson, Kevin Jeffery, Michael Leaman and Nick Smart for commenting on an earlier draft. None is responsible for any errors that follow, nor do they necessarily share my views. It is a great pleasure to dedicate this book to a good friend and much-respected fellow historian.

Chapter 1

The Triumph of Consumerism

'Do you realise you have a legal obligation to keep a record for Sales Tax and Purchase Tax? You do? Where is your till roll then? A cash book, a day book, your invoices in order? Would it be impertinent of me to enquire why you bother with a cash till at all when you have no record of your business?'

The tax inspector to the Chinese restaurateur in London, in *Sour Sweet* (1983) by the Anglo-Chinese novelist Timothy Mo

'I spend therefore I am' was the motto of these decades. The consumer, and industries geared to consumerism, drove the pace of social change. The citizen thought of himself as a consumer in all sorts of spheres. This was related to a range of factors in the political culture of the period including the dominance of the individual and individual preferences in social mores and practices, the political ethos of the house owner, and the decline of 'elitist' and Reithian public-spirited notions of culture, in favour of a public culture focused on consumer preferences. To critics, there was a disengagement with social concerns as part of a breakdown of civil society.

This was a world centred on the shopping centre, which increasingly played a greater role in individual and family leisure time. Government policy combined with the impact of the car to re-mould the spaces in which people shopped. The abolition of resale price maintenance (RPM) in 1964 by Edward Heath, when he was President of the

Board of Trade, was a significant moment in the shaping of modern British retailing. RPM had obliged shops to sell goods at standard prices set by suppliers, and thus prevented the search for more business through undercutting. This helped small independent shopkeepers in their resistance to multiples. 'Manufacturer's Recommended Price' was often still on goods. Once RPM was abolished, it became easier for supermarkets benefiting from economies of scale, such as mass purchasing, to offer pricing structures that drove competitors out of business. A form of RPM continued for books and medicines, and that was important to the survival of small bookshops and chemists. However, the situation for them similarly changed in the 1990s, although government concern about the availability of chemists led, in 2003, to measures to limit the provision of in-house pharmacies in supermarkets.

The rise of the supermarket in the 1950s, and of the hypermarket, mainly out of town, and of out-of-town retail centres in the 1980s, led to new shopping patterns. One of the earliest arose from the opening, in 1973, of Sainsbury's out-of-town Coldham's Lane superstore in Cambridge. By 1992, 16 per cent of the total shopping space in Britain was made up of shopping centres, such as Brent Cross in north London, Lakeside Thurrock in Essex, the Glades in Bromley, south London, Meadowhall in Sheffield and the Metro Centre in Gateshead. The openings of such centres were local events and great interest was shown in which stores they contained. This was important to developers and councils, leading to practices that were legal – rent or rate 'holidays' (exemptions), and developers funding facilities from roads to schools as a result of deals with local authorities – and illegal: corruption linked to planning permission. Suburban and out-of-town locations helped to ensure the rapid supply by large lorries that outlets required for profitable turnover.

The Metro Centre was the epitome of this new world. Applauded by Thatcher, its development made the fortune of John Hall, enabling him to become the leading entrepreneur of north-east England and to transform the fortunes of Newcastle United football club, whose chairman he became: the way to wealth was through selling, not making. This was displayed in 1987 when Hall bought Wynyard Hall, an estate near Teesside that had been developed by former local potentates, the Marquesses of Londonderry.

The construction of hypermarkets continued. In 1999 two centres that claimed to be the biggest in Europe were opened: Paisley's 900,000-square-foot Braehead development, and the Bluewater centre in London's Kent suburbs. At a smaller scale, towns across Britain, including relatively small ones such as Axminster and Langport, saw their high streets decline, or at least change, as large stores were built at locations that could be reached by car and with plentiful parking provided on-site. Supermarkets such as Asda also ran their own bus services. The impact of such stores on retail services elsewhere was accentuated (and marked) as products that they had not previously sold, such as alcohol and petrol, became available.

City centres sought to respond and avoid the decline of high-street shopping by constructing glazed-over shopping precincts, such as St Enoch Centre and Princes Square in Glasgow, and Eldon Square in Newcastle. These developments kept shoppers in the city centre, but frequently had a detrimental impact on shopping outside the precinct: Eldon Square, opened in the 1970s, hit nearby Pilgrim, Clayton and Grainger Streets.

Big shopping centres were the moulders of taste and provided spheres of spending activity at the centre of the consumer society. Almost all their customers came by car, abandoning traditional high-street shopping, with its gentler pace and more individual service. Mobility thus brought access to wider shopping opportunities, but the net effect was less beneficial, as many shops on high streets closed. This was despite the fact that, for some products, especially fruit and vegetables, they were less expensive. However, the convenience of purchasing all household requirements under one roof was more significant for many consumers, particularly for working mothers, whose time was under greater pressure and who were trying to fit shopping into a life dominated by work and childcare.

Dunmow in Essex demonstrated the general impact. Following the opening of Tesco on the outskirts at the beginning of the 1990s, the High Street became almost entirely charity shops, where once were grocers, newsagents, ironmongers, butchers, bakers and greengrocers.

The pattern was similar in many other high streets, with only occasional boutiques, health-food shops and antique shops providing opportunities for old-style shopping; although, especially outside the cities and the poorer suburbs, most high streets still offer a range of shops. The fate of local shops was linked to that of local economies. Far from purchasing from local suppliers, superstores bought their food only from very large producers, and it was moved by lorry from central warehouse sites. This hit local wholesalers, thus reducing the availability of fresh food for local shops.

The fate of high-street shopping became the focus of planning disputes, especially from the 1980s, and, also, was increasingly important in contested senses of local identity. In Leominster, for example, in 1996 the town launched a shopper 'loyalty card' as part of a 'fightback' against a Safeway out-of-town superstore and its loyalty scheme.

Convenience became a key term of the period in both word and thought; and it was adopted as a description, as in convenience foods. This concept was linked to particular forms of packaging, such as wrapping in plastic. It was also linked to a marked decline in the mending of clothes and shoes. This led not only to the closure of cobblers and other outlets, but also to a decline of domestic skills such as darning. The latter was part of a major shift in female activity, in particular. Thus cooking, preserving food, knitting and needlework were seen as less important than hitherto as accomplishments, and this was also linked to the decline of traditional voluntarist activities.

By 1999, 88 per cent of all the food purchased in Britain was bought from big shopping chains. The previous year, the preponderant role in food marketing of just four retailers, Asda, Safeway, Sainsbury's and Tesco, appeared sufficiently monopolistic to trouble the Office of Fair Trading. In the period of this study, supermarkets also expanded into products they had hitherto not sold, such as alcohol, newspapers and magazines. By 2000 Tesco had 7 per cent of the magazine market. There was also an increasing stratification of supermarkets with their markets having different social profiles.

As a result of their expansion, takeover battles for supermarkets in the early 2000s were of great importance to the national economy and to local economies. The takeover of Asda by the American chain

Wal-Mart was important to the further Americanization of British shopping patterns. In 2003 Tesco, with its 200,000 staff, was the largest private-sector employer in Britain, while Morrisons' bid for Safeway was valued at £2.3 billion.

Such shopping was also a prime cause of pollution. Aside from the petrol used to drive to supermarkets, they were responsible for large numbers of plastic bags. In addition, supermarket trolleys came to litter surrounding streets and were dumped in nearby waterways. Supermarkets and superstores also played a role in the liberalization of aspects of society. In the 1990s their pressure was important in introducing Sunday shopping and round-the-clock stores. Alongside the liberalization of drinking laws in the 1990s, the last was an aspect of the emergence of the 24-hour city. Leeds as much as London marketed itself in these terms from the late 1990s.

Travel was a major focus of consumerism and one that was actively catered to by newspaper supplements and television programmes. Thanks to high levels of disposable income, and the absence of any restrictions on taking money abroad, the numbers travelling overseas rose, while more of the population took more than one holiday a year. The number of those taking holidays abroad rose from 4.2 million in 1971 to 13.1 million in 1981, 20.8 million in 1991 and 32.3 million in 1998. The number of passengers at Scottish airports trebled between 1975 and 1996, while, between 1995 and 1998, passenger traffic through airports in the London area increased at a rate of 7 per cent a year; in part, also, a testimony to the importance of foreign tourism in Britain to the economy. In 1999 Heathrow handled 62 million passengers, making it the fourth busiest airport in the world and the busiest outside the USA. In 1999 foreign visitors were estimated by the British Tourist Authority as spending £12.5 billion in Britain: the largest percentage (20.3 per cent) was American, followed by German (7.4 per cent) and French (5.7 per cent) visitors. In addition, foreign visitors paid £3.2 billion in fares to British carriers, with Americans spending the largest share.

Although much of the population never travelled abroad, and large numbers still travelled to Blackpool and other traditional destinations or went caravanning, domestic tourism became relatively less important. This led to a changing sense of place for many. Glaswegians who went to Majorca, rather than Largs, and Londoners who travelled to Cyprus, not Cornwall or Southend, now had a different experience of their own countries, and mental maps altered accordingly. As tourists went abroad, many formerly important domestic destinations, particularly seaside resorts, came to be particularly sad and drab.

For many, from the 1980s, foreign travel was linked to the owner-ship of property abroad. This was a matter either of timesharing, which became particularly popular in seaside destinations, such as the Canaries, or of owning second homes, although these also became far more common in Britain. The most popular region for second homes abroad was France, especially, but not only, Brittany, Normandy and south-west France, and this was an aspect of an important bridging of the Channel in lifestyle terms. This bridging was furthered by the increasing numbers who chose to retire abroad, particularly near the Mediterranean. This was an aspect of the convertibility of the rising prosperity of the 1980s and '90s and, more specifically, of the cashing in of the benefits of the growth in property values in Britain, and of the freedom to move money.

Foreign lifestyles and travel were also related to the marked growth in cut-price air travel in the 2000s, although the government pushed the cost up by taxing air tickets. By November 2002 EasyJet alone was offering two million seats each month. Prices were cut in part by the more efficient use of planes and staffs and, in part, by removing the need for travel agents by encouraging the direct purchase of tickets, by credit card, over the phone or via the internet. This method, which was also adopted by more established airlines, hit travel agents hard. It was an aspect of the move away from a face-to-face society. Cut-price air travel led to a new geography of communications, as airports that were its centres, such as Bristol, East Midlands, Liverpool, Luton and Stansted, became more important. Such air travel was not only a British phenomenon. Similar airlines developed elsewhere, including in Ireland and the USA.

The character and destination of domestic tourists also changed. One of the most striking shifts was the growth of tourism to former industrial sites. Thus, the South Wales coalfield is now a tourist attraction, rather than the centre of a productive industry. On the Durham coalfield, Beamish became the site of a museum that sought to recreate the local world of 1913. In 1980 Bradford received its first official package holiday tourist and became the first northern city to appoint a Tourism Officer.

WE ARE WHAT WE EAT

Purchasing might centre on a narrow range of outlets, but also reflected an eagerness to reject established patterns of consumption. This was reflected in diet, with the greater commodification of food and the fashionability of particular foods. From the 1960s the national diet was increasingly affected by new ingredients and by dishes introduced from foreign countries. As more people ate out, Chinese, Indian and Italian meals came to dominate the restaurant trade. By 1998 there were more than 8,000 Indian restaurants alone. As an indication of wider cultural shifts, Bradford's Bombay Brasserie was not unique in being located in a former church or chapel, in its case a former Presbyterian chapel.

There was also a major shift in takeaway food, which, in the 1970s, was overwhelmingly either fish and chips or what was provided by the Wimpy chain. There were only 38 branches of McDonald's in Britain in 1979, but by the 1990s American fast-food chains, such as Kentucky Fried Chicken, were ubiquitous, and in 1997 McDonald's had over 750 branches. In his novel *Money* (1984), Martin Amis describes his part of London 'going up in the world. There used to be a third-generation Italian restaurant across the road . . . It's now a Burger Den. There is a Burger Shack, too, and a Burger Bower'. Pizza takeaways also became very important. 'British' cooking came to mean curries, chop suey, chilli con carne, spaghetti and pizza, as much as steak and kidney pies, or fish and chips. In homes, traditional breakfast dishes, such as bacon and eggs or kippers, became less common, as did the entire notion of a cooked breakfast. Instead, the amount of time spent on breakfast decreased. Tea also became less prominent as a meal, and this was linked to a decline in teatime dishes such as crumpets, scones and teacakes. Snacks and food taken on the move became more important: by 2002, £5 billion was being spent annually on crisps.

Supermarkets increasingly stocked foreign dishes, including Indian and Chinese food. By 1998 one supermarket chain alone, Waitrose, stocked sixteen regional Indian dishes. In the 1990s there was growing consumption of Continental-style breads, a marked contrast to the dominance of sliced white bread in the 1970s. Such breads also found their way into cafés and train buffets, particularly in the 2000s. Aside from Continental-style breads, there was a greater emphasis on granary and wholemeal loaves. In fruit, avocados, mangoes, and passion, star, Sharon and kiwi fruit, all largely unknown in Britain in the 1960s, became widely available in supermarkets. Similarly, decaffeinated hot drinks, speciality teas and bottled water all became popular, and the range on offer increased.

These shifts in consumption reflected a widespread willingness to embrace change, and the seductive impact of marketing and fashion. By the 1980s cookbooks themselves, the pornography of the kitchen, had become a consumer product. Lavishly published, with full-colour photography and printing, they catered for households that were no longer prepared to accept inherited recipes or one biblical cookbook. Instead, consumers purchased several, and some of the more popular focused on the food of foreign, even exotic, areas such as Provence and India.

Cookery programmes also became more prominent on the television, and shared with fashion or house-makeover programmes an ability to combine aspirations and entertainment. Thus Delia Smith was matched by Rick Stein, Ainsley Harriott, the Two Fat Ladies and Jamie Oliver. Social respectability was enhanced with the role of fashionable figures such as Nigella Lawson. Top-selling books in early 2002 included Delia Smith's *How to Cook* and Jamie Oliver's *Happy Days with the Naked Chef*. The ability and willingness of supermarkets to stock a wider range of ingredients, and to do so throughout the year, increased the potential for such programmes. There was a run on products, such as goose fat, when they were endorsed by celebrity cooks.

The educational role of television was not restricted to the preparation of food. It included presentation and the 'total package'. This was not an aspect of a state-driven didacticism, but, instead, a can-do empowerment that was presented as entertainment and where the viewer was seduced by presentation into feeling that they could, and therefore should, do better.

Technology also played a major role. The increased consumption of ready-made meals, generally stored in deep freezers and reheated rapidly in microwave cookers, provided a major market for new dishes and for meals for one or two. Wine boxes were designed to enable drinkers to have less (or more) than one bottle without spoiling the rest. In typical British fashion, there was a snobbish overlay with some changes, such as wine boxes, seen as less acceptable than others, for example the use of olive oil and balsamic vinegar.

Consumerism and fashion also interacted as diet changed in response to concern about healthy eating. Appetite and fashion, rather than hunger and custom, came to dominate eating. Red meat, such as beef, mutton and lamb, became less popular in favour of chicken, and the consumption of fats, such as butter and cheese, dropped, in favour of low-fat spreads. The consumption of eggs also fell. Grilling became more common than frying, and there was sensitivity about what food was fried in: butter became less popular and olive oil more so. A traditional diet, which had been formed largely in accordance with the needs of men, became less widespread, both for men and for women. Cheap, filling foods, especially bread and potatoes, became less important in home eating. Thus, the average consumption of calories fell. Concern about calories was supplemented by anxiety about cholesterol.

As well as 'looking good and feeling great', convenience played a major role in the changing fashions seen in the diaries kept for the Expenditure and Food Survey begun in 2001 by the Office for National Statistics. These led in 2003 to the dropping from the retail prices index of tinned spaghetti and brown ale. Entries added instead included take-away burgers, kebabs, café latte and diet drink powders.

By 2002 there were about four million vegetarians in the country, three-quarters of whom were women. This reflected the role of choice, as did the extent to which individuals adopted their own definition of vegetarianism. Some were vegans, others ate no meat or fish, and others ate fish and still called themselves vegetarians. The halfway house options included eaters of chicken but no other meat. The increased popularity of vegetarianism did much to make the publication of cookbooks a growth industry. A range of enticing recipes was pioneered and sold on the back of endorsements from celebrities such as Linda McCartney. Gender differences were not limited to the preference for vegetarian food. Women were also readier than men to abandon potatoes for fresh vegetables.

This approach, with its focus on national trends, and on 'discourses' or languages that seek to approach all, for example that for healthy eating, risks underrating the ineluctable facts of social and geographical variation, more specifically issues of class that both the Conservatives and 'New' Labour sought to ignore or underplay. Thus, consumption of fresh fruit and vegetables, and fresh (as opposed to fried) fish, is higher among affluent groups, while the poor tend to have less variety and fewer fresh ingredients in their diet. The general practice of purchasing prepared foods, which are more expensive, rather than cooking from ingredients, further reduced the nutritional value of what was spent by the poor. Issues of cost and access are important. Healthy foods, such as fresh vegetables, fruit and fish, cost more, in part because it is easier to mass produce and preserve foods high in fat, sugar and salt. Furthermore, neighbourhood shops in poor areas respond to the poverty of their market by offering only a limited range of goods. The supermarkets that offer a wider range, including healthier ingredients, tend to be in suburban or out-of-town areas; and access to them is difficult for the poor, many of whom lack access to cars. The 1999 British Medical Association report *Growing Up in Britain* revealed that poor children were far less likely to drink fruit juice and eat fresh fruit and vegetables.

This was an important aspect of a more general crisis in obesity. In 1997–2001, over a fifth of ten-year-olds were regarded as obese, or at least overweight; and the rate was increasing, as it also was for adults. In 2002 this contributed to the first known cases of white children in Britain being diagnosed with type-two diabetes. Aside from the problem for individuals, the resulting ill-health and early deaths posed serious issues for the NHS and for society as a whole. However, while 6 per cent of the population in 2000 were members of health clubs, concern about health was very much linked to social indicators.

Social contrasts were linked to regional images, such as the 'pie and pint' male food culture in Northern cities, although, within cities such as Newcastle, the local pattern in food consumption, shops and restaurants reflected social differences. Per capita, meat consumption was highest in Yorkshire. In addition, the overall differences between England and Scotland were significant. The Scots consumed more salt, sweet things, carbonated drinks, animal fats, sausage rolls, meat, butter, chocolate, alcohol and tobacco per head than the English and less salads, green vegetables, wholemeal bread and roughage.

These preferences were directly linked to health differences. Figures released by the Office of National Statistics in 2003, based on data collected in 1991–2001, revealed that – measured by life expectancy at birth – Glasgow was the unhealthiest place for men and women, with Inverclyde, West Dunbartonshire, North Lanarkshire and Renfrewshire among the ten worst for men and women. In contrast, none of the best ten for either were in Scotland, while the areas for the top ten for both were north Dorset, east Dorset, Purbeck and Christchurch (both in Dorset) and South Norfolk.

Social differences were also found among smokers. Stronger brands and roll-your-own cigarettes were more common among the poor than among the wealthier segments of society. This became more pronounced from the 1970s as the anti-smoking message was disseminated. Tobacco products were increasingly slanted towards the poor as smoking became less common among the affluent.

A FASCINATION WITH BRICKS AND MORTAR

The social dimension also plays an understated role in the presentation of Britain as a property-owning democracy. After the Housing Act of 1980 allowed local authority tenants to buy their houses, the sale of council houses was explicitly pursued by the Conservative government in order to break up what were presented, often with considerable accuracy, as the fiefdoms of local councils, and to help create a property-owning society based on individual opportunity. It was hoped that such a society would be naturally Conservative.

The policy had a major impact. By the late 1980s three-quarters of trade unionists owned their own homes. In Scotland, where public housing had been more prominent than in England, the percentage of the population in owner-occupation still rose from 36.4 in 1981 to 52.8 in 1991. In England and Wales, the figure (to nearest percentage) rose from 54 in 1977 to 62 in 1985 and 67 in 1990; while the percentages for those renting from local authority were 32, 27 and 24. The number of houses built by the private sector rose from 736,000 in 1980–85 to 904,000 in 1986–90.

The Prime Minister from 1979 to 1990, Margaret Thatcher, who had a marked preference for freedom and market mechanisms, as opposed to planning and state pricing, refused to allow local authorities to use the proceeds of sales in order to embark on new building projects. As a result, the number of new homes built in the public sector fell dramatically, from 542,000 in 1975–9 to 226,000 in 1980–85, and 156,000 (including by Housing Associations) in 1986–90. An absence of newly available, affordable accommodation was a result, and this helped push up the number of homeless people. In Scotland it rose from 16,034 in 1978–9 to 30,859 in 1986–7.

The lack of accommodation in the public sector put great pressure on local authorities, not least as they had statutory housing obligations. As a result, councils were forced to put people into bed-and-breakfast accommodation. Renting property to local authorities became a growth business, altering the character of streets and even neighbourhoods, for example certain seaside resorts, such as Paignton. The situation in housing provision helped to ensure that the asylum issue in the early 2000s was even more difficult, and also accentuated pressure on local authority finance.

There was, from the 1980s, a rejection not only of council housing but also of post-war urban rebuilding, which was blamed for a host of social problems. In Basingstoke in 1999, the 'deprivation index' of the Office of Population, Census and Surveys remained highest in Popley, the grim area of housing estates built in the 1960s to accommodate London overspill. Across the country, there were many demolitions, not only of high-rise estates, but also of low-rise, deck-access blocks, such as the Chalkhill area in Brent, London, demolished in the 1990s. Such estates were frequently the lot of those who could not find anywhere else to live, and were characterized by social problems, such as family breakdown, crime and high levels of indebtedness. They were the stamping ground of the unlicensed, not to say illegal, elements of the community, such as pawnbrokers and unlicensed lenders and bookmakers. When English Heritage, in 1998, refused to share in the general theme of renewal through destruction and, instead, listed the tower blocks of Park Hill, Sheffield, and others on the Alton Estate in Roehampton, London, as architectural masterpieces, the decision was mocked by the press and widely deplored by the tenants

The last was important. Those tenants who could afford to, bought. Aspiration focused on home ownership, which was seen as crucial to social mobility. So also, for many, was the move from inner city to suburban estate, a trend that had existed throughout the century but remained pronounced, leading to estates of 'executive homes', each house narrowly separated from the other and each with a garage and driveway for the owner's car or cars. Conversely, inner-city regeneration did not attract those who aspired to leave the inner city. The detailed local geography of social mobility was largely set by such aspirational factors.

Home ownership appeared to focus aspirations far more than wider political movements, and it survived the restrictions on tax relief for mortgages introduced in 1974 and the withdrawal of relief in 2000. The high rate of house price inflation in 2001–3 reflected the strength of demand, although speculative investment was also a factor, since house purchase offered a better return than shares. This encouraged the purchase of additional homes, as by the family of the Prime Minister, Tony Blair, in 2002. Earlier, his close ally Peter Mandelson had gained unwelcome attention over the way in which he had financed the purchase of an expensive London house.

Home ownership brought more of the population in touch with estate agents, an occupation that became much more important and prominent in the 1980s and was seen by its critics as quintessentially Thatcherite. Estate agents were subject to greater regulation after scandals in the 1990s. Surveyors also became more important, while another profession regarded as particularly of its time was accountancy. House purchase linked every street to the 'enterprise culture' seen with deregulation in the City of London and privatization. The values of the period were captured in Dunfermline when what was once the biggest linen damask factory in the world, that of Erskine, Beveridge and Co., closed and was converted to flats in 1983–4.

Home ownership was matched by a determination to improve the comfort of home living, and tenants also expected higher standards. Thus, the percentage of houses with central heating and, later, double-glazing rose, as did those that were carpeted throughout. This had many unexpected consequences. It was argued that carpeting and better insulation, by reducing draughts, led to homes that had less fresh air, and that this was related to rising levels of asthma. Double-glazing, however, did lead to a more efficient use of energy.

The cult of DIY (Do It Yourself) work was closely linked with home-ownership. With television, DIY was the main leisure pursuit of men according to polls in the 1970s, '80s and '90s. It led to a 'win both ways' economy: when prosperity enabled people to move and buy new homes they did, and then altered them, while, in times of downturn, the DIY boom kicked in as people improved the properties they could not sell. Very substantial sums were spent on DIY, and this was linked both to home makeover programmes on the television, which were very pop-ular in the 1990s and 2000s, and to the growing consumer importance of DIY and home improvement suppliers, such as B&Q, whose stores were generally located 'out of town'. The two combined in fashions such as loft conversions, the construction of conservatories and the installa-tion of en-suite bathrooms, including in student accommodation. In addition to home makeover television programmes, which stressed how to increase the value of property, there were programmes to guide house-purchasers. By 2003, when total mortgage lending rose to the unprecedented height of £25 billion, the range included *Escape to the Country*, *Grand Designs*, *Hot Property*, *House Doctor*, *Selling Houses*, *Property Ladder*, and *Location, Location*.

ANOTHER NATIONAL FASCINATION: GARDENING

The installation of water features was the comparable development in gardens in the 1990s and 2000s. It was linked to the ready availability of small electric pumps. The scale of the consumer demand was such that measures had to be taken to stop the removal of boulders from beaches. As with home makeovers, this fashion owed much to the popularity of gardening programmes on the television. These programmes were aimed at non-specialists and were designed to satisfy what was correctly seen as a widespread desire to use affluence and leisure in order to create attractive gardens.

As with home makeovers, which made Laurence Llewelyn-Bowen a celebrity in the late 1990s, gardening programmes exemplified many important aspects of the social and cultural history of the period. These included the creation of celebrities by television. To be successful, these celebrities had to be accessible figures who conveyed knowledge in a relaxed fashion. Alan Titchmarsh and Monty Don were particularly successful in this. This was an approach far removed from the authoritative style of the past, and it was one particularly suited to a democratized age. There were obvious parallels in the presentation of cookery programmes. The move towards a more accessible style can be seen in the shift from the technicalities of the radio programme *Gardeners' Question Time* to Geoff Hamilton's presentation of BBC2's *Gardeners' World* (which in 2003 had run for 36 years), and then to Titchmarsh, Don and others.

Secondly, the television programme and celebrity came before the book, as visual was placed before written culture. Nevertheless, the market created by reader interest was also met by a host of lavishly illustrated books, the publication of which indicated the nature of the commercial possibility. Thus, in 2001 an edition of Stefan Buczacki's *Essential Garden Answers* was produced for the high-street chain Marks and Spencer. The theme throughout was on making everything seem possible, as with the title of Jane Fearnley-Whittingstall's *Gardening Made Easy* (1995), published by the major imprint of Weidenfeld & Nicolson. The spread of colour photography, both in magazines and in newspaper supplements, was also important.

From the point of television companies, gardening, house and cookery programmes made cheap television in part because they engaged with the real world rather than the costs of fantasy. The sets were bare pieces of earth or run-down houses. Tackling these and making them attractive, and, in the case of houses, adding value, addressed the desire for improvement that was widespread, including among the large numbers who claimed to have no wish for social mobility. Looked at differently, social mobility had changed. Instead of being gained by leaving the working for the middle class, there was a greater sense of fluidity involving both, while it was also regarded as desirable to improve living standards irrespective of social classification.

Gardening also indicated the variety of social developments. The number of gardeners for hire reflected the continued role of personal service, which was also seen in the boom in the number of cleaners and home-helps. At the same time, statistics are of little value as many of these gardeners preferred to work for cash in order to evade taxation. Nevertheless, most gardening was not done by professional gardeners. Instead, it reflected shifting leisure patterns, which, for women, included the decline in the amount of time spent cooking. For both men and women, the rise in gardening was also an aspect of the greater fitness of many of those in late middle age and of many of the elderly.

At the same time, many people did not wish to garden. Gardening and home makeover programmes sought to address this constituency. There was a greater interest in other aspects of the use of outdoor space, ranging from rising sales for barbecues to the development of decking, patios, conservatories, hot tubs and other seating or activity areas. Technology played its role, not just with hot tubs but also with outdoor heaters.

For those who still wished to garden, there was a shift in emphasis, with a decline in interest in mowing lawns. This was linked to a shift in the visual character of the conventional garden, away from rectangular lawn surrounded by flower-beds, and toward more sinuous shapes and varied layouts. Water features provided another aspect of changing consumer demands. They were sold in part as means to reduce stress, and thus responded to one of the more important consumer demands of the period, one also seen in the growing sales of aromatherapy products and of medical or paramedical methods such as the Alexander Technique.

Like other aspects of the consumer economy, aspirations were focused on image and leisure, the entire process expressed through expenditure, in the case of gardening in the large number of out-of-town gardening centres that were opened. Car-borne consumers not only went there to buy but also to eat, part of the process by which shopping became a leisure activity. By the standards of the 1950s, much of this expenditure was non-necessary. Money was being spent on flowers and shrubs, not vegetables. The trees planted were decorative, not fruit trees.

Similarly, in other areas of consumption, non-necessary products became staple goods. Thus, in the first half of the century, toiletries meant soap for most of the population, but the use of other products – conditioners, moisturisers, lotions – spread greatly from the 1960s. This was followed by an expansion in the range of male toiletries. The production and sale of cosmetics and toiletries became far more important in terms of turnover, employment and profitability, and the leading products and stores in the field became household names. From the 1980s, the Body Shop (a chain opened in 1976), with its bright colours, fragrances and novel products, and 'eco-friendly' image, came to play a role on most high streets. Established providers, such as Boots, came to offer similar products. The battle for customers became so intense that advertising campaigns would stress how environmentally friendly a company's products were, which was a response to public sensitivity about animals. Once started, the pace of innovation increased and the product range interacted with developments in other fields of society. Thus, in the 1990s, both the Body Shop and Boots offered ranges of toiletries and products linked to aromatherapy.

Standards of toilet paper also rose, in large part because of the success of the market leader, Andrex, in creating a product that other manufacturers found they had to match in order to meet consumer expectations. Compared to earlier brands, there was an expectation of softness, while, as another aspect of fashion-consciousness, consumers sought colours that matched their bathrooms. Thus, the variety of colours on offer rose, and the manufacturers had to take careful note of fashions in bathroom tiling. The latter was another sphere in which consumer expectations led to a far greater range in product, including in colour, pattern and texture. Home makeover programmes and the lavish colour photography of magazines contributed to this shift. The bathroom was no longer considered simply as a functional room, or, looked at differently, its function in the consumer society changed considerably. As such it matched the kitchen.

AFFLUENCE AND DEBTS

All this cost money. For those in work, a growing percentage of the population, this was a period of affluence that would have amazed their predecessors. The number of those employed rose from 22.5 million in 1979 to 26.9 million in 1989, in part due to the expansion of the female workforce, before falling, in the recession of the early 1990s, to 25 million in 1992. Average disposable income rose by 37 per cent between 1982 and 1992. A combination of rising real earnings, lower inflation and taxation, and easier credit, encouraged spending. The standard rate of income tax fell from 33 per cent in 1979 to 25 per cent in 1988, and, thereafter, governments, both Conservative and Labour, felt it important to sustain this fall.

North Sea oil revenues helped to underpin this fall. Their proceeds were used to subsidize consumption, rather than to fund infrastructural improvement or, indeed, a fundamental reform of public services such as healthcare, or the particular ends that Scottish nationalists claimed their oil should be used for. By 1986, oil production constituted 5 per cent of British GNP. This was a major windfall for the Conservatives. Scholars of the future will debate the wisdom of the uses to which it was put, but there is little doubt that it helped give an additional margin to Thatcherite economics. It was also important to this that private companies played the major role in the industry, while Britoil was privatized. Foreign capital and expertise played a crucial part in the development of the North Sea oil industry.

Thanks to the strong electoral focus on tax levels, the rate of taxation became an important test of Conservative success in the 1990s, and there was considerable disappointment in the budget of November 1995 when the cut in the standard rate announced to come into effect the following April was only one penny in the pound. The determination of the Conservatives to cut public spending was closely linked to their commitment to low taxes. In January 1996, John Major, the Conservative Prime Minister, announced that he wanted to cut it to 35 per cent of national income. Blair, who became Labour Prime Minister in 1997, was very careful to promise not to increase Conservative direct tax rates, although other forms of taxation rose markedly.

A marked decline in the birth rate, which owed much to the spread in the use of the contraceptive pill, to higher levels of female employment, and to changing assumptions about marriage, and family structure and size, was also important in increasing disposable income. Shifts in costs were also important for trends in expenditure. In 1971 food took one-fifth of the average family budget, but in 1993 only one-ninth, freeing disposable income for other forms of expenditure. The Office of National Statistics' Expenditure and Food Survey for 2001–2 indicated that the average UK household spent £398 per week: of this £41.70 was on food and non-alcoholic drinks, but £54 on recreation and culture and £57.70 on transport.

In a society that was focused on individual and, to a lesser extent, collective living standards, if not happiness, as a goal, domestic consumption became far more important to the economy, and exports proportionately less so. As a result, manufacturers had to concentrate on the domestic market, rather than on metal-bashing. As elsewhere, this led to a responsiveness to higher expectations for comfort. For example, whereas the condoms of the 1930s were supposed to be re-usable and, due to a high rate of breakage, were thick, those of the 1990s were disposable, more sensitive, quality kite-marked by BSI, and marketed with a full understanding of the nuances of a modern consumer society.

One aspect of consumerism, however, was a greater exposure to high levels of debt, in absolute terms and as a percentage of household income. This reflected the relaxation of credit controls. The consequences, however, were serious. Downturns in the economy led to a large-scale failure to manage debt, especially mortgage repayments. In 1980–89 private household debt rose from £16 billion to £47 billion, and mortgages from £43 billion to £235 billion. In the recession of the early 1990s, large numbers were affected by repossessions against a background of 'negative equity' caused by a fall in the value of their houses, in many cases below the mortgage they had borrowed to purchase them. By June 1992 repossessions of houses by creditors were at an annual rate of about 75,000, while 300,000 mortgage-holders were six months or more in arrears. This helped to undermine the appeal of the Conservative government.

The crisis and the more general fall in house prices, combined with the rise in interest rates in 1992 that made mortgages more expensive, helped reduce the appeal of house purchase in the early 1990s. However, the growing absence of new public provision reduced alternatives to purchase. Furthermore, the Conservatives sought to maintain incentives. Thus, the 1995 Queen's Speech promised an extension of the right-to-buy to Housing Association tenants. The recession and the reduced appeal of house purchase of the early 1990s were to be followed by a marked rise in house prices at the close of the decade and, even more, in the early 2000s.

House purchase contributed greatly to debt, although other factors also played a role. The growing amount of debt was, in part, a product of general creditworthiness in a period of rising house values and low unemployment; hence the plethora of home-owner loans. Debt levels also reflected the willingness to take risks; as was also seen with the popularity of the National Lottery launched in 1994. This was a dramatic success, with over 70 per cent of the population regularly playing by 2001 and over 90 per cent having played at least once by then. In the financial year 1997–8 ticket sales totalled £5.5 billion and, though they continually dropped thereafter, the figure for 2001–2 was still £4.8 billion. Another form of gambling followed the demutualization of building societies and life insurance companies as they entered risky financial sectors, only in some cases, such as Abbey National, to lose heavily. The demutualization of building societies owed much to carpet-bagging speculators and to members voting for short-term payouts over long-term advantage. This led some societies to introduce a stockade mentality of periods of membership before voting rights were gained.

Many found debt difficult to manage. By 2001 average household debt was at about 120 per cent of disposable income, a figure greater than Germany, the USA and France. In January 2003 the Financial

Services Authority warned, in its *Financial Risk Outlook* for 2003, that six million families – one in five – were encountering debt problems, and this despite very low interest rates and high employment. This suggests that there may be very serious problems in future when the economy hits greater difficulties. A large number of loans are secured on people's houses. Aside from the long-term risk factor with debt, there is also the short-term problem of obtaining money in order to meet existing obligations.

As the economy hit growing problems in the early 2000s, and public expenditure rose considerably at the same time, government revenues were put under greater pressure, leading to a need to raise taxation. National Insurance payments rose in April 2003, but this did not suffice. This fiscal pressure particularly threatened individuals in debt.

Technology was also important in financial transactions, with the rise in electronics leading to a marked fall in the centrality of paper products and records, and in the need for cash transactions. People were increasingly paid by BACS, bank automatic credit. Credit cards and cheque guarantee cards proliferated and encouraged purchases on credit. Credit cards facilitated telephone purchases and helped to limit the importance of face-to-face commercial transactions from the 1990s. Purchasing was increasingly divorced from shops and other retail premises, a process taken further with internet shopping. The same shift affected other branches of the economy. Telephone banking was introduced in 1989, and was followed, from the late 1990s, by internet banking.

THE WORLD OF THINGS

The internet was a system particularly appropriate for a society focused on choice. Many people chose to purchase machines that improved their access to communications. Telephone ownership had already risen to a high level, but it continued to do so. As a consequence of a greater emphasis on consumers that followed the privatization and deregulation of telephone services, it became easier and quicker to have phones installed. By 1991, 90 per cent of households had a telephone, compared to 42 per cent in 1972, and by 2002 the percentage was 98. This was linked to the rise of telephone sales and centres. This expansion was supplemented by the mobile phone, which became the present of choice in the 1990s, when they were the country's fastest-selling consumer good of the century, as well as the target of preference for muggers. Such phones were also developed for 'texting' messages. From 1999 there was serious controversy over the alleged effects of the use of mobile phones on users' brains. In 2000 a British firm, Vodafone, became the world's largest mobile-phone company and the most valuable company in Europe. However, too much money was spent by the companies buying licences for 'third-generation' wireless networks, a quest that brought a windfall to government finances. This was also a heavy 'stealth' tax. The popularity of telecom shares played a major role in the stock-market boom that peaked in early 2000 and was followed by a collapse in 2000–01. This was an international rollercoaster that was followed by a more general slump in stock markets in 2002–3.

The mobile phone was not alone. Television channels multiplied, with the number of regular terrestrial channels rising to four in 1982, and subsequently to five. This was supplemented for many, first by satellite transmissions, which began in 1989, and then by cable television. More outlets meant more advertising, and this central facet of the consumer society helped to finance the expansion of media outlets, while television rights helped to finance the growth in sport, such that Manchester United had a turnover of £110 million in 1998–9. The receiving dishes of satellite televisions altered the appearance of many houses, as television aerials had earlier done. By 1992 more than a million Sky Television dishes had been sold in Britain, and by 1999 BSkyB had 3.5 million subscribers, while cable had 3.2 million. By 2003 nine million out of the twenty-five million homes had multi-channel televisions. The digging up of roads and pavements in order to permit the laying of cable links was a major disruption, and led to the death of many trees as their roots were cut. Among the machines of choice for the consumer society, there was also the video recorder, with the video itself followed in the early 2000s by DVD. By 2000 over 50 per cent of British households had video recorders, giving them even greater control over what they watched, although critics claimed that this control was an illusion.

In part, and in contrast to the spread of 'white goods' in the inter-war period, the diffusion of such goods reflected and encouraged a growing degree of classlessness in which many jobs ceased being so closely identified with a specific social class, while men and women from working-class backgrounds gained middle-class jobs. Others benefited from rising real incomes and the greater availability of credit, and shared in middle-class lifestyles. Classlessness was also seen in the widespread popularity of computer games. However, compared to many other Western countries, social divisions and, even more, a consciousness of class remained strong. Thus, the survey of educational achievement for 15-year-olds carried out by the Organisation for Economic Co-operation and Development in 2000 revealed that in Britain the gap in reading levels between the poorest quarter and the wealthiest quarter was particularly big.

The spread of computers and electronic mail ensured that more messages were sent and more information stored than ever before. By 1999, 42 per cent of UK workers were estimated to use the internet in what was increasingly a knowledge economy, with information a key product and 'messaging' a major form of work. Indeed, the overload, management and accessibility of information became major problems for both institutions and individuals. Greater expenditure on Information Technology was seen as a solution to problems in institutions such as the NHS. The internet also acted as a focus for concerns over morality. From 1999 there was serious controversy over access to pornography over the internet, and this was heightened by concern about its alleged links to crimes against children.

In 2003 Britain was placed seventh in the 'network readiness index' drawn up by the World Economic Forum. This assessment of infrastructure, usage and regulatory conditions put Britain above Germany, France and Japan. The pressure of individual usage was important, as in Britain it was from this level that much of the pressure for network improvement stemmed. It was met by servers and suppliers keen to attract custom and thus reducing the cost of access; a situation that also characterized the mobile phone industry.

Consumerism also played a major role in the democratization of politics and society. Democracy – government by freely elected representatives of the people and the use of the franchise – was incomplete without the responsiveness to the popular will and accountability to the public entailed by democratization. However, hostility to accountability was widely demonstrated, not least, albeit in an implicit manner, by the unwillingness of (often largely self-selecting) elites, such as the judiciary and town planners, to accept popular beliefs and pastimes as worthy of value and attention, and their conviction that they were best placed to manage society and define social values. In December 2002 Lord Woolf, the Lord Chief Justice, issued sentencing guidelines for burglary that clashed with popular views. He argued in favour of a community sentence rather than a custodial one for most first-time convicted burglars. More generally, paternalism was a powerful attitude in what the novelist and former official C. P. Snow termed, in 1964, 'the corridors of power'.

The extension of the scope of government during the century exacerbated this tendency, because much of it entailed social policing. Behaviour deemed anti-social in the spheres of education, health, housing, personal conduct, and law and order all became a matter for scrutiny, admonition and, in some cases, control by the agencies of the state. The expansion of government agencies and extension of state control also brought income and status to those who ran, or benefited, from government. This had a powerful class component, and was linked to the prestige of 'white-collar' over 'blue-collar' occupations. Thanks, in large part, to the growth of state power, the twentieth was the century in which the frequently discerned rise of the middle class reached its apogee. A resistance to consumer expectations played a role in the state sector as the 'providers', employees such as teachers, academics and doctors, sought to define what was appropriate for their institutions and to control them; thus acting as a counterpoint to trade union resistance to managerial reform and government direction.

More generally, middle-class social and cultural condescension was linked to contempt for popular views on such matters as capital punishment and immigration: these views were in favour of the re-introduction of capital punishment and of severe limits on immigration. British society, government and culture are nowhere near as demo-cratic as their American counterparts. Instead, the British pattern had become more similar to that in Western Europe, where the notion of a political class, a paternalism born of a conviction that the state knew best, and a hostility to populism, were strongly ingrained in adminis-trative culture. In America, elections are far more numerous, and many public offices, for example judges, are filled by elected candidates. In Britain, in contrast, from the 1980s there was a rise in the power of quangos (government-appointed bodies) and, in the mid-1990s, it was estimated that Wales had more Quangocrats – unelected officials – than it had local councillors. Under Thatcher and Major, the govern-ment transferred former central and local authority responsibilities to quangos, helping it to control or, at least, appear to cut spending, but lessening responsibilities for the delivery of services.

Paternalism could also be seen in politics, especially in the hostile response to what was presented as Thatcherite populism. Thus, in January 1996, Emma Nicholson, a Conservative MP who had defected to the Liberal Democrats, complained that John Major, the Conservative Prime Minister, was relying increasingly on the 'worst, hard-faced, populist instincts of people'. As with other defectors, her sense of moral superiority ensured that she did not think it appropri-ate to offer her constituents the right to pass judgement in a by-election. A similar unwillingness could be seen in hostility in the mid-1990s to a referendum about joining a European single currency. The support for low taxation that was a crucial aspect of political consumerism and consumer politics met with only limited support from established interests, not least those who directed the public sector.

There was also administrative and political resistance to the ability of individuals to choose to spend their money on private health and on private education for their children. This resistance could draw on an often bitter public envy of the wealth and opportunities of others that was particularly, but not only, apparent on the Left. Both issues exposed fault lines in British society. Thus, Conservatives accused Labour politicians of hypocrisy when they sent their children to grammar (selective state) and public (i.e. private) schools, as when Harriet Harman was supported by Tony Blair in her decision in 1996 to send her son to a grammar school.

Democratization did not imply one social agenda or political programme, but it gave vitality to democracy, translating it, in particular, from politics to society. Yet, at the same time, the focus on customers/voters/members, and the emphasis on their rights, not their responsibilities, combined to make it harder for institutions to operate.

All were affected by public scrutiny and demands. In 1992, for example, Windsor Castle suffered a serious fire that caused major damage to the state apartments. It was initially suggested that the cost of the repairs be met from public funds, but this led to an outcry on a scale that would have been inconceivable when Queen Elizabeth II came to the throne in 1952. Indeed, in 1992 the Queen felt it appropriate to decide to pay income tax on her private income. Five years later, *Britannia*, the royal liner domesticated as a 'yacht', was not replaced when it ended service. In 2003 a critical report over the handling of presents by the Prince of Wales was published. The public nature of the controversy was again very different to the situation a half-century earlier. So also was discussion of who was staying in royal palaces and at what cost.

Government bodies were also subject to greater scrutiny. A Police Complaints Board was established in 1979 and, in 1984, the independent Police Complaints Authority followed. The National Audit Office and its parliamentary equivalent, the Public Accounts Committee, directed a critical look at public bodies and at policies such as the Public Private Partnerships and Private Finance Initiatives of the early 2000s. The incorporation of the European Convention on Human Rights into British law in October 2000 provided individuals with greater opportunity to take public bodies to court.

Businesses were also subject to scrutiny on behalf of consumers. Thus, the industries privatized by the Conservatives were overseen by regulators instructed to limit costs and foster competition. From the 1990s democratization contributed to a stress on the importance of individual customers, which affected both business and the public sector. This administrative pressure was linked to a so-called quality revolution, with training and education being intended to improve the quality of management in the public and private sectors. Major argued that 'quality', rather than subjects such as productivity, was going to be the issue of the 1990s. The endless satisfaction surveys/market research/focus groups of the 1990s and 2000s promoted a sense of responsive and democratized businesses and public services. As a consequence, the failure of the NHS to offer adequate treatment to individual patients became a press and political issue, as in the 2001 election campaign, and again in February 2002.

Politicians responded by carefully charting public opinion. Political parties devoted greater attention to public opinion polls, while Tony Blair was particularly interested in the opinion of focus groups. Politicians such as Thatcher, who, anyway, had an instinct for populist remarks and gestures, received 'make-overs' to make their image more television-friendly, and Parliament itself was televised from the 1990s. The role and ability of public relations companies, such as Saatchi and Saatchi, M. and C. Saatchi, Lowe Bell Communications and Shandwick, were seen as important to political success. Saatchi and Saatchi, the advertising agency for the Conservatives in the general elections of 1979, 1983, 1987 and 1992, was important in giving Thatcherism a particularly adroit edge in public relations, and between elections Tim Bell was used as a speech-writer.

Politicians were anxious to woo the support of television and the popular press. Thus, Thatcher made a successful effort to win over *The Sun*, giving the Conservatives powerful support in the popular press in the 1980s. *The Sun* played a major role in the attack on Labour's leader Neil Kinnock during the 1992 election. The ability of Blair, in turn, to win over *The Sun* was seen as important, not least by the paper which claimed, after the 1997 election result, 'It's *The Sun* wot swung it'.

Once in power, Blair made major efforts to retain the support of the press, wooing Rupert Murdoch, the owner of *The Sun*, and other owners, editors and journalists. In 2001 *The Sun* was told the date of the election before the Prime Minister informed the Queen. Blair's official spokesman, his Director of Communications, Alastair Campbell, a former tabloid journalist, was regarded as particularly influential, as Bernard Ingham had been under Thatcher. Ministers who fell foul of the media, such as Stephen Byers, the Transport Secretary, in 2002, had to resign even though Blair would have been prepared to keep them: the hostility of the press was more important than parliamentary criticism.

Aside from wooing the media, both Blair and his opponents sought to propagate the notion of an active civil society that they could make an active partner in government and social renewal. Thus, Blair talked much of communitarianism and community. His Conservative opponent, William Hague, responded to the 1997 defeat by undertaking to 'listen to Britain' and, in the 2001 election campaign, promised an Office of Civil Society as part of the structure of government, an Office drawing on 'charities, faith communities and family groups'. Both Blair and Hague were interested in the role of 'community leaders' and in religious activism in community life. Much of the public, meanwhile, was sceptical about such activism and lost interest in politics, with the percentage voting in the 1997 and 2001 elections showing major falls in participation.

Responding to public concerns, the Labour Party promised at its 2002 conference 'schools and hospitals first'. However, although politicians might chart the public mood, there was only a limited willingness to give the public a choice in the 'public services'. Aside from the minority able and willing to afford private health and education, there was a need to rely on a type of state provision that left the consumer with few choices and only limited redress. This was particularly marked under Labour, a party that talked about public service reform but was unable to provide much of it. Thus measures to allow certain, so-called foundation, hospitals to win limited independence were strongly resisted from within government, as well as by much of the Labour Party, in 2002–3. In part, the opposition was political, but there was also a prioritization of the governmental objective of Treasury control over possible financial commitments by hospitals above the prospect of better services for patients.

These administrative proposals, anyway, still left patients with scant choice, and their needs only framed provision in so far as they were interpreted by government. This was in accord with the centralist decision-making and authoritarian inclinations of Labour's Chancellor of the Exchequer, Gordon Brown. Funding, and the setting and monitoring of goals and standards, were highly centralized. Public Service Agreements were used by Brown to set quantitative and qualitative goals for individual ministries. Partly as a result of excessive centralization and a lack of financial incentives, the productivity of the NHS, in terms of the relationship between expenditure and activity, declined after Labour came to power in 1997. Thus, although waiting lists declined, a large infusion of extra expenditure did not produce commensurate benefits. Instead, it simply contributed to higher public spending, which rose to £418 billion in the fiscal year 2002–3 and was scheduled to rise to £511 billion in 2005–6. Furthermore, there was particular concern among consumers about waiting lists for hospital treatment and in accident and emergency departments. In addition, the government's promise to ensure access for all to dental care from NHS dentists was not implemented. .

More generally, consumer demands were not satisfied by the performance targets offered by Blair or, earlier, by the charters provided by Major. Instead, both led to new bureaucratic demands on workers in the public sector without ensuring the fundamental reforms necessary to match standards elsewhere.

Consumerism can be presented as a triumph for the people, indeed as another form of democracy, but its expression was greatly affected not only by government, but also by the structures of economic power. A powerful pressure against democratization was provided by globalization, specifically the rise of multinationals in the economy and their extension into the service sector. This was very much seen in the media. A new generation of foreign ownership began in 1969 with the purchase of *The Sun* newspaper by Rupert Murdoch, an Australian (he later bought *The Times* from the Canadian Thomson family, while, in 1985, another Canadian, Conrad Black, acquired control of the *Daily* and *Sunday Telegraph*. The role of private ownership in satellite and cable television was dramatized in the 1990s and 2000s when private companies purchased the right to broadcast sporting events, emphasizing the degree to which the BBC had lost its pre-eminence as the moulder of national memories and images. Instead, these events were open only to those who could pay, although there was now more choice among providers. Murdoch controlled BSkyB, the satellite television company, and in 1999 tried to buy Manchester United, the country's leading football team, only to be blocked by regulators.

The privatizations of the 1980s and '90s also opened new fields for foreign ownership. French companies came to play a major role in the water industry, and American and German companies in the electricity generating and supply industry: thus Powergen, created in the 1990 privatization, was bought by a German utility EON. With their foreign bases and ownerships, such concerns were in part removed from British opinion, as was seen in 2003 when the Dutch-based company Corus, which had taken over British Steel, decided to shut one of its three remaining British steelworks. Nevertheless, in many fields the breakdown of monopoly provision, and the emphasis on customers in an age of fast-changing consumer preferences, ensured a degree of responsiveness.

This was also seen with the development of referenda. Held in Scotland and Wales in 1997, in order to endorse the Labour government's creation of a Scottish Parliament and a Welsh Assembly, and in Northern Ireland in 1998, in order to win backing for the Good Friday Agreement, these were also promised in order to determine whether there should be regional assemblies in England and the replacement of sterling by the Euro. Thus, consumerism, in the shape of democracy, however manipulated by government and other interests, looks set to make choices that will be crucial to the national identity.

Politics and consumerism came together with the petrol price revolt in 2000. This indicated how concern about prices arising from the government's increases in indirect taxation could provoke a profound political crisis in the sense of a serious questioning of the ability of government to enforce the law. The government 'toughed it out', but then backtracked on the Petrol Tax accumulator, which had been introduced by the Conservatives. The seriousness of the demonstrations derived not only from concern about petrol prices, but also from a wider sense of distrust of the Blair government. This, in particular, focused on a breakdown of relations between the rural community and the government.

In the face of the blockades of petrol depots in September 2000, the government faced uncertainty about the likely response of the police and the troops in the event of it being decided to try to use force to reopen supply routes. This was not a tangential issue in British history, for the role of the forces of 'law and order' was integral to the structure of government, as it is in other countries. The 'Troubles' in Northern Ireland led, in the 1970s, to the development of new tactics of crowd control, which were then employed in Britain during the inner-city disturbances of the 1980s. Furthermore, the deployment of large numbers of police in the East Midlands during the 1984–5 miners' strike focused attention on the role of force in domestic history. Nearly 12,000 miners were arrested during the strike. In late 2000 the government responded to the possibility of a resumption of the petrol depot blockades by training 1,000 soldiers to drive oil tankers so that picket lines could be breached. There were also plans to use troops if strikes, such as those of early 1979, became more serious in their impact. The ability of the government to turn to the army to provide coverage during the firemen's strike of 2002–3 was important in enabling it to resist the challenge to pay restraint.

The 'Troubles' in Northern Ireland also led to disputes over media coverage, and to government attempts to control it. In 1971 there had been a clash within the BBC, when Lord Hill, the Chairman of the Board of Governors, made it clear that the BBC could not be impartial between Army 'and the gunmen', the IRA. The controversy over the programme *Real Lives: At the Edge of the Union* led, in 1986, to the first one-day strike by journalists in the history of the BBC. Two years later, the Conservative Home Secretary, Douglas Hurd, announced a ban on the use of the direct speech of terrorists on radio and television. Defended as an opportunity to prevent the dissemination of attempts to justify 'criminal activities', the ban captured the dilemmas arising from a strange situation of what was at once war and peace, a deadly struggle but also one conducted in a peacetime democracy, most of whose inhabitants were not directly affected. The absurdity of the ban was shown by the use of actors to speak the words of IRA leaders.

A very different aspect of the relationship between consumerism and politics was thrust into prominence in 1997 following the unexpected death in a car accident of Diana, Princess of Wales. Like the use of force for domestic purposes, the monarchy was an understated aspect of the government process. This was particularly so under Elizabeth II, who reigned from 1952. An experienced and skilful adviser of successive Prime Ministers, she had political opinions, not least a belief in the Commonwealth, but was careful not to take a public political stand, and to maintain constitutional conventions. Politicians helped to preserve the monarchy's neutrality. Under Elizabeth, the royal family maintained their important charitable role as patrons of good causes, especially voluntary organizations, both at community and national level. This played a part in the maintenance of social harmony and in the nation's sense of continuity, and contributed to the widely held feeling that the royal family had an important purpose.

From the 1980s, however, the royal family, like other national institutions, such as the Church of England, was affected by increasing public criticism and had to consider how best to respond to the pressure of change. This problem was accentuated by the position of the Queen's children, especially the role and matrimonial difficulties of the heir, Charles, Prince of Wales, who finally divorced Diana in 1996. He sought to make the monarchy more 'relevant' and, indeed, played a major role in addressing and highlighting issues of national concern and some that had been marginalized, not least the environment, inner-city problems, alternative medicine and the excesses of Modernist architecture, but his private life was the issue of public concern.

The 1990s saw an upsurge in anti-monarchical sentiment and a more critical press. This was focused when the death of Princess Diana unleashed a wave of national grief that the royal family seemed totally unable to comprehend. This was popular consumerism on terms. Instead of accepting royalty on the terms offered, a large section of the population showed that it was determined to take the image of monarchy it liked. This was skilfully exploited by Blair, who read a lesson at the princess's funeral service, in order to advance his call for modernization. He presented Diana as someone who was in touch, compassionate and inclusive, all goals that Blair sought. Indeed, he told the Labour Party conference in 1997 that the Labour government represented a 'giving age' of greater compassion.

Diana, somewhat improbably, became the 'People's Princess' in Blair's phrase, and this perception was such that in 2002 she came close to winning the BBC's Great Britons competition; although, in the event, this poll was convincingly won by Winston Churchill. The use of celebrities, rather than experts, to present the candidates for greatness to the television audience; the choice, throughout, by public vote, rather than expert opinion; and the possibility of voting by internet and interactive television, as well as telephone; were all symptomatic of the changing nature of British society in which perception merged with reality.

Yet, as a reminder of the variety that was an important aspect of consumer democracy, the response following Diana's death in 1997 was far more divided than is generally appreciated. Demonstrations of grief and protestations of concern were stronger among women, homosexuals and those under 40, than they were among non-homosexual men, especially if working class, as well as people over 40, and Scots. Indeed there was considerable controversy over the curtailment of sporting fixtures on the day of her funeral.

Diana's death was followed by an attempt by the monarchy to modernize in response both to the public mood and to encouragement from Blair, a self-proclaimed modernizer. Royal visits became more informal and there was a conscious effort to link royalty with the younger generation. The Queen's Golden Jubilee in 2002 was carefully organized to that end, with the garden of Buckingham Palace thrown open for a popular concert that was televised. A million people took to the streets of London to celebrate the jubilee.

At the same time, the far more eulogistic tone following the death of the Queen Mother earlier that year highlighted the shift in the public mood over the last sixty years. She was largely remembered in a golden glow that cast a conscious contrasting light on a more troubled present. This present was made more troubled later in 2002 when the trial of Paul Burrell, Diana's butler, provided fresh fodder for those seeking sensationalism in the royal family. The willingness of Burrell subsequently to sell his story to a newspaper indicated the pervasive pressure of publicity. Conversely, according to Burrell, the Queen had told him 'there are powers at work in this country about which we have no knowledge'.

No golden glow was cast on the House of Lords. Having promised, in its 1997 manifesto, to make the second chamber 'more democratic and more representative', the Labour government failed to do so, but it did remove the automatic right of the hereditary peers to sit there with no public fuss: only 92 were left in the Lords.

Meanwhile, the Conservative opposition was giving Party members, rather than simply MPs, the right to make key decisions on Party policy: on the Euro (1998) and on the leadership (2001).

CONSUMERISM AND SOCIETY

The vague and nebulous character of consumerism does not make the concept less valuable, but it does make it difficult to employ. How, for example, is consumerism to be related to Britain's favourable position in international rankings of corruption? Transport provides an apt illustration of the problem in using the concept of consumerism. The public wants personal mobility, in the shape of cars, inexpensive petrol, uncluttered roads and, for most, the absence of any need to rely on public transport, as well as car prices that are no higher than those elsewhere in Europe; but it does not wish to be consumed by cars. Phrased differently, there is an expectation of air quality and of an absence of road-building that clashes with the goals of cheap personal mobility. Thus, since 1989, when a bold White Paper proposing road-building was thwarted by popular hostility, there has been much reluctance to propose new roads. Newbury's second bypass was opened in 1998 only after bitter struggles with anti-road protesters in 1995-6.

Similarly, as never before, people wished to fly, but there was a marked reluctance to accept the building of new runways, let alone airports. This is an important instance of nimbyism, a term coined in the period from the use of NIMBY: 'Not in my back yard'. In the case of landowners and farmers seeking to block public footpaths, this was often literally true. It also often reflected a hostility to outsiders. In contrast, the authoritarian tendency of the Blair government led to interest in reducing the roles of public inquiries and local authorities in major planning decisions.

The culture of rights, and the empowerment of individuals' claims through legislation or judicial ruling, also clashed with the interests of the collectivity of consumers. Thus, granting rights of access to disabled consumers could make expensive arrangements necessary that led to the closure of facilities. The flexible working rights, extended maternity leave and paternity leave introduced in April 2003 also helped to price jobs and services out of Britain.

Similarly, despite the protectionism and price support of the European Union's Common Agricultural Policy, there is an expectation of inexpensive food, more so than in most of Europe. At the same time, there is a widespread reluctance to accept agricultural developments, such as genetically modified plants. This issue caused a controversy in 1998 and, subsequently, government-authorized field trials of herbicide-resistant crops faced disruption by protesters. At the same time, as with the Diana furore in 1997, it is unclear that the concern was as widespread as was suggested. Consumerism can look, or be made to look, faddist.

A different set of responses to example, admonition, and the risk of disease was provided by the range of issues raised by sexual freedom. Individual demands and expectations clashed with social norms, posing problems for legislation and policing. Thus, prostitutes, more open in their trade than their predecessors in the 1950s, faced neighbourhood complaints about their presence and those of curb-crawling clients. Government interest in regulation, such as the 2002 proposal to make sex with a prostitute under 18 an imprisonable offence, failed to give due weight to the issue of knowledge on the part of the offender. This issue was fought over in controversies over rape trials and related policing and sentencing policies. Conviction rates for rapes reported to the police fell from 24 per cent in 1985 to 7 per cent in 2001 as those implementing these policies struggled to respond to shifts in sexual mores, specifically the difficulty of determining when what had been a sexual relationship became date rape, a new term that itself reflected these shifts. The competing expectations of legal practitioners, in the shape of established standards of proof, juries, who were ready to differentiate stranger rape from date rape, and feminists, made this issue especially vexed.

Another form of variety in response was provided by the relationship between trade union reform and consumerism. Anger with union power and restrictive practices, such as pre-entry closed shops, led many union members to help vote Thatcher into power in 1979 and to keep her there thereafter: the Conservatives were clear in their determination to restrict union power. The subsequent Employment Acts met opposition, but there was also acceptance and a measure of co-operation from within the union movement. Thus, when, in 1986, Rupert Murdoch and News International broke the restrictive practices of the print unions by moving from Fleet Street to a new plant at Wapping, they were able to do so in part by turning to the electricians. Trade union membership fell from 13.5 million in 1979 to 6.7 million by 1998: an important indication of what people were willing to do when they had the choice.

Weaker trade unionism helped make it easier for companies to respond to consumer demands, not least by providing services at more flexible times. The attacks on restrictions on employers, for example the abolition of 26 wage councils in 1993, were part of the 'bonfire of controls' under the Conservatives. In 1986 the City of London was deregulated in the 'Big Bang'. Building societies followed by 'demutualizing' (ceasing to be owned by policy-holders) and, instead, becoming banks that pursued traditional banking strategies and had publicly traded shares.

Thatcher's support for market-orientated measures helped to characterize the 1980s with its pronounced individualism. Tax-cuts were the means to this goal. Thatcher believed in the right of individuals to spend their money as they saw fit. The growth of private education and health-care was one major result. Sticking to her guns and harmfully castigating her successor, Major, Thatcher announced in a lecture in January 1996 that the unpopularity of his government was due to a feeling among those who wished to join the middle class that they no longer had 'the incentives and the opportunities they expect from a Conservative government', and which she, in her view, had helped provide.

In turn, as Thatcher had predicted, the European Union brought renewed controls in the shape of business regulation and labour inflexibility. Thus, the Working-Time Directive, which became law in Britain in 1998, was followed by a drop in the average weekly hours in full-time jobs and in the proportion of employees working more than 45 hours. Once the opt-out from the social chapter of the Maastricht treaty negotiated by Major had been relinquished by the Blair government in 1997, other regulations also affected employers, including the need to establish works councils. By limiting economic growth, these rights made it harder to respond to consumer demands.

By the 2000s the Conservatives were debating their response to consumerism, particularly in the shape of social interests and practices, in a very different fashion to their predecessors in the 1980s. An influential wing of the party, which called itself the modernizers, sought to respond to the character of contemporary society, not least the role of women, ethnic minorities and homosexuals, and to the process of social change. In contrast, the more traditional wing offered consumerism in a different form by explicitly seeking to satisfy core supporters.

A less politically charged instance of the clash between general interests and those of a smaller number was provided by the growth, particularly in the 1990s and 2000s, of a compensation culture that left scant role for individual responsibility and the acceptance of risk. Instead, the allocation of blame and the demand for compensation helped place a heavy burden on public life. Yet, as a reminder of the role of judgement, the compensation culture was also an aspect of institutional accountability.

More generally, there is a problem with the understanding of risk. This is related to powerful demands for safety and security, without much understanding of the resulting costs. Consumers are concerned with their own or their family's safety, for example with rail safety or the autism allegedly linked to immunization against measles, mumps and rubella; they also expect the costs to secure it, by automatic braking mechanisms and other means, or immunization, to be borne by others. As an instance of the complexities of the issue of risk, children die traumatically in large numbers in road accidents, but that is accepted by public culture with far less concern than the relatively minor risk of death at the hands of sex-offenders.

On the whole, the state acted to seek to lessen risk. This was seen, for example, in legislation making seatbelts compulsory, as well as in measures to ban the ownership of handguns and cigarette advertising. However, gun ownership and use by criminals increased: the government's authoritarianism hit law-abiding handgun owners and did not prevent the criminal use of guns. In other spheres, however, for example sexual practices, the government has not sought to rely on the law to deal with issues of risk and responsibility arising from specific consequences of individualism.

Individuals also acted to lessen risk by investing time and money heavily in healthcare. This involved a range of activities from exercise and the large-scale consumption of vitamin pills to alternative therapies and pseudo-religions. Respectable alternative activities, such as yoga and homeopathy, stand at the start of a continuum that moves through 'holistic therapies' to paganism and 'white' witchcraft.

An important aspect of consumerism, divorce, became easier after the Divorce Reform Act of 1969, and the rate rose considerably, to one for every two marriages by 1992. The annual divorce rate per 1,000 people rose from 2.45 in 1979 to 3.25 in 1999, the highest rate in the European Union. Divorces affected the highest in the land, including the Queen's sister, Margaret, in 1978, and three of the Queen's four children. In Scotland, there were 13,133 divorces in 1994 and 31,480 marriages, the latter the lowest figure since 1926. High divorce rates reflected increasing expectations of marital harmony and higher standards for this harmony. There was a decline in the economic need for marriage, and there was less toleration than hitherto for adultery and wife-beating. Divorce thus replaced stoical or angry acceptance. It was also seen as the way out of unhappy and celibate marriages.

Due, in large part, to divorce, the percentage of single-parent, female-headed households rose: from 8.3 per cent of households with children in 1971 to 12.1 per cent in 1980. This was linked with the breakdown in the relationship between sex and marriage. So also was the increase in sexual activity by those who had never been married, by both adolescents and adults. This activity was the subject of novels, films and television programmes, providing the basis for 'reality' TV programmes. In turn such material, for example the film *Bridget Jones's Diary* (2001), helped to create models for behaviour, or, at least, discussion. The rise in the number of long-term young singles certainly influenced consumer behaviour, and retailers had to come to terms with the fracturing of conventional markets.

To critics, high divorce rates, and the accompanying single-parenting, were an aspect of social breakdown and selfish individualism, especially when children were involved; others saw the high rate as a response to individuals' refusal to accept unhappy relationships. The sensitivity of the issue was shown in March 1996 when the government's Divorce Bill was attacked by right-wingers who presented it as a blow to family values. In particular, there was sensitivity about the notion of no-fault mediation and speedier divorces. In the event, the social conservatism seen in such episodes was to become far weaker after the Labour victory in 1997, although that led to a new and more modish authoritarianism. Divorce also contributed greatly to the housing crisis, alongside the larger number of young singles, greater longevity and higher immigration, leading to a need for more homes. With more single-person households, there was increasingly a demand for more flats and for smaller homes. The greater prominence of homosexual relationships accentuated this trend by contributing to the increase in childless households.

In addition to these shifts, there were other broad currents that helped to give a character to the age. The decline of formality in all its respects was a major one that was more important and far-reaching than is generally appreciated. Informality in means of address and conversation became far more pronounced. So also did informality in dress. The spread of informal clothing was linked to the erosion of social differences, at least in appearance. The wearing of suits and sports jackets declined, and that of casual wear increased. Thus, the sportswear fashion industry grew in importance. Trainers, for example, became a fashion choice, while, more generally, brand and designer labels became more important. This was an aspect of the expression of personality (or conformity) not through personal convictions, such as religion and politics, but through spending.

Chapter 2

Culture

Weeds flourished in the crevices between the paving-stones, a number of which had evidently been ripped out; others, several of them smashed, stood in an irregular pile. Elsewhere there was a heap of waterlogged and collapsed cardboard boxes and some large black plastic sheets spread about by the wind . . . along with after-shave cartons, sweet-wrappers, dog-food labels and soft-drink tins.

Kingsley Amis's description of urban neglect in Mornington Crescent, London, in his novel *Jake's Thing* (1978)

Television linked consumerism with culture. It had played a major role already from the 1950s, but this link became more important as television increasingly set the idioms and vocabulary of public and private life. For example, on 14 July 1989 the Prime Minister, Thatcher, was attacked by Denis Healey of the Labour Party for adding 'the diplomacy of Alf Garnett to the economics of Arthur Daley'. This attack was based on the assumption that listeners would understand the reference to prominent television characters. It was also an aspect of the blending of image and reality that was to become more insistent with the reality television shows of the early 2000s.

Prior to that, through programmes such as *Coronation Street* and *EastEnders*, viewers experienced life as they themselves lived it, or could at least identify with. Television was the central determinant of the leisure time of many, a moulder of opinion and fashion, a source of conversation and controversy, a cause of noise, an occasion of family cohesion or dispute, and a major feature of the household. A force for change, which demanded the right to enter everywhere and report everything, television also became, increasingly, a reflector of popular taste. As such, it faced accusations of 'dumbing down'. The impact of television was increased by the introduction first of 'daytime' (i.e. morning and early afternoon) television and then of round-the-clock broadcasting. Television also contributed to the increasingly noisy nature of life, although other consumer goods, such as the Walkman, were also a problem.

Television was certainly responsible for making football more central to public life, such that the sport became a motif of consumerism. The public and private lives of star players such as Manchester United's David Beckham were extensively reported, and the iconic status of the players was celebrated by their role in advertising and by discussion of their alleged cultural significance. New or enhanced football grounds were important symbols of the age, combining seating for large audiences with plentiful opportunities for television coverage. Football was not alone. The Millennium Stadium in Cardiff provided a setting for rugby and other activities.

Sport drew on, and encouraged, combative instincts. Thus, during the 1996 European football championships, England was drawn against Germany in the semi-final, and much of the popular press employed martial language. *The Sun* declared 'Let's Blitz Fritz', while the *Daily Mirror* of 24 June carried headlines such as 'Mirror Declares Football War on Germany' and 'Achtung! Surrender . . . For you Fritz, ze Europe 96 Championship is over'.

By 1994, 99 per cent of British households had televisions, with 96 per cent having colour televisions. Both the BBC and ITV were expected not to broadcast material that was deemed obscene, cruel or blasphemous, or to encourage people to break the law. There was a period when challenging television drama did have a popular audience, for example the plays of Dennis Potter, such as *Pennies from Heaven* (1978), but, on the whole, television helped ensure not only that popular culture was the dominant culture, but also that popular culture set out to offer few challenges. 'Difficult' work was marginalized. Potter's

Brimstone and Treacle (1977) was banned by the BBC. Potter himself claimed that, thanks to television, the real national theatre was to be found in the corner of the sitting room, rather than on the banks of the River Thames, the site of the National Theatre. Ministers and newspapers expected television to set an appropriate tone. In 2002 the Secretary of State for Culture, Tessa Jowell, called its celebrities 'role models'.

Television also led to a more homogenous culture, with millions of people across the country watching the same programme at the same moment, and then discussing it subsequently: in Ian Rankin's Edinburgh novel *Set in Darkness* (2000), 'now it was Hogmanay, and everyone was talking about how bad the television had been'. Cult programmes acquired clubs of followers who dressed like their heroes. Television advice affected lifestyles and consumption patterns, leading for example to the fashion for water features in gardens. *What Not to Wear*, a book by two fashion advisers who had become prominent due to television, was one of the more successful books of 2002.

Yet, this homogenization was challenged by the multiplication of channels, beginning with the establishment of Channel 4 in 1982, and followed by satellite and cable television, by the spread of the video recorder, and by the development of digital television. This weakened the relatively narrow range of cultural references that had arisen from the very popular television programmes of the 1960s and '70s that provided shared experiences. The fall in the size of what was considered a good audience indicated this. The resulting loss of shared experience was possibly linked to the nostalgia for the television successes of the earlier period, such as Morecambe and Wise and *Dad's Army*. Aside from the multiplication of channels, the growth in the number of television sets per household led to compartmentalization and isolation within the family, particularly as more children possessed sets in their bedrooms.

Television culture was also a powerful aspect of the Americanization of aspects of British life. The USA dominated television and film imports, although Australia was responsible for the successful soap opera *Neighbours* and for *Home and Away*. When 'J.R.', the leading character in the American-import television series *Dallas*, was shot, it was reported on the BBC news, the fictional world displacing its less exciting real counterpart. Whereas, in the 1970s, entertainers such as Mike Yarwood impersonated people who appeared on television, such as Harold Wilson and Edward Heath, now they increasingly focus on the personalities from television soaps.

The British film industry was hit when quotas were abandoned in 1983. In 1998 over 20 per cent of films shown were British productions, but their American counterparts still dominated the market. In the early 2000s many of the most successful television programmes were American, such as *Friends*, *Seinfeld*, *The Simpsons* and *The Sopranos*, and there was a widespread conviction that the British no longer made better television programmes. The attempt to use National Lottery money in order to help create a strong British film industry led to some commercial and critically successful films, such as *Gosforth Park*, *Calendar Girls* and *The Importance of Being Earnest*, but some other works were less successful.

The role of American programmes was complemented by that of American and American-derived consumer products, and both contributed to the more diffuse, but still very important, mystique of America as a land of wealth and excitement. The suburban culture and society that had become prominent in Britain from the 1950s, with its focus on the car, was particularly accessible to American influences. Indeed the combination of mobility and the private space that the car brought helped to define the aspirations and lifestyle of most of the population. Greater car use combined with suburban home ownership led to a living environment that was closer to that of the USA, Canada and Australasia than to most of continental Europe.

Cars were a democratizing mechanism, making work and leisure more accessible. Greater mobility for most, but not all, of the population, however, exacerbated social segregation. Car ownership brought a sense, maybe an illusion, of freedom, and an access to opportunities and options for many, but not all. The division of the population into communities defined by differing levels of wealth, expectations, opportunity and age was scarcely novel. Indeed, in most towns it had developed considerably since the eighteenth century. However, it became more pronounced during the twentieth century, and an obvious aspect of what was termed the 'underclass', in both town and countryside, was their relative lack of mobility. This was doubly important because of links between cars, status, independence and notions of virile masculinity. The theft of cars reflected their appeal.

The response of the cultural world to the changing nature of British society was a vexed one. There was a culture war between the criteria and ranking set by the artistic Establishment that influenced and directed government funding and those that made sense in the vernacular culture of popular taste. This led to issues of taste and influence that divided commentators. The use of governmental patronage on behalf of the artistic Establishment was regarded as normal in the corporatist 1960s and '70s, leading for example to the establishment of the publicly subsidized National Theatre in a new complex on London's South Bank in 1976–7. However, from the 1980s this use of patronage caused more anger, while avant-garde works were regarded by some critics as ridiculous. Thus, the National Lottery grant in 1997 of £78.5 million to update the Royal Opera House in Covent Garden was very controversial, while difficult works of art, such as those of Damien Hirst in the 1990s and Tracey Emin in the 2000s, were criticized.

Conversely, there was also criticism of the ready response to public taste, particularly in the media and other aspects of popular culture. In the play *Comedians* (1975) by the left-wing playwright Trevor Griffiths, those comedians who remain true to their trainer's ideals, and believe that jokes should not exploit prejudices and sustain stereotypes, are rejected by the agent, who is 'not looking for philosophers but for someone who sees what the people want and gives it to them'. In the 1990s there was criticism of the 'dumbing down' of culture, and critics, such as William Best, in his *The Strange Rise of Semi-Literate England* (1991), blamed institutions, such as public libraries and the BBC, for failing to maintain cultural standards. After the National Lottery was introduced in 1994, the BBC gave it publicity by screening the weekly results. Criticism of the BBC for 'dumbing down' was accentuated in 2000 when Blair's ally Greg Dyke became Director-General. For the BBC, modernization seemed to mean a level of accessibility that was equated by critics with crudity and stupidity. However, this accessibility also helped the BBC's ratings. In 2001, for the first time since ITV, the leading terrestrial commercial channel, was launched in 1955, BBC1 replaced it in the top position, in part because of its successful deployment of soaps, especially *EastEnders*, game-shows and reality TV, none of which matched the aspirations of the early days of the BBC when Sir John Reith, the first General Manager (1922–6) and then Director-General (1927–38) had shaped the BBC as a public institution with a social and cultural mission to enlighten as well as entertain, a process helped by the BBC's monopoly position.

The 1960s had destroyed a cultural continuity that had lasted from the Victorian period. This reflected the impact of social and ideological trends, including the rise of new cultural forms as well as a new agenda moulded by shifts in the understanding of gender, youth, class, place and race. That left, however, a cultural world of bewildering complexity. Alongside the apparent continuity in popular culture of works such as *The Mousetrap*, the James Bond films, the novels of Dick Francis and the radio soap *The Archers* appearing throughout the period, there were also important shifts, for example in popular music. Furthermore, works that appeared during the period also changed. *The Archers* responded to social shifts, while, with *GoldenEye* (1995), the Bond films acquired a female 'M', who described Bond as a 'sexist, misogynist dinosaur, a relic of the Cold War', and a Moneypenny who could not remember whether she had 'had' Bond.

Alongside change in continuity, there were major attempts to stress new beginnings, in both style and content. For example, and dramatically so, in the mid-1970s the punk style set out to shock and transform popular culture in reaction to the commercialized world of popular music. Punk was a conscious reaction against the technical wizardry and excessiveness of 'glam rock'. It championed a more archaic approach where the only rule was that there were no rules, an approach that was far from restricted to punk. The most famous punk group to emerge was the Sex Pistols, whose anarchic behaviour soon attracted as much attention as their music. Yet, to reach a wider audience, punk itself had to be taken up by record companies and television, who, in the case of the former, then exploited it for their own financial ends. Tamed in the interests of commercial viability, punk ultimately entered the cultural mainstream, giving birth to new and positive music such as 'two tone' bands, and affecting style in fashion and design. Vivienne Westwood, who first came to prominence because of her links with the Sex Pistols, was, by the 1990s, one of the country's leading fashion designers. The respectability of popular music was also seen when the National Centre for Pop Music opened in Sheffield in 1999, with National Lottery funds, although lack of success led to its closure in 2000.

A different form of transformation was attempted by Virago, an imprint for women's literature, which in 1973 published its first book, *Fenwomen* by Mary Chamberlain. From 1976 its books carried a quotation from *Women, Resistance and Revolution* (1972) by the feminist historian Sheila Rowbotham:

> It is only when women start to organise in large numbers that we become a political force, and begin to move towards the possibility of a truly democratic society in which every human being can be brave, responsible, thinking and diligent in the struggle to live at once freely and unselfishly.

The following year, Virago also set out to recapture an obscured female past with the launch of the Virago Reprint Library. The Virago Modern Classics followed in 1978. Virago played a major role in the careers of a number of feminist writers and thinkers, taking a particularly prominent part in the publication of the works of Margaret Atwood and Angela Carter.

The leading outlines of avant-garde culture were not always easy to discern. In architecture, in a stiff reaction against earlier trends, Modernism was increasingly criticized by conservation movements and on aesthetic grounds. Buildings such as Denys Lasdun's National Theatre (1965–76) and the Institute of Education (1970–78), both in London, were attacked as a 'New Brutalism' lacking a human scale. This attack was popularized by Prince Charles in the 1980s and '90s, not least with his description of the initial plans for the extension to the National Gallery as a 'monstrous carbuncle [facial growth] on the face of an old friend'. He also condemned the plans for the new British Library as 'a dim collection of brick sheds and worse'. By the 1980s

Modernism was also being challenged by a neo-classical revival pioneered by Quinlan Terry.

However, a determination to embrace modern shapes and materials and to focus on functionalism was seen in important works of the late 1990s and early 2000s, such as Nicholas Grimshaw's Eurostar rail terminal at Waterloo and work at Bristol and Stansted airports. Far from being seen as a redundant form, skyscrapers were built and projected in London in the early 2000s, including the one termed the 'erotic gherkin' designed by Norman Foster. Richard Rogers's Millennium Dome and his plans for Terminal 5 at Heathrow airport, Norman Foster's Millennium Bridge in London and his egg-shaped Greater London Assembly, David Libeskind's Imperial War Museum in Manchester, and the award-winning Canary Wharf Tube station, were far removed from neo-classicism, as was the successful Tate Modern. The award of peerages to both Rogers and Foster indicated political interest in architecture.

The prestige of British painting and sculpture remained high. It was recognized and celebrated with prominent exhibitions, such as the Hayward Gallery's account of British conceptual art, 'The New Art', in 1972. Established figures, such as Francis Bacon, Barbara Hepworth and Henry Moore, were joined by younger ones such as Patrick Heron and Peter Howson. Furthermore, with increased interest in performance art, there was a growing determination to break down the gap between performer and audience. Especially true of sculpture, this culminated in 1998 with Antony Gormley's *Angel of the North*. Situated on a panoramic hill south of Gateshead, overlooking both the A1(M) and the East Coast railway line, this work was seen by over 90,000 people daily. It is the most viewed piece of sculpture in Britain.

The *Angel of the North* was a product of public patronage. Gateshead Urban District Council was keen on sculpture as a way to raise artistic consciousness and improve the quality of life. There was also money available in the 1990s from a number of sources, especially the National Lottery. The Arts Council of England Lottery Fund provided £791,000 for the *Angel*. This was a very different cultural context from the working men's clubs, which were especially prominent in northern England, and in the 1990s still numbered more than 3,000, with a total membership of three million. Entertainers there had to be immediately responsive to their audiences, and they tended to focus on traditional themes. It is too easy to overlook such institutions and also forget that, for example, Sheffield's Crucible Theatre was best known from 1977 as the venue for the World Snooker Championships.

The use of public money ensured that, in the 1990s, culture became increasingly a political issue, although it had scarcely been free from controversy in the 1970s and '80s. Then, although there was no consistent widespread popular interest in the place of the arts in society, individual artists had taken political positions. Influenced by Brecht, Howard Brenton probed the nature of power in plays such as *The Churchill Play* (1974) and *The Weapons of Happiness* (1976), and caused controversy with his criticism of government policy in Northern Ireland in *The Romans in Britain* (1980). Edward Bond attacked from a Revolutionary Socialist perspective in his play *The Worlds* (1979). In *Bingo* (1973), Bond had also attacked the nation's cultural icon by presenting Shakespeare as colluding in agrarian exploitation and committing suicide in self-disgust. David Hare's powerful play *Plenty* (1978), which was subsequently made into a film, was a striking account of disillusionment with life in Britain, and this was matched by Howard Barker's *The Hang of the Gaol* (1978). Plays were not the sole forum of criticism. Poetry was used, as by the Glaswegian poet Tom Leonard, while he also turned to prose, as in his *On the Mass Bombing of Kuwait, Commonly Known as the 'Gulf War'* (1992).

A different form of disillusionment was provided by the Bond film *Never Say Never Again* (1983). The porter at Shrublands greeted Bond with the remark that they no longer made cars like his; the new 'M', the head of the intelligence service MI6, had little use for the 00 section, which he saw as redundant, and, instead, was intent on purging toxins from the body by means of a strict diet; and 'Q' complained of slashed budgets, dullness, and rule by bureaucrats and computers. Another aspect of criticism was seen with the popular comedy series *Blackadder*, which closed in 1989 with programmes presenting the First World War as futile, cruel and unheroic.

While the Conservatives were in government, in 1979–97, many critical, radical and anti-authoritarian works included them among their targets. Music was a feature of popular political feeling and was used by New Labour. Labour under Kinnock and Blair has deliberately created a youthful image, compared certainly to the fairly elderly, working-class image it had under James Callaghan, Prime Minister in 1976–9. By appearing in a pop video, Kinnock distanced himself from cloth-cap 'manufacturing' industry in favour of the new industry of music entertainment. The song 'Things can only get better' was used by Labour in 1997 and helped it by creating youth support for change.

In turn, after Labour had returned to power, they received a measure of criticism, especially once the 'honeymoon' period of New Labour had worn thin. Thus, Mick Martin's play *The Life and Times of Young Bob Scallion* (2003) presented Tommy Marchbank, a Bradford crook, willing to turn to pimping, smuggling, extortion and, if necessary, murder, who, having welcomed Thatcherite individualism, becomes a Labour parliamentary candidate in 1997, accurately parroting New Labour-speak and dispensing with his long-term mistress to fit in with Tony Blair's desire for a 'squeaky-clean' image.

Culture was a highly political matter for Thatcherites and they attacked publicly subsidized 'left-wing' theatre. Community theatre, which had flourished in the 1970s, was hit, as subsidies were withdrawn from companies like 7:84, Joint Stock, and Belt and Braces. Conversely, many arts figures, such as the playwright Harold Pinter, attacked the Thatcher and Major governments; meanwhile, the appointment of businessmen as trustees to national museums and galleries led to controversy, although there was no issue comparable to that of the use of Lottery funds in the 1990s. Nor, despite questioning its value, did the Conservatives end the BBC licence fee, which, by 2002, thanks to increases under Labour, brought in £2.5 billion per annum.

The 1990s saw a fierce controversy over whether it was appropriate to charge for entry to museums. This was related to concern about the social position of culture. The Labour government elected in 1997 attacked what it termed cultural elitism, and sought to redirect public patronage in line with its 'Young Country' image. The government quickly found itself embroiled in controversy, not least over the major commitments of public funds to the Royal Opera House. The geographical location of culture was also an issue. There was strong criticism of London's dominant position, not least over the decision to locate the Millennium Dome at Greenwich. Although its subsequent failure led Labour to seek to distance itself from the Dome, the project was seen as an affirmation of the government's determination to modernize Britain, despite its genesis under the Major government. Indeed, in December 1999 Blair rounded on critics of the project whom, he claimed, 'despise anything modern' and stated that the Dome was a 'triumph of confidence over cynicism, boldness over blandness, excellence over mediocrity'. The opening ceremony was similarly used to affirm an image of modernity, but the entire project revealed the folly of Labour's claims.

National institutions were important cultural investments. Thus, the opening of the Tate Modern in London provided a showcase for modern art. Despite the focus on London, there was also a move towards the provinces. A part of the Tate Gallery opened in Liverpool in the 1980s; another part opened in St Ives in Cornwall; there were major developments in Birmingham and Glasgow; the National Museum of Photography, Film and Television opened in Bradford in 1983; and the Royal Armouries moved to Leeds, although it went on to lose a lot of money. The New Art Gallery was opened in Walsall in 2000, and the Lowry Centre, an art gallery and entertainment complex, was established in Salford. Nearby, an Imperial War Museum opened in Manchester. Gateshead gained the Baltic Mill, a contemporary art gallery opened in 2001, with National Lottery funds following for a regional music centre; and Leicester received a National Space Science Centre. The opening in 1997 of a National Museum in Edinburgh devoted to Scottish history was linked to a strengthened sense of national identity.

Such developments were seen as important to local economic regeneration. Museum admission charges were abolished in 2001, in part to the benefit of tourists, but in line with the Labour preference for charges to be born by the taxpayer rather than by service users. Aside from museums outside London, there was also the development of cultural festivals, such as the Orkney Festival, which began in 1976 and became the showcase for the talents of the composer Peter Maxwell Davies.

Debate did not only focus on institutions. There was also concern about the content and morality of modern culture, especially the 'conceptual' Britart that played a prominent role from the late 1980s. The presentation of parts of animals, fixed in formaldehyde, by Damien Hirst, including *The Physical Impossibility of Death in the Mind of Someone Living* (a dead tiger shark), *Away from the Flock* (a dead sheep) and *A Thousand Years* (the head of a slaughtered cow being assailed by flies), and the display of the cast of a house by Rachel Whiteread did not strike everyone as art. This reached a height with the 'Sensation' show at the Royal Academy in 1997, which led to unprecedented media attention on British art. Although Hirst's animals were on display, much of the controversy related to Marcus Harvey's large portrait of the sadistic murderess of children, Myra Hindley, a portrait painted in 1995 with the template of a child's hand. The painting led to controversy within the Academy, with the resignation of four Academicians, while two artists threw ink and eggs respectively at the painting. The range of printed opinion over the exhibition indicated the ability of the arts to focus attention. On the one hand, there was the clash between social convention and individualism, a clash that resonated throughout the century. Other critics saw the show as part of the rhythm of cultural change, with the former rebels having stormed the bastions of the artistic Establishment. This was an aspect of a long-term process in which genres that would not have been considered art, and once-banned works, became lauded classics. Whole areas of experience that had been expressed covertly, such as homosexuality, were given prominence. E. M. Forster's novel about homosexuality, *Maurice*, written in 1913–14, was finally published in 1971, a year after his death, and filmed in 1987.

The debate over fashionable art was given an annual outing in the popular media with the award of prizes to works that did not strike most of the population as art. This was particularly so with the Turner Prize, which was won in 2001 by a light installation. Tracey Emin, an artist not apparently obviously talented in a conventional artistic sense, displayed her unmade bed in an exhibition. In 2002 Ivan Massow, the Chairman of the Institute of Contemporary Arts, was made to resign after he described most conceptual art as 'pretentious, self-indulgent, craftless tat'. He was particularly unimpressed by Emin's work.

Much art, however, was far less controversial. Marcus Harvey's painting tells us less about the possibilities of painting in the 1990s than Howard Hodgkin's explorations of colour and its use to depict emotion. Winner of the Turner Prize in 1984 and knighted in 1992, Hodgkin was a member of a group of British painters who began exhibiting in the 1960s, including Patrick Caulfield and David Hockney, who were of international significance.

Alongside the rhythm of cultural change can be seen a continuing fissure between elite and popular cultural forms, a wide disjuncture between 'high'- and 'low'-brow works. Thus, although Harrison Birtwistle wrote *Grimethorpe Aria* (1973) for the Grimethorpe Colliery Band, a piece still recognized as one of the biggest tests for any brass band wanting to make its mark, the world of most composers played on Radio 3 was different to that of the brass band culture of northern England, while self-consciously intellectual novels such as those of Iris Murdoch, for example *The Sea, The Sea*, which won the 1978 Booker Prize, *The Message to the Planet* (1989) and *The Green Knight* (1993), were a world away from the easy style and clear narrative of the novels of Jeffrey Archer, which followed the model of his accessible first novel *Not a Penny More, Not a Penny Less* (1976). The intellectual interests seen in plays such as Tom Stoppard's *Arcadia* (1993) were far removed from the continued strength of pantomime. The themes and attitudes that characterized critical movements variously termed post-modernism, deconstruction and post-structuralism greatly influenced 'high'-brow works, frequently at the expense of accessibility.

In contrast, the popular fashion for the past led to the 'heritage industry', to period styles, as seen in clothes, furniture, decorations and architecture, and to works such as the film adaptation of classic novels by the Merchant Ivory film company, including E. M. Forster's *A Room with a View* in 1985 and *Howard's End* in 1992. Nostalgia was powerfully presented on television with programmes such as the hugely popular *Dad's Army*, *It Ain't Half Hot Mum* and *Hi-De-Hi*.

There were also parallels between 'high' and 'low' brow. For example, both detective fiction and children's literature from the 1960s tackled issues that would have been generally regarded as inappropriate prior to that decade. In doing so, they lessened the gap in content between them and more 'high'-brow works. By the 1990s, the surrealistic stories of Roald Dahl were the most popular children's works in Britain. His subversion of nursery stories was seen in his *Revolting Rhymes* (1982). In a different tone, Philip Pullman's novels dramatized the closing gap between children's literature and the established canon when his *The Amber Spyglass* (2001) won the Whitbread Prize, the first time a children's book had gained this honour. Like Dahl, Pullman ignored the conventional simplistic morality of the genre and offered an ambiguity more in keeping with life.

J. K. Rowling's Harry Potter novels, which succeeded to Dahl's popularity, were more conventional in their narrative structure and morality. Their success and the revived appeal of J. R. R. Tolkien's *Lord of the Rings* trilogy when films were released in 2001–3 indicated that British culture did not have to ape that of the USA in order to succeed in domestic and foreign markets. The popularity of fantasy worlds was also seen in the novels of Terry Pratchett, such as *The Light Fantastic* (1986).

Dahl was an experimenter, but the overwhelming characteristic of popular 'low'-brow works was a reluctance to experiment with form and style. This division in approach was more widespread than fiction. It also affected other arts, such as architecture, music, painting and sculpture. As a consequence, a pattern of contrast that was set earlier in the century, with the impact of Modernism on 'high'-brow art, remained important to the cultural life of the country. It ensured that there were very differing understandings and experiences of culture and the arts.

This difference was more than a matter of stylistic pluralism. It also reflected the wider cultural politics of a society containing very different levels of income, education and expectation. While there was no automatic link between these different levels and artistic developments, they were very important to the configuration of the cultural life of the people. Gender also played a growing role in cultural identity, not least with the rise of girl bands, especially with the Spice Girls and Atomic Kitten, and with the 'lad lit' and 'chick lit' of the early 2000s.

These different levels of income, education and expectation (as well as gender) were important to other aspects of culture, in its wider sense. In 1990 the death rate for social class 5 males was 26 per cent higher than for social class 1 males. In place of a mid-century stress on a (then) sexy form of consumption – alcohol, cigarettes and gambling, all made glamorous in films – came healthy eating and an emphasis on firm stomachs, gyms and personal trainers. This was partly due to a (middle-class-dominated) shift from enjoying things that were supposed to be bad for one towards the vanities of trying to look good. Smoking (and not going to the gym) was very much part of a dwindling working-class culture, although there was also an increase in the number of women smoking.

Social differences such as these were in part expressed through geographical contrasts, although these were less prominent than in the past. National broadcasting, state education and employment, nationwide companies, unions, products and pastimes, had all brought a measure of convergence that can be seen in the decline of dialect and of distinctive regional practices, as in cooking. Cultural developments were also national, if not wider, in scope. Youth culture for example was universal. Alongside 'soaps', clothes and consumer products that were particularly successful for teenagers, came children's obsessions such as Teenage Ninja Turtles, Teletubbies, Tamagotchi and Pokemon. It was particularly through popular music that Britain contributed to this global culture. This was not only a metropolitan contribution. Scotland, for example, produced bands that had a wider impact, such as the Bay City Rollers in the 1970s, and Wet Wet Wet in the 1980s and '90s. Irish 'boy bands', such as Westlife and Boyzone, rehabilitated Ireland's reputation with the young as not completely full of folk bands and Celtic culture. The role of radio, television and the record industry helped to ensure the national, indeed international, character of popular music, for example the Britpop explosion in the 1990s with groups such as Oasis and the Spice Girls.

Yet, alongside commercially induced homogeneity, there was also a diversity of cultural roots. This was seen in interest in ethnic music, for example, in the 1990s, Bangra, the revival of Irish traditional music via Riverdance, and the greater performance of Scottish traditional music that led to the foundation of a Piping Centre in Glasgow and the launch of an annual Celtic Connections festival there. The extent to which such ethnic or national consciousness would contribute to, or define itself as separate from, more mainstream British elements was an important aspect of the tension over identities that became increasingly apparent in the 1990s and 2000s. Nevertheless, an acceptance of different cultural traditions was seen in June 2002 when the celebration of the Queen's Golden Jubilee brought carnival dancers and gospel singers into the Mall in London.

The strength of Scottish and Welsh cultural distinctiveness was important to their sense of separateness. A distinctive Scottish viewpoint, frequently opposed to that of London, was encouraged by the activities of the two Scottish independent television companies: Scottish Television (1958–) and Grampian Television (1962–). Unlike the BBC, they operated only in Scotland, and also took at least half the viewing audience there. On the other hand, in the mid-1990s, 50 per cent of the Scottish sales of tabloid newspapers were of London titles and 75 per cent of those of the 'quality' press. James Kelman's novel *How Late It Was, How Late* (1994), a prominent Scottish literary declaration of cultural self-determination, was published in London by an English publisher and won the Booker Prize, a national award. The novel was an account of a drunken former convict stumbling along the main streets of Glasgow, which, four years earlier, had been the 'European City of Culture'. Another comment on Glasgow was provided by the television series *Taggart*, which depicted it as very violent.

In Wales a campaign of public protest forced the Thatcher government to honour its promise to establish a Welsh-language television channel. This was yet another example of the extent to which Wales took a disproportionate share of national expenditure, although it took Gwynfor Evans's threat to starve himself to pressure the government into honouring its pledge to set up the channel, s4c (which began transmitting in 1982). It carried English subtitles on some of its more popular programmes. Language in Wales carries with it an emotional force denied most political issues other than religion, and, in the case of some, there was a transfer of energy from religion to language.

A consensus around a compromise about the place of the Welsh language emerged in the 1980s. The compulsory teaching of Welsh in schools has been accepted with relatively little opposition, and Welsh-language schools have developed in anglicized areas.

Language was far less important as an issue in Scotland, although efforts were made to encourage Gaelic and Scots. The Western Isles Council began a bilingual English/Gaelic policy in 1975, but its impact was hampered by the dominant role of English, especially on television. Although Gaelic-medium schools were established in 1985 in the Highlands and in the Western Isles in the 1980s, the 1991 census revealed a pronounced fall in the use of Gaelic by children, and in 2002 only 1,900 pupils attended such schools. By then, Gaelic was spoken by only 60,000 people, about 1 per cent of the Scottish population.

A more direct form of identity was provided by the naming of children. In 1997 and 1998 the most frequently chosen names for newborn children registered in England and Wales were Jack and Chloe, the names of the oft-discussed children of the presenters of the television programme *This Morning*. Other television- and film-linked names whose popularity rose in 1998 included Courtney, Caitlin, Phoebe and Ethan. That year, John, the most common name earlier in the century, was no longer in the top 50. The following year, the great event, as far as the popular press were concerned, was the marriage of the footballer David Beckham and the popular music personality 'Posh' Spice, a marriage carried out as if they were an alternative crowned couple. Reports that Beckham might move to play for a Spanish team, as he in the event did, kept journalists busy in 2003.

The impact of the media was not restricted to names and faces. There could also be political consequences in terms of shifting identities. Thus, an error-strewn American film like *Braveheart* (1995), which depicted opposition to Edward I of England in the 1290s and 1300s, could help to energize an already strong sense of national distinctiveness in Scotland. Films, novels and other works also commented on the changing nature of British society. The most readily apparent characteristic was the number of works published, which was a commentary on the strength of British literary life, the breadth of the domestic book-reading public, the ability of publishers to respond to new interests, and the role of English as a universal language. Indeed, many of the works published in Britain were by foreign-born authors, whether resident or not. This was true, for example, of the works of Salman Rushdie.

As an indication of variety among the chroniclers of British life it is possible to point to Joanna Trollope (1943–) and Martin Amis (1949–). The former was noted for what were unkindly termed 'Aga-sagas', novels about rural life among the comfortably off that focused on personal relationships, for example *The Best of Friends* (1995) and *Marrying the Mistress* (2000). Her sales testified to the appeal of rural themes, which were also seen in the popularization of images of rural and provincial England in the long-running BBC radio soap opera, *The Archers*, and in the BBC television comedy series *Last of the Summer Wine*. Launched in 1973, the latter had audiences of up to 16 million by the early 1980s. Filmed in the Yorkshire town of Holmfirth, it depicted an attractive countryside around a small Pennine town in which people could readily wander. Furthermore, this celebration of northernness and the Pennine environment was presented in terms of a comedy of character that played on another aspect of the national self-image, tolerance of eccentricity. In the series the disreputable, grubby, poorly dressed, ferret-keeping Compo was presented positively.

Amis is the son of the novelist Kingsley Amis (1922–95), who had shown a criticism of modern social developments in books such as *Jake's Thing* (1978). London provided the unsettling backdrop for Martin Amis's novels *Money* (1984), *London Fields* (1989) and *The Information* (1995). His was a depiction of a society and cityscape under strain, buckling under the pressure of change. A troubled view of London, specifically the docklands, can also be noted in Iain Sinclair's novel *Downriver; Or, The Vessels of Wraths* (1991), while the ambiguities of the city's past emerge from the novels of Peter Ackroyd (1949–), for example *Hawksmoor* (1985), *The House of Doctor Dee* (1993) and *The Clerkenwell Tales* (2003). Some of the films of the period, such as *Mona Lisa* (1986), showed London as patterned by crime, with class, sex and race suffused by themes of individualism that some critics linked to Thatcherism. Even in *Sliding Doors* (1997), a romantic film set in London, an attack by a mugger plays an important role in the plot.

An even bleaker eye was cast on Edinburgh by the detective writer Ian Rankin (1960–). His is a city of gangsters and corruption, where development, whether of Leith's dockside or the new Parliament, is inseparable from violence and the malaise of the ignored, such as the 'greasy Venetian blinds and kicked-in passageways of the tenements in Easter Road or Gorgie' (short story 'Playback'). The drugs aspect of Scottish youth culture was emphasized in Irvine Welsh's novel about the grim Glasgow drug scene, *Trainspotting* (1993), which was filmed in 1996, and drugs returned as a theme in his *The Acid House* (1994) and *Marabou Stork Nightmares* (1995). Drugs also played a role in the lyrics of popular music.

A different form of bleakness, one not lit by the distorting, self-absorbed light of drugs, was the account of life on Glaswegian buses offered by James Kelman in his novel *The Bus-conductor Hines* (1984). The harshness of urban life and environment was also captured by playwrights such as Mike Leigh and Stephen Poliakoff; although it was not all gloom. Humour also played a major role in the depiction of urban life. This could be seen in *The Full Monty* (1997), a film that clearly showed unemployment and urban decay in Sheffield, and in works that engaged with issues of inter-racial relations, such as Zadie Smith's novel *White Teeth* (2000), which was set in London, and the film *Bend It Like Beckham* (2002).

More generally, the largest city (or cities) in any region, for example Bristol, Leeds, Newcastle and Norwich, remain very important to cultural horizons. Manchester in the 1990s was compared with Milan (although not by many Milanese). Manchester was not alone in developing cultural and other aspirations, but London's long-held position remained strong. The new world of 'executive' houses, out-of-town shopping centres, industrial parks and cars, always cars, has attracted less attention from writers, but it is an Americanized landscape and sheen best captured on, and by, television. Consumerism has made this world a shared aspiration and lifestyle for many. Instead, it is the city, especially the inner city, that dominates most fiction, for it is there that change plays through the human drama with most intensity and pungency.

Chapter 3

Environment under Strain

Westway had, after all, been relatively prosperous, a comfortable enclave of the respectable, reliable, law-abiding lower middle class who owned their houses and took a pride in clean lace curtains and carefully tended front gardens, each a small triumph of individuality over the drab conformity. But their world was crashing down with their houses, rising in great choking clouds of ochre dust. Only a few houses were now left standing as the work on the road-widening went inexorably ahead ... Soon there would be nothing but tarmac and the ceaseless roar and screech of traffic thundering westward out of London. In time even memory would be powerless to conjure up what once had been.

A Certain Justice (1997), novel by P. D. James

The major pressure on the environment seen earlier in the twentieth century, as technological change, particularly the car, and greater disposable wealth pressed home the human impact, did not abate in its closing decades. Indeed, in some respects, these pressures gathered pace, both then and in the 2000s, not least as estimates of the anticipated need for the number of dwellings were revised upwards to take note, first, of social changes, especially the rise in the percentage of single-parent families, and, secondly, of higher than expected rates of immigration. Demands for new housing led to a remoulding of the visible environment, and also contributed to a sense of excessive change, if not crisis. This was important as the landscape was central to images of place and, indeed, for many, nationhood. Thus, the sense of environmental challenge was significant to a wider angst about identity.

WILDLIFE

House building and road construction represented particularly potent assaults on the environment, diminishing the possibility of animals and humans sharing territory. By the 1990s between 3,000 and 3,500 barn owls were killed on UK roads each year, joining large numbers of rabbits, hedgehogs, badgers, deer and other animals. Pressure on animal habitats also became more insistent as a result of changes in agricultural practice, which radically altered the way in which the remaining land was farmed. The loss of grassland was significant, but changes in grassland management, especially more intensive stocking of pastures and the switch from hay to silage making, which destroys nests, were also very important.

Birdlife was hard hit by agrarian change. The number of skylarks fell by about 50 per cent in 1976–98, while that of grey partridge fell by about 80 per cent, due in large part to the destruction of nesting sites when hedgerows were grubbed up, and the reduction in insect food. Hedgerows also provided birds with food supplies and cover. The falling number of rooks gave cause for concern from the mid-1970s: it was partly blamed on chemicals, specifically the pesticides used extensively in agriculture. On the whole, lowland species of birds were more seriously affected than their upland counterparts by housing developments and agricultural changes, in large part because more upland was protected and because agriculture there was less intensive. Nevertheless, upland species were also affected by these changes, in part due to overgrazing as sheep density rose in response to the farm subsidy regime for marginal farmland. In the lowlands, the drastic reduction in wetland habitats as they were drained was a particular problem for birdlife. For example, the fall in the number of reed-beds hit the number of bitterns and reed buntings in the Fens. Among common birds, there have been major declines in the number of swallows, house sparrows and starlings. 'We don't hear the birds anymore', was a frequent comment made to me by city-dwellers when I was discussing this book.

Other forms of wildlife were also badly affected by human action. The destruction of hedgerows and wetlands ensured that more than 78 per cent of the breeding colonies of the pipistrelle bat, the most numerous bat, were lost in 1979–98; while bats as a whole were hit by the increasing use of timber preservatives in the old buildings they used as breeding sites. The loss of habitats in sand dunes, salt marshes and heathlands largely wiped out the natterjack toad; and the filling-in of ponds, in which they bred, badly hit the great-crested newt. The rise in underdrainage has reduced the amount of water in surface water channels, hitting the frog. Like other animals, it has also been affected by the impact of herbicides and pesticides on its food supplies. The brown hare is in chronic decline due to changing agricultural methods, especially 'prairie farming', with its destruction of hedgerows, and an increase in the fox population.

Far from being inconsequential, such changes made rarer many sights and sounds that had once characterized the country. The diminution (and even disappearance) of the dawn chorus in several parts of the country, and the decline in the number of butterfly species, was a particularly poignant indicator of loss to changes in land use, as well as pollution and pesticides. The spring became more silent thanks to the massive decline of common garden birds like song thrushes, although their numbers were also hit hard by predators, especially sparrow-hawks.

Human pressure on wildlife was not all one way. The Welsh red kite was brought back from the brink of extinction. In addition, the numbers of some species, especially the otter, great spotted wood-pecker, the stock dove and the magpie, have risen, while the numbers of many species in the 1990s were stable, sparrow-hawks for example.

Efforts were made to protect animals. The breeding sites of creatures such as bats and the nests of hornets became protected. The cleaning up of rivers such as the Mersey and the Thames led to the return of fish, including, after £1 billion of expenditure over two decades, salmon to the Mersey estuary. However, the pressure was mostly one way. The designation of particular protective areas was generally linked to a deterioration of the situation elsewhere, and was, indeed, commonly a response to it. This was also true of National Parks. Alongside the ten in England and Wales created in 1951–7 after the 1949 Act, came measures to add comparable protection to the Norfolk Broads (1998), the New Forest (1999) and the South Downs (1999).

FORESTRY

Plants were also badly hit by environmental pressures. Wild plants were affected by the use of more powerful chemical fertilizers and herbicides, while hedgerows were grubbed up, the latter an issue mentioned by John Major. The aggregate figures for acreage under trees, which, unlike the length of hedgerows, did not decline, nevertheless concealed a major shift. The dominant tree cover became coniferous. This was linked to an increase in the area of woodland, which rose to 9 per cent of the UK in 2000. Scotland was the major area of planting, but there is a plan for an increase of woodland to 15 per cent of England by 2050, in part by planting 30 million trees in a 'National Forest' in the Midlands. This would improve the measure of 'Ecological Footprint' in Britain and the country's position on the Carbon Index, because Britain's absorption of carbon dioxide would improve. Currently, the figures for Britain do not compare well with the international averages.

The 1981 Forestry Act encouraged private planting by increasing tax incentives. As a consequence, actors, football stars and others seeking tax-breaks were attracted into forestry. In environmental terms, it had an impact comparable to that of the better-known 1980 Housing Act in the cities. The rationale of the Thatcher government was the same: harnessing private enterprise by tax incentives, and the target was similar. Public ownership, in the shape of the Forestry Commission, was to play a smaller role as a consequence of the Act, after which the overwhelming majority of upland plantings was by private enterprise. The government also forced the Commission to sell off part of its estate.

However, afforestation had serious environmental consequences in terms of wildlife, plant variety and visual amenity. The tree monoculture and the absence of undergrowth hit the bird population and the range of bird species, while the numbers of plant species declined. Open land was forested to the anger of walkers and others. There have also been consequences for water availability and soil fertility, with the soil often becoming more acidic.

At the same time, in marked contrast to timber policies in authoritarian societies, such as the Soviet Union, there has been a welcome responsiveness to concerns and criticism. This is particularly the case with the sensitive issue of visual amenity, and also in response to concern about monoculture. The two problems have been tackled by the use of deciduous belts in lowland areas, which provide more diffuse and varied forest edges.

The local impact of forestry policy has been considerable. This is particularly true of afforestation, both in established areas of woodland and in others such as the new Community Forests. The most sensitive issue is that of access and recreational use, which are more restricted under private owners. In addition, there has been particular concern about the effect of afforestation in specific environments. The Flow (peat bog) Country of Caithness and Sutherland was an important instance, as afforestation there hit drainage patterns and soil structure in a very vulnerable environment, with major impact on the peat and on local wildlife. More generally, peat bogs were hit by the demand by gardeners for peat for compost. This led the National Trust in 2003 to move to selling peat-free compost.

Terrains were also altered by other human actions during the period, especially by road building. The Skye road bridge and the Channel Tunnel linked islands to the mainland. The Tunnel was opened to rail travel in 1992. With an overall length of nearly 2,200 metres, the Humber Bridge, built in 1972–80, was the longest single-span bridge in the world until the Akashi-Kaikyo bridge in Japan was opened in 1998. The A9 was taken across the Dornoch Firth on an 800-metre bridge.

More generally, economic growth, greater affluence and more people posed major environmental problems. Coastal waters were heavily polluted by sewerage outflows and this led the bacteria found in human waste, such as faecal coliform, to thrive. Oil spills, such as that by the *Braer* in 1993, in which 85,000 tonnes were spilt, and one on the Pembrokeshire coast in 1996 from the beached tanker *Sea Empress*, in which 76,000 tonnes were split, did terrible damage. Lead emissions from traffic seriously affected air quality, as did emissions from aircraft. Industrial pollution was responsible for 'acid rain', which damaged woodland, rivers and lakes. High-stack emissions from power stations spread pollution far and wide. Although sulphur dioxide emissions were reduced by the use of cleaner techniques at power stations, there was a rise in nitrogen oxides, ammonia and photochemical smog. One consequence was a problem with ozone levels.

The extent to which legislation was able to keep up with contaminants in the air varied. Thus, the burning of stubble after the harvest became a major problem in the 1980s, as it increasingly replaced ploughing the straw in. The resulting fires pushed up ammonia levels, but they were banned from 1993. Car emissions and greenhouse gases will not be so easy to tackle.

WATER

Environmental pressure took many forms. It affected, for example, water availability, noise and light. Increased use of water, thanks, in part, to the use of hosepipes for washing cars and watering gardens, more toilets, baths and showers, and appliances such as washing machines and dishwashers, placed great demands on water reserves, and led to the depletion of natural aquifers and to restrictions on water use. In 1990 hosepipe bans affected 20 million customers. Greater demands for water exacerbated droughts, such as that of 1995, and encouraged water-metering. Government plans for regional development in the South-East were criticized in 2003 for their failure to take note of problems in water supply, for example near Ashford.

There was a powerful regional dimension to water supply. Development in the South-East exacerbated the strain on water supplies and emphasized the problems stemming from the absence of a national water grid. As a result, the reuse of water is particularly high in the South-East, with recycled water, on average, flowing through several people as a result of the system of treatment plants. Some new reservoirs have also been built in the last thirty years, particularly Kielder and Rutland Waters, and the Cow Green Reservoir in Upper Teesdale. Kielder on the North Tyne, completed at a cost of £150 million in 1982, and filled in 1983, is the largest reservoir in northern Europe and, via pipelines, it can supply demand in the Wear and Tees valleys. Ironically, the Teesside chemical industry, which had been seen as a major consumer of this water, became less important after the reservoir was opened. Tension over reservoir flooding has remained a major issue in upland and lowland valleys, and is a reminder of the close relationship of local with national politics.

Ground water levels were put under pressure from the use, by means of pumping, of ground water sources (in addition to surface waters, reservoirs and rivers). This led to a notable drop in the water level across much of the country, causing the seasonal disappearance of rivers or sections of rivers from the 1980s, for example part of the River Ver in Hertfordshire. Recharge schemes, involving replenishment by surplus water when available, have had only limited success in tackling this problem and are expensive. Ironically, under London the water table has been rising as industrial extraction, for example by breweries, has declined. As an instance of major projects for environmental change, concern about water availability has led to interest in estuarine barrages, for example the Cardiff Barrage project.

Water quality (purity) was also an issue, and one of greater sensitivity as growing public concern encouraged a huge boom in the sale of bottled water. The marked increase in nitrogen levels in ground water was in part due to the greater leaching of artificial fertilizer run-off from agriculture. Industrial effluent and sewage were also problems. An indication of the potential consequences was provided by the increase of oestrogens in river water, which appears to have resulted in changes in the sexual characteristics of fish. Water quality in lakes has also been an issue, while the cleanliness of inshore waters has concerned the European Union. This led to directives and proceedings in order to reduce outflows of raw sewage. Industrial waste is also a problem in coastal waters and nearby seas, with high levels of metals flowing into the sea from rivers, as well as material being deposited and leaching from oil rigs. Effluent from the Sellafield nuclear processing plant in the Irish Sea is of particular concern around its coasts, although public attention led to a decline in the quantity of radioactive caesium in the Irish Sea, especially from the late 1980s.

AGRICULTURE

Agricultural practices have also been linked to far higher rates of soil erosion. Agriculture has become more heavily mechanized, and rising land values, and the reliance of many farmers on loans, have led to a greater determination to use every scrap of land to the maximum short-term profit. In particular, the grubbing up of hedgerows in order to facilitate the use of farm machinery has helped exacerbate run-off, while the change to crops such as maize has increased pressure on soil fertility. The shift from organic to easier-to-apply chemical fertilizer is another problem, while the ploughing up of grassland has exacerbated the issue of soil retention. Soil erosion has been linked to the flooding of houses and roads: both reflect greater rates of run-off. Urbanization has also increased run-off as water has not been able so readily to move down through the soil.

Other agrarian shifts driven by the nature of the fiscal-economic context include the rise of specialization and the consequent decline of mixed farming. Arable farmers now buy their milk and meat in supermarkets: most have no farm animals. In addition, new crops reflected financial opportunities and made an impact, not least visually. This was especially true of maize, of the striking yellow colour of oil-seed rape, particularly from the 1970s, and of the pale blue of European Union-subsidized flax in the 1990s.

The larger scale of production, not least the factory farming of chickens, and the greater use of machines also ensured that farm buildings became larger and more obtrusive. Old barns, built with local building materials, were replaced by the utilitarian factory designs of modern barns, silos and other buildings.

A sense of malaise became especially strong in many parts of rural Britain in the 1990s and 2000s. Much of this malaise was economic – a combination of low agricultural commodity prices, greater foreign competition, a strong pound (which hit exports and helped imports), a public health crisis in beef production, falling consumption of dairy products, decreasing domestic and foreign markets for British pork, and the major role of supermarket chains as purchasers. In addition, the abolition of the statutory Milk Marketing Board for England and Wales in 1994 changed the regulation of the dairy industry from a state-controlled producer corporatism to control by retailers, and thus to a buyer's market, which adversely affected dairy farmers.

Pressures on farming hit, or at least influenced, the rest of the rural economy, as well as that of small towns. A more general sense that government and urban society no longer cared about rural society was also important. A survey of adults in 2003 indicated that two-thirds had never met a farmer, while nine out of ten people had no direct connection with British agriculture. Given the role of the countryside in sustaining traditional images of Englishness, this was particularly striking.

The cash nexus is such that it is through subsidies that attempts have been made to protect the rural identity. The Wildlife and Countryside Act of 1981 established Sites of Special Scientific Interest, which were partly protected from 'damaging agricultural operations'. Under the Agriculture Act of 1986, farmers were paid to 'set aside' land from farming or to adopt less intensive farming methods: £900 million was spent as a result in 1994 alone. This indicated the subordination of the traditional rural role of producing food. In addition to these 'set-aside' schemes, Environmentally Sensitive Areas, Countryside Stewardship schemes and Nitrate Sensitive Areas have been introduced or designated.

Development pressure led to tension over planning regulations, both in designated areas, such as National Parks, and elsewhere. Close to cities this pressure was affected by Green Belt legislation, although this generally simply led to development beyond the belt and to a rise in commuting, as with Cambridge, London and Oxford.

All of these measures reflect a human-based approach to environmental developments, but many changes to the land surface, instead, reflect geomorphological processes. This is true of slope erosion and of the frequency of landslides, as on the Dorset and Holderness coasts and at Scarborough.

ENERGY

The production and consumption of increasing quantities of material goods meant a greater use of energy, despite increases in energy efficiency. In 1987 each person was using an average of the equivalent of 6.2 tonnes of coal per year, although the use of coal in fact declined, especially from the 1980s, while oil, natural gas and nuclear power became more important in meeting British energy needs. In 1990, 158 million tons of carbon dioxide were dispersed into the environment above Britain. The position of the nuclear power industry, which by 2003 was producing about 25 per cent of the country's electricity (including a far higher percentage in Scotland), added to the contentiousness of energy issues. In the 1950s this industry had largely been seen in a positive light, with nuclear power as a clean fuel of the future that would replace coal and oil. From the 1970s, however, there was increasing criticism of the safety and environmental threats posed by the industry. This even resonated in popular culture. In the Bond film *The Man with the Golden Gun* (1974), 'M' referred to the energy crisis and told James Bond that the depletion of coal and oil and the dangers of uranium ensured that Britain had to think of solar energy. The reprocessing of nuclear fuel at Sellafield was a particular cause of public and governmental concern. In addition, the decision in 1985 to study the feasibility of four sites as near-surface radioactive waste repositories led to strong public protests that caused the end of the study in 1987 and the decision, instead, to look at deeper repositories.

Renewable energy sources were the most politically acceptable, and in 2003 a White Paper set out the goal of a 60 per cent fall in greenhouse gas emissions by 2050, a figure far greater than that agreed under the Kyoto Protocol of 1997. It was intended that renewables, such as wind turbines on wind farms, would provide 20 per cent of the country's energy by 2020, but it was also hoped to achieve a cleaner use of fossil fuels. By requiring electricity generators and suppliers to purchase some of their power from renewable sources, the Blair government helped the development of this, otherwise, uneconomic source of energy. It also ignored aesthetic concerns about the ugliness of the massive wind turbines, as well as environmental concerns about the disruption that resulted from digging their foundations.

The rise in interest in renewable energy, as an aspect of the increasingly prominent goal of sustainability, was the latest stage in what had been a very fast-changing energy sector that responded to domestic and international shifts, not least those in government policy. Politics played a major role: the National Union of Miners and Arab oil producers both posed problems for energy providers and planners. This made reliable domestic sources of power more economically attractive. Aside from North Sea oil and natural gas, this encouraged a search for both in Britain and nearby waters, for example in Dorset and the Irish Sea. In addition, the lower cost of open-cast coal-mining and the less militant nature of its workforce led to a major shift towards this form of production. When the 1984 miners' strike began, one of the first acts of the militants was to damage vehicles at open-cast workings.

Pressure to reduce global warming stemmed from the evident rise in temperatures from 1976. When periodic falls in temperature occurred after 1976, in every case they were to a higher level than the temperature in the mid-1970s. Global warming was also an accelerating process. It ensured that climatic zones moved geographically, leading to predictions of major environmental changes in Britain. These included alterations in climate, vegetation and disease, as well as water shortages, coastal flooding due to higher sea levels, particularly on the south and east coasts, more extreme weather conditions and, possibly, a fundamental shift in the Gulf Stream leading to a far colder Britain. At the present, however, the trend is toward bouts of heavy rainfall and higher summer temperatures, the latter seen particularly in 2003. This trend has indirect as well as direct consequences: decreased summer run-off from the rainfall that occurs then will lead to higher concentrations of pollutants in surface water and to a reduction in oxygen in the water.

RUBBISH

Aside from higher temperatures, the consumer society also produced greater and greater quantities of rubbish, much of it non-biodegradable and some of it toxic. By 1999 up to 76 million tonnes of commercial waste and up to 29 million tonnes of industrial waste were being produced annually. By 2002 about 30 million tonnes of garbage were being generated, with the figure growing at an annual rate of 3 per cent. Only about 8 per cent of the household waste was recycled, although the percentage for other types was higher. The rise of rubbish was a product of rising affluence and of the transformation of material culture, including major changes in packaging.

Kitchen and garden waste, and newspapers and magazines, were the largest categories of household waste, but other types also posed major demands. In Devon alone, by 1999, 80,000 disposable nappies were being buried each day. Rubbish disposal was increasingly a problem for both local government and business, not least because of greater public sensitivity about the means and locations of landfill. Finding suitable landfill sites became a serious problem, but there was widespread opposition to the alternative of incineration due to fears about the production of toxic chemicals. As a consequence, there was increasing pressure by the early 2000s to encourage recycling, which, indeed, hitherto was limited by the standards of most Western European countries, and to use charges in order to get people to separate out recyclable material.

NOISE AND LIGHT

Noise and light pollution also became serious problems. The Countryside Commission's map of tranquil areas showed that an area five times the size of Kent was lost to tranquillity in England between the early 1960s and the early 1990s. This was especially a problem in lowland areas, although in upland areas, such as the Cheviots and the Brecon Beacons, and moorlands, such as Dartmoor and Woodbury Common, military training can be very noisy. Concern over noise divided communities, with some rural 'incomers' complaining about the noise of weekend harvesting, while others also remonstrated about farmyard smells. Across the country, traffic was a particularly potent source of noise. By the late 1990s noise was the biggest source of complaints to local authorities, ahead of rubbish or litter, and, in 1996, the Noise Act made it possible to confiscate offending hi-fi equipment.

Light pollution, a new concept, ensured that it was difficult across much of the country to see stars in the night sky. The Council for the Protection of Rural England and the British Astronomical Association reported in 2003 that light pollution spread during the 1990s, so that the area of the English countryside with pure dark skies fell by 27 per cent; and by 2000 only 11 per cent of England was free from light pollution. More locally, sleep was affected by continuous lighting.

A problem that fused visual amenity and health concerns was that created by the construction of high structures in rural areas, especially electricity pylons, and television and telephone masts. Anxiety about their consequences for health led to much stronger opposition to the erection of such structures in the early 2000s, when, in turn, the pace of new schemes was dramatically increased by mobile telephone operators and the particular requirements of the police for coverage. The resulting local agitations and hearings were a ready register of concern about development, and its ability to bridge social divides. In 2003 the regulars at my favourite pub were vexed by this issue, and a mast at another nearby site was destroyed one night.

TRANSPORT

Tranquillity was particularly affected by the continued rise of the car. There were 12.2 million in Britain in 1970, and over 20 million in 1995, a rise far greater than that in population. Car ownership rose from 224 per 1,000 people in 1971 to 380 per 1,000 in 1994. Two-car families became more common: 40.3 per cent of households in affluent South Cambridgeshire in 1991 had two or more cars. Whereas there was one car for every five Scots in 1978, in 1996 there was one for every two. In 1997 John Prescott, the minister in charge of transport, claimed that by 2002 more people would be taking public transport and fewer using cars. The former, but not the latter, was to be proved correct.

The greater use of cars was linked to a major shift in energy use: whereas, in 1950, oil had provided an equivalent of one-tenth of the calorific value of coal, by 1970 they were equal. This reflected changing demand as well as a fall in the relative price of oil to about three-quarters of that of home-produced coal. Although the OPEC price rise of petrol in 1973 increased the cost of driving, and it was always greater than in the USA, pre-tax British petrol prices were then held down both by the discovery of oil under the North Sea and by a major fall in the world price in the 1980s and '90s.

People not only bought cars; they also used them for work and leisure. The average distance travelled each day per person rose to about 39 km (24 miles) by 2000, an increase of three-quarters over a quarter-century. This helped drive a demand for more space, for both roads and associated infrastructure, such as garages: in 1985–90 an additional 15,000 hectares were used for these ends. A fictional reference was offered in Douglas Adams's radio series and novel *The Hitch-Hiker's Guide to the Galaxy* (1979), which rested on the idea that Earth had been demolished to further an inter-stellar bypass.

In rural areas, it has been particularly hard to resist the impact of the car. This has facilitated the mobility of most rural consumers, but in turn this has led to the closure of many rural schools, shops, pubs, churches and post offices. By 2000, 42 per cent of rural parishes had no permanent shop, 49 per cent no school and 75 per cent no daily bus service. Central government attempted to assist bus transport by offering Rural Bus Grants from 1997, and the deregulation of bus services outside London in 1986 led to investment by big operators, especially Stagecoach, but the buses were increasingly used only by the poor, the elderly and the young. Park and ride schemes, such as that introduced in Cambridge in 1999, mean, however, that buses are likely to play a greater role in urban transport as an adjunct to cars.

Car culture affected, and was affected by, other aspects of social development. It was linked to changes in employment patterns. In place of factories or mines dependent on large labour forces, most modern industrial concerns are capital intensive and employ less labour. They are often located away from the central areas of cities on flat and relatively open sites with good road links. Car-park space is considered as important to the attraction of sites as access routes. This is also true of business, science and shopping 'parks'.

Related changes in location have also been of great importance in such areas as education, health, shopping and retirement. Whereas, in 1971, 14 per cent of junior schoolchildren were driven to school, by 1990 the percentage had risen to 64. Conversely, the percentage walking, cycling and going by bus fell, an aspect of the declining use of public space and one related to the increase in obesity and unfitness among children.

The car had a direct impact on the environment, producing carbon monoxide, black smoke and photochemical smog. This toxicity helped poison the air. It also contributed to the new geography of air pollution. This was not the sole impact. For example, the space occupied by cars was accentuated by the development of car dealerships occupying large sites on suburban and out-of-town 'industrial' parks, most of which were, instead, devoted to car-borne retail.

Rising levels of car use put major strains on the national network and on local road systems. At the national level, growing congestion and increasing delays led to pressure to supplement existing roads. The Oxford to Birmingham section of the M40, opened in January 1991, was designed to supplement the overstrained M1 as a route between London and the Midlands. In 1997 a second road bridge was opened across the Severn. The M25 around London became the busiest route in the country and, because of frequent traffic jams, there were soon plans to add more lanes. There were also major improvements on other routes, as roundabouts and junctions along trunk roads such as the A1 and the A30 were replaced by slip-roads. In turn, new roads and infrastructure were heavily used, as traffic responded to new opportunities, particularly new links in the national road system, which were fewer than in Western Europe and the USA. In Cambridgeshire, between 1982 and 1995, traffic on the mostly new A14 and the new M11 increased by close to 300 per cent; in the same period, it grew by over 100 per cent on the older-established A10 between Ely and Cambridge.

There was no comparable expenditure on new rail infrastructure, with the exception of the 110 kilometres (70 miles) of Channel Tunnel rail link. Thus Britain lacked the new high-speed rail links increasingly being developed on the Continent, although there were improvements to rolling stock. The InterCity 125, a high-speed diesel train capable of travelling at 200 km/h (125 mph), was introduced in 1976. The tilting Advanced Passenger Train did not prove a success, but, on the East Coast main line from London to Edinburgh, fully electrified 225s, capable of travelling at 225 km/h (140 mph), were introduced in 1991.

Although there was a steady growth of passenger traffic on major rail routes in the 1990s and 2000s, train travel has become relatively more marginal as a consequence of the continued rise of the car and lorry, while the development of low-cost air traffic added competition for long-distance routes, especially between England and Scotland. The rail system did, however, avoid the dramatic cuts proposed in the Serpell Report of 1983. This would have reduced the system to 2,600 kilometres (1,600 miles), essentially a few major routes. Instead, the system has stabilized at about 17,700 kilometres (11,000 miles), just over half the inter-war network. Given the greater use of road transport, problems with rail were less significant for the bulk of the population than increased congestion on the roads.

This is even more the case with freight transport, most of which moves by road as a result of improvements in the road network and problems with rail transport, not least the limited flexibility of the system. Warehousing increasingly responded to road-based supplies. In 1999, 5 per cent of British freight was moved by rail, a figure well below that in Germany and France.

Nevertheless, the failure to improve the rail system, which was privatized in 1996, helped to accentuate concern that the British were unable to improve their infrastructure, as an aspect of a wider failure to fulfil grand projects. In 1998 the government's Comprehensive Spending Review declared that the country suffered from 'an overcrowded, under-planned and under-maintained transport system'. In 2000 grave limitations in the safety of the network and its ability to respond to bad weather were revealed, and an emergency programme of track replacement was launched to tackle broken rails after a fatal crash at Hatfield in October. Passenger numbers rose considerably after privatization, by 20 per cent in 1997–2001, but this was at the cost of overcrowding. Punctuality has diminished, and much of the rail system is in need of replacement.

Transport infrastructure improvements faced major problems due to the crowded nature of Britain and the cost of projects; but these were not the only issues. In London, it proved difficult to ensure backing for the rebuilding of an increasingly obsolete Underground system through a public–private partnership. The difficulty of ensuring such a partnership, for example by establishing an effective performance regime, discouraged investment, and delay helped to push up costs.

At the neighbourhood level, major road routes became obstacles, as high streets, such as Crediton's, became increasingly busy through routes. This encouraged the building of new through routes unrelated to existing neighbourhoods, but these also caused blight and damage. Those neighbourhoods that were not bisected in this fashion were still affected by the car. Side streets became 'rat runs', quick shortcuts linking busier roads, and the sides of all roads filled up with parked cars. Parking space came to take a greater percentage of city space, and a more dominant role in townscapes, and the problems of parking became a major topic of conversation. So was the digging up of roads, a process facilitated by the New Roads and Street Works Act of 1991. The repeated digging up of the same stretch of road by utility companies seemed to show, at the local level, the same failure to execute policies successfully that was more widely held to characterize British administration at the national level. Road schemes were politically contentious and led to opposition between local interests, most obviously over proposals for bypasses, for example that at Newbury, which finally opened in 1998.

Car and home ownership, both aspects of consumerism and public culture, had a major impact on the environment, but the effect of this on government policy was limited. Government, both national and local, was constrained by public unwillingness to accept restrictions on individual freedom. Thus, in 2000, the attempt to push up fuel duties was resisted by demonstrations of anger that led to the blockade of petrol storage depots, and to the Conservatives briefly passing Labour in the public opinion polls; in 2003, however, it proved possible to introduce a congestion charge in central London. Motorway tolls appeared a more serious challenge, but, on a systematic basis, were ruled out by the government until at least 2011. Despite its proclaimed wish to discourage road use, seen in a White Paper in 1998, the Labour government found it difficult to take meaningful steps to shift the balance towards public transport, and thus, in the face of congestion, had to respond to pressure not to abandon road building. In 2002 Alistair Darling, the newly appointed Secretary of State for Transport, rejected the idea of toll motorways in parallel with free ones: 'Britain isn't big enough for us to be pouring more and more concrete over its green and pleasant land'. But that was what happened.

HOUSING

In housing, government encouraged 'brown-field' building within existing urban areas, and pressed for greater housing density, but these wishes were at variance with public demands for space, which led to the low-density sprawl planners disliked. Furthermore, the move to rural or suburban areas, counter-urbanization or dispersed urbaniza- tion, or to gated urban neighbourhoods, represented a rejection not only of what appeared to be the hostile nature of crime-ridden town- scapes, but also of government views of the desirability of high-density mixed populations. A survey of British Social Attitudes in 1999, by the National Centre for Social Research, showed that those who lived in big cities were the group keenest to move. For some, these moves repre- sented a British equivalent of what the Americans termed 'White Flight'. At the very least, the move away from the social problems of inner cities, particularly their higher rates of crime, linked social issues to the environmental pressures posed by regional expansion in housing. In addition, 'Towards an Urban Renaissance', the 1999 report of the government-created Urban Task Force, drew attention to serious problems in urban planning, development and governance.

The move from the cities ensured that commuters came to dominate many villages. This reflected the appeal of an idealized image of the countryside, but also led to a shift in the nature of rural life, as well as the effective erosion of any significant boundary between rural and urban society. This was less the case with villages that were distant from major towns.

FOOD SAFETY

Public concern over pollution and the environment was heightened as a result of anxiety over the safety of food. Changes in agricultural practice had become controversial before the scandals of the 1990s and 2000s. 'Factory' farming was a matter of concern, especially the treatment of 'battery hens', but also that of pigs. Characteristically, discussion of this issue focused on the conditions of the animals and on food safety, rather than on the environmental consequences of large usage of electricity and massive production of waste products. When a government minister, Edwina Currie, claimed in 1988 that much of Britain's egg production was contaminated by salmonella, she created an outcry and resigned.

In the 1990s a crisis over bovine spongiform encephalitis (BSE) in the cattle herd, and its transmission to humans through meat, causing variant Creutzfeldt-Jakob disease, drew attention to the consequences of agricultural practices, especially feeding dead animals to those that were alive, for animal and human health. In 1998 it was predicted that as many as half a million people could die of the neuro-degenerative disease by 2080, although five years later, in large part due to a fall in the number of deaths from 2001, this was revised downwards to 7,000. BSE accentuated public concern about food safety and led to alarmist rumours, in Britain and abroad, of the dangers posed by British beef. Alongside fatal outbreaks of E.coli, including one in Scotland in 1996 that killed twelve people, this led to the establishment of a food safety agency in 1997. The BSE crisis also led to a prohibition on meat-

and-bone meal fodder, which raised costs for animal, especially pig, farmers. There were also health scares over levels of mercury in farmed fish.

Concern over agricultural methods, and food standards and safety, continued. A controversy in 1999 over genetically modified (GM) crops reflected fear about the impact of science, although the genetic modification of the raw materials of farming and forestry was nothing new. Thus, the use of more nitrogenous chemical fertilizer was accompanied by the development of plant strains that responded well, while there was a general emphasis on producing strains with a greater yield. Anxiety about GM foods captured the pessimistic and anxious character of the public mood towards science, a mood that was very different to that in the nineteenth century. It also acted as a symbol for an anti-globalization that was increasingly pronounced. As a result, Britain lost an early advantage in biotechnology, and agriculture remained heavily dependent on pesticides. The know-nothing and self-righteously destructive character of the critical public response was symptomatic of a wider combination of willing the ends (high living standards) but not the means, alongside the role of a minority of violent militant activists. At the same time, the threat that GM crops allegedly posed to 'organic' farming was a sensitive issue, as the diversity offered by the latter appeared to offer an alternative to the economics and methods of agri-business.

The foot-and-mouth crisis of 2001, in which at least six-and-a-half million animals, about one in eight of the livestock in the country, were slaughtered, further heightened concerns about the environment. The crisis, which cost the country £8 billion, led to horrific scenes of large numbers of animals being slaughtered, followed by dense clouds of smoke rising from funeral pyres. It also posed a serious crisis for an already weak agricultural sector, while hitting tourism very hard. Less dramatically, the pig industry was hit by rising costs, as well as by disease (Postweaning Multisystemic Wasting Syndrome), and the size of the breeding herd in Britain fell from 800,000 at the start of 1998 to 550,000 four years later. The prohibition on the tethering of pigs in narrow stalls that came into force in 1999 increased costs. The low-density individual dwellings constructed as a result impressed a group of American tourists with whom I took a coach excursion through Oxfordshire and Wiltshire in 2000 – 'these are just like hotels'.

Already, in 1971, there were only four counties in Britain where more than 30 per cent of the male workforce was involved in agriculture, and the national average was under 2 per cent. By 1999 agriculture's share of the GDP had fallen to 0.9 per cent and it employed only 1.5 per cent of the workforce, although these figures minimize its regional importance, for example in Cumbria, Mid-Wales and the south-west of England.

Fishing was also in crisis. The fisheries were hit by overfishing and competition from European Union (EU) countries, particularly Spain. The EU manages fishing within the 200-mile economic zone of its members and sets quotas for catches within it. The numbers of British boats and fishermen have declined greatly, and landings have also fallen. As a result of the decline of fish stocks, established fish dishes such as cod, herring and mackerel have become scarce.

POLITICS

Although there is a widespread consensus that the environment is one of the central issues of our time, this co-exists with forces of untrammelled consumption and selfishness. What, in 1987, became the Green Party was founded in 1975; it won 15 per cent of the vote in the 1989 elections to the European Parliament (which, given the first-past-the-post system, was still not enough to win it any seats as it would have done under the subsequent list system). This percentage of the vote was exceptional. In the 1999 elections to the Scottish Parliament the Greens gained only one of the 129 seats, although in 2003 they won six seats.

Despite the continued activity of Friends of the Earth and Greenpeace, the energy that was building up behind the environmental movement in the 1980s seems to have been diverted into more self-centred concerns like organic foods (based on anxiety about personal health, rather than sustainable farming). Mainstream politics co-opted some of the language of the 'Greens', but was unwilling to, or incapable of, taking on society's unbounded sense of material entitlement, which is the main driver of environmental pressures. This contrast was also apparent elsewhere. The Eden Project, the biomes in Cornwall opened in 2001, designed to stress sustainability and extensively supported by the National Lottery, were largely visited by car.

HEALTH

Rather than concern about the environment, public anxiety was more heavily focused on health in the shape of medical care. The health system was under increased pressure, in part because of a major increase in life expectancy. For men, this rose from 68 (for those born in 1961) to 75 (for those born in 1999–2001), and for women from 73 to 80; the median age of the population rose to 37 in 1998, and continued to rise thereafter. As a result the number of pensioners increased, which made it hard for governments to contain welfare expenditure. The improved health of people in their sixties and seventies was a worthwhile goal, but they did not contribute much to the economy or to public finances; in addition the growing number of those aged over 80 put pressure on the social services, made care for the elderly a more important political issue and contributed to the pensions crisis.

At the other end of the age spectrum, infant mortality fell by nearly two-thirds between 1971 and 1994. This owed much to improvements in midwifery, in hospital facilities and conditions, and in the ability to deal with premature deliveries. Birth in hospital became the norm. In addition, the possibilities of conception extended. In 1978 Louise Brown, the first 'test-tube' baby, was born. This was a success for in vitro fertilization (IVF), in which egg and sperm were mixed in a glass dish, and the embryos created inserted in the womb. By the end of the century about 1,400 IVF babies were being born each year. In 1994 there appeared the first baby born as a result of the use of a frozen embryo. Far from being left to scientists and entrepreneurs, these activities were heavily regulated by government. There was greater public concern in the early 2000s about the cloning of human tissue in order to permit experimentation designed to help tackle genetic conditions that led to disease.

On average, people became healthier and longer-living in the period, in part because of improvements in nutrition and, in part, because the hazards of drinking to excess and, particularly, of smoking became generally appreciated and were addressed by government action. The Clean Air Act and other environmental measures, safety at work awareness, and the Health and Safety at Work Act, as well as a growing understanding of the dangers of working in smoke-filled buildings and with asbestos, all contributed to changes in health, not least to the decline of chest illnesses. Immunization programmes were extended, covering mumps after 1985 and German measles after 1990.

Health, however, was affected by the relatively long hours worked, certainly compared to France and Germany. In part these hours were necessary in order to ensure living standards, as productivity in terms of output per hour was relatively low, certainly lower than France, Germany and the USA. Long working hours, for both men and women, may have been partly responsible for poor 'parenting' and for the rise in juvenile crime and other bad behaviour. Stress levels among the workforce reflected not only the number of hours worked but also the very challenging nature of the work environment. As with many other indices, it was also affected by greater public awareness of the problem, and the decline of stigmas about owning up to it. This decline is linked to shifting conceptions of masculinity.

As well as public health measures, there were also developments in healthcare. From the 1970s limited population screening was introduced for the early detection and treatment of diseases such as breast and cervical cancer. The 1980s saw the increasing development and use of anti-viral agents for the treatment of viral infections. There were also major advances in the treatment of the heart, especially bypass and transplant surgery. The first heart transplant in Britain was performed in Harefield Hospital in 1980.

Research and development continues. It has come to encompass skin grafts and artificial knee joints. Technological advances solved technical issues, but, in turn, created ethical and legal problems. In 1989, for example, it was necessary to pass the Human Transplant Act because the Human Tissue Act of 1961, which specified the ways in which organs could be taken from the body for research, teaching and transplantation, had related only to dead humans; by 1981 organs could be transplanted from live people. In 1997 Dolly, the first cloned animal, was born: the nucleus of an adult sheep cell was transferred to an egg cell from which the nucleus had been removed, and the egg developed to become a mature sheep. For many, however, insulin from pigs, 'donor cards' and stem-cell research pushed against the boundary of morality and health.

There is evidence of a deterioration in some areas of health, and there has been public concern over such issues as antibiotic-resistant 'super-bugs' in hospitals: methicillin-resistant staphylococcus aureus is so resistant to normal antibiotics that it is treated by either toxic-level antibiotics or washes of high-dose antiseptic fluids. Although the more thorough collection of statistics is in part responsible for a more compre-hensive coverage of problems, there are also clear signs of greater, as well as new, problems. Possibly as a result of increasing car ex-haust emissions, and general pollution, and justifying the positioning of health in the chapter on the environment, respiratory diseases such as asthma are definitely more common. Some other respiratory diseases may also be increasing. Eye irritation has become more ser-ious. Allergies and food intolerances are more frequently reported, while diarrhoeal diseases, as recorded in food poisoning, and virus-related infections have risen since 1940. Tuberculosis and malaria have made a comeback, although for different reasons: tuberculosis from general health problems focused in particular on poverty and immig-ration, while malaria may be climate-related. The growth of ethnic minority communities led to an increase in particular conditions such as sickle-cell anaemia.

The products of economic activity have been held responsible for a range of problems. The massive increase in the importation, treatment and burying of hazardous waste in the 1980s led to concern about poss-ible health implications. More generally, pollutants have been linked to hormonal changes among the population, including declining sperm counts and the acquisition of female characteristics by men.

Social issues are also important to some diseases. Thus the major increase in venereal disease in the 1990s and 2000s reflected, in particu-lar, the high rate of sexual activity among people in their teens and the failure to take sufficient heed of government advice on 'safe sex', particularly the use of male contraceptives. This has been linked to notions of masculinity, not least the widespread assumption that contraception was the responsibility of women. The major increase in venereal disease affected both men and women, but awareness of it was influenced by a focus on the HIV virus and its frequent consequence, AIDS (Acquired Immune Deficiency Syndrome). The impact of the disease hit home when it claimed the lives of stars in the fields of popular music, such as Freddie Mercury; and AIDS had a major impact on culture, featuring frequently in television and radio plays and in other works, such as Paul Bailey's novel *Sugar Cane* (1993). Although heterosexuals were also infected, the disease was popularly perceived as largely a product of homosexuality or drug abuse. Furthermore, as antibiotics dealt with most other sexually transmitted diseases, there was a failure to realize their potential consequences, which includes infertility in the case of chlamydia, a (non-fatal) disease that affects far more people than AIDS.

If the rise in certain illnesses was a problem, so also were some of the cures. The belated realization that blood transfusion could induce new disease resulted in the 1970s in the routine screening of blood products for hepatitis B. It took time before the hazard of HIV transmission through blood products was realized, with tragic consequences, in particular for haemophiliacs. In the 1990s concern rose about the overprescription of antibiotics and their decreasing effectiveness. Similar concern had for long been expressed about the use of tranquillizers and the resulting addictions. This provision was itself a product of the sense that patients were entitled to treatment and a cure. This attitude led to controversy in 1999 over the government's attempt to limit the prescription of the anti-impotence pill Viagra on the NHS.

By the end of the period, the causes of death were very different to those a century earlier when infections were a major cause of death. Today, infections generally only kill people who are suffering from associated disorders and who are at the extremes of life. Now, later-onset diseases, especially heart disease and cancers (most of which are not curable), are far more important. Each was responsible for more than a quarter of the deaths in Scotland in 1994.

Healthcare became a greater burden on state and society, and the rise in life expectancy led to greater problems of dependency. Once introduced, state welfare was seen as a right, and there was little interest in making direct personal contributions to the cost of healthcare or pensions, despite governmental encouragement for the latter. The cost of the NHS rose from £26.2 billion in 1989 to £42 billion in 1997.

There was also much resistance to public health campaigns, for example the attempt to discourage underage smoking, which actually rose, especially among women, in the 1990s. There were 138,000 smoking-related deaths in the United Kingdom in 1990. A Department of Health survey in 1993 suggested that half the adult population was clinically overweight or obese, helping to explain high rates of heart disease. Furthermore, the percentage of the population judged severely overweight rose, for example from 8 to 13 among men from 1986 to 1991. Death rates from coronary heart disease in Scotland and Northern Ireland are among the highest in the world for both men and women, and England and Wales are close behind. This is a comment on public health, if not the NHS. In another sign of resistance, there was opposition in 2002 to the MMR vaccine, given to children to protect them from measles, mumps and rubella, because it was claimed that it increased the risk of autism. As a result, many parents preferred three single vaccines. The failure to give all three led, in some areas, such as part of south London, to a fall in the vaccination rate and increased risks of the diseases.

The persistence of class differences in British society was seen in the limited impact of public health education among the poor. By the late 1990s those from low-income groups generally died about five years sooner than the better-off. Gender issues and politics both also played a role in health provision. For example, whereas uterine and breast cancer attracted major attention from the 1980s, prostate cancer, which affects men, appeared relatively underrated by the 1990s. More generally, the rising cost of dental and optical treatment in the 1990s, especially the difficulty of obtaining dental treatment on NHS terms, was held responsible for a deterioration in the dental and optical health of sections of the population.

The combination of longer life expectancy, and conditions and diseases of affluence, such as obesity, have altered life experiences and created the context for social changes. The move towards a more elderly age structure has an importance in terms of consumer demands. As a result, there has been a greater concern with the health service, and this has been in part at the expense of education. Although the elderly, on average, are less likely to be victims of crime than young men, their anxiety about it has also helped drive the issue up the political agenda.

Greater life expectancy contributed to a larger population, helping to mitigate the impact of falling birth rates, which in 2001 reached an average of about 1.64 children being born to each British woman; the figure was as low as 1.48 in Scotland. In 1994 there were only 61,656 live births in Scotland, the lowest figure since records began in 1855. Combined with emigration, this led to a fall in the Scottish population by 152,000 in 1976–86 alone, or, measured on a different index, by 4.3 per cent in 1987–95. The impact of falling British birth rates was further mitigated by immigration, such that the British population rose to 59.8 million in 2001, with further growth anticipated. Combined with high rates of divorce and, in some areas, rural depopulation, especially by the young, this led to a demand for housing, particularly in southern England, that created the sense of an environment under strain.

This sense was also an aspect of concern about the impact of immigration which, by the early 2000s, was running at above 100,000 people per year from non-European Union countries. Furthermore, the figure was increasing. In 2002, 110,000 asylum-seekers arrived, 20 per cent more than the figure for 2001. As the bulk of asylum-seekers in fact sought to live in cities, especially London, they were not, in practice, a factor in the building over of the countryside, other than through contributing to higher population projections and encouraging movement from the cities, both of which were very important. Already, by 1996, about 10 per cent of the land of the United Kingdom was urban.

Human beings thus have made the major impact on the environment, but it is as well to be reminded that they are not alone. The great expansion in population, in the man-made environment, and in man-made products, ensured that animals benefiting from contact with humans also increased in number. In part this was a matter of animals that humans wished to see, whether as farm animals or as pets. Thus, the increased consumption of chicken and the farming of fish, especially of salmon in Scottish sea lochs, led to increases in numbers, although environmental problems followed, not least due to the quantity of waste-products. Fish farms gave off very large quantities of ammonia, and this appears to be toxic to other organisms.

Demand for pets spawned a major industry that recorded many of the processes of social change, including consumerism, fashion, growing trade, specialization, and the importance of developing and satisfying the sensibilities of children. Social and environmental trends also affected the composition of the pet population. The trend from dogs to cats reflected the growing percentage of the British population living in small dwellings, the decreased ability or willingness to take dogs for walks, which, in part, was a product of other leisure options (such as the cult of the gym), and the greater role of women and female self-images in the choice of pets.

In large part, the animals that benefited from humanity were less welcome than pets. The pigeons fed by tourists in London's Trafalgar Square were judged unacceptable by the elected mayor, Ken Livingstone. More generally, rats, cockroaches and other wildlife benefited from the growth in the volume of rubbish. Animals such as foxes and squirrels altered their activity patterns in order to exploit bins and other sites of rubbish accumulation and disposal. Indeed, foxes became increasingly urban. At a more local level, wastewater emissions from power stations and factories raised water temperatures and led to greater animal and plant activity nearby. Sewerage flows into lakes such as Windermere led to an increase in algae. The general rise in temperature may have been more widely beneficial for animal life. It was certainly held responsible for an increase in the badger population in the 1990s, and their potential role in transmitting disease to cattle led to pressure for culls.

Animals that are not native to Britain, notably coypu, mink and American bullfrogs, have escaped into the wild, creating colonies that have been pernicious to other species. Wild boar, porcupines and wallabies have also escaped in numbers big enough to create colonies, while there are persistent reports of big cats living wild, presumably panthers or lynxes that were one-time pets whom their owners did not choose to register. The ecosystem in the Norfolk Broads altered when coypu escaped from local fur farms, and had an impact on other wildlife. Coypu also damaged the drainage system and destroyed sugar beet. They were exterminated in the late 1980s. Four mink that escaped from a fur farm on the Isle of Harris in the late 1960s created a colony of about 12,000 that attacked both rare seabirds and chicken farming. In the New Forest in 1998, 'animal rights' activists deliberately freed mink from fur farms with, unintended, devastating consequences for the local wildlife. Whatever their source, mink succeeded in cutting numbers of the indigenous water vole. In addition, American bullfrogs killed British frogs, which are smaller. Foreign diseases also hit British wildlife.

The period saw an accelerating race between humans and other animals for profit from what humans saw as their habitat, but which was of course shared with animals. Thus, the shallow drilling of cereal seeds provided opportunities for birds such as starlings. There was also a parallel tension between humans and plants, as in the spread of bracken fern. This is toxic to sheep and can also harbour the ticks that are the vector of Lyme disease. The spread of the latter is a reminder of how the environment can become hostile.

The major human remedy against unwanted animals, plants and microbes was chemical, in both houses and fields. This had unwanted side-effects, not least the development of immunity among animals such as rats.

At a different level, the limited control of humans was driven home by the climate. In part this was a matter of global warming, which in 2003 was seen as threatening the fruit industry because traditional British fruits need a sustained cold period chill. The challenge from the climate was more brutally displayed in spectacular episodes, such as the hurricane of 1987, the floods of 2000 and the storms of 2002. In the first, about 15 per cent of the timber east of a line from the Isle of Wight to Norwich was brought down, nineteen people were killed and about £1 billion was spent to clear up. The floods exposed the extent to which building in floodplains, for example near York, drainage policies and agricultural practices combined to make large areas vulnerable to particularly heavy rainfall. The limitations of the human response were shown as reliance was placed on sandbags. In turn, the expectation that government could, and should, cope with the impact of unexpected climate was an aspect of the dependency culture that, in part, arose from the commitment of politicians to provide such coverage. Thus, drought and floods called forth interventions, while cold snaps, as in January 1987, led to controversy about the extent of special cold-weather payments to the elderly. Such demands would have been dismissed as nonsense in the early decades of the century.

A more seminal, but less dramatic, warning of the limited capabilities of humans was provided by crustal movement from long-term structural adjustments to the removal of ice cover during the latter stages of the Ice Age. While Scotland, together with north-west and north-east England, is experiencing uplift leading to raised beaches on the west coast, to the south of these areas there is a downwarping that is particularly apparent in East Anglia and the South-East. This exacerbates the region's vulnerability to flooding, a measure that led to the construction of the Thames Barrage, a major feat of civil engineering. Long stretches of the English coastline are vulnerable to a rise in sea level, and in some areas, such as the Fens, the Ouse valley in Yorkshire and the Somerset Levels, this vulnerability extends far inland.

As a different reminder of vulnerability, the inroads of Dutch elm disease on tree numbers had a major impact on the landscape, especially in southern England; the planting of new trees, meanwhile, was greatly affected by browsing by deer, which doubled in numbers between 1965 and 1995. Although the Red Deer Commission favours a major cut in the number, the current culture is not amenable to mass shooting (there is, however, a marked preference for shooting foxes rather than hunting them with hounds).

The crowded character of the British Isles reflects not only the rise in population but its varied demands and its ability to seek to fulfil them. Thus, this crowded character was a product of the consumer pressures already referred to. Aside from housing, there were powerful demands from recreational desires. These were readily apparent on crowded beaches, but the range of leisure activities also ensured that pressure was felt across the country. This is increased by greater mobility, although its consequences vary: four-wheel-drive vehicles and mountain bikes make more of an impact on the environment than car-borne walkers, and lead to the need for conservation work in order to counter erosion. Most domestic tourists use cars, and these often tow or carry other means to increase tourist mobility, such as dinghies and canoes.

The role of landscape and the countryside in the national psyche was shown by the success of the Royal Society for the Protection of Birds, which had more than a million members by 1999, and the National Trust. The latter throws interesting light on modern British society. The Trust has more members than any political party: in 1997–8 its membership rose above 2.5 million, whereas there had been only 278,000 in 1971. The Trust is also the largest private landowner in England. The list of its most frequently visited properties reflected the popularity of gardens. In the year March 1997–February 1998, the most popular was Wakehurst Place, a 500-acre estate in West Sussex that contains the national collections of birch, southern beech, hypericum and skimmia. The second, Fountains Abbey and Studley Royal, contains Georgian water gardens, and the third, Stourhead Garden, is a masterpiece of Georgian landscape design. Other popular garden destinations include Sissinghurst, Lanhydrock and Sheffield Park, while gardens and grounds provide much of the appeal of many of the more popular building properties, such as Cragside. In 2000 Wakehurst and Fountains were again first and second.

The National Trust was not the sole custodian of much-visited gardens. Other sites received much attention, and the number of gardens that were open was increased, for example with the recovery of the ruined Lost Gardens of Heligan in Cornwall, and with the opening in 2000 of the National Botanic Garden of Wales in Carmarthenshire.

National Trust gardens offered a sanitized version of landscape, one welcome to a population much of which felt stressed, and one removed from the pressures of modern economics. A more accurate vignette of life was the rising cost of burials, which, in part, reflected rising urban land values. This encouraged cremation, a fitting reference to close the chapter.

Chapter 4

An Ungovernable People?

The Leaderene [Mrs Thatcher] is most distinctly 'not amused' by
the latest antics of Peter Walker, the Minister for Agriculture and
Asset Strippers.

   The leaking of his heretical and counter-revolutionary speech
to the Tory Reform Group . . . in which he deeply questioned the
Government's economic theology has led to a rich reprimand from
the Headmistress for daring to doubt her infallibility. 'Asset Stripper'
is dutifully writing out his 1,000 lines: 'I DO, YES I DO, believe in
Monetarism and Market Forces'.

Private Eye, 1 August 1980

The sense that Britain was in a state of collapse was captured in Lindsay
Anderson's satirical film *Britannia Hospital* (1982). This presented
Britain as a collapsing NHS hospital with overly powerful anarchic
trade unionists careless of the consequences of their actions. This sense
of malaise drew on a variety of causes, but union militancy was a
potent one. The labour-relations crisis of the 1970s ensured that far
more working days were lost in strikes than in the 1960s, and this
discouraged investment and made it harder to maintain productivity
increases and economic growth. This situation discredited the post-
war social democratic consensus.

The Conservatives fought the 1979 election pledged to change aspects of labour relations, including the 'closed shop' and secondary picketing, and to enforce the use of secret ballots before strikes. Their 1980 Employment Act banned secondary picketing and offered funds for secret ballots before strikes. A second Act of 1982 banned pre-entry 'closed shops' and allowed 'closed shops' to exist only where a ballot revealed 85 per cent support. These changes were not achieved without opposition, but it was unsuccessful. A 'Day of Action' (i.e. strike) in 1980 in protest at government policies achieved little. Three years later, the National Graphical Association was fined and had its assets sequestered following its attempt to enforce a closed shop at the Warrington printing plant of the *Stockport Messenger*. In 1984 another 'Day of Action' failed to shake the government's decision to ban unions at the Government Communications Headquarters (GCHQ), a branch of the intelligence services.

After the failure of the miners' strike in 1984–5 (see next chapter) and the unsuccessful, violent picketing of News International's new printing plant at Wapping in 1986–7, additional Employment Acts were passed in 1988, 1989, 1990 and 1993. These successive Acts proved far more effective than Edward Heath's earlier attempt at one-stage total change. The Acts of 1988–90 gave trade union members the right to ignore a union ballot on industrial action; banned strikes to establish or retain 'closed shops'; introduced restrictions on industrial action, election ballots, and cases going to full industrial tribunals; and forced unions to repudiate unofficial action. This incremental approach towards union reform proved to be very successful, as it created a series of new status quos that were given time to establish themselves before being bolstered by further measures. In turn, such an approach made it more difficult to undertake concerted opposition to the reforms that were introduced. The Major governments (1990–97) kept the momentum of trade union reform going: the Trade Union Reform and Employment Rights Act was passed in 1993. It established the principle that pre-strike ballots should be by post and decreed that strike action could not begin until seven days after the result of a ballot was known.

The legislation had an impact not only on high-profile disputes but also on the general climate of labour relations. In the late 1980s trade union militancy became less common, and the level of industrial action continued to fall in the early 1990s, especially in the private sector. The number of stoppages beginning in a year fell from over 2,000, throughout the period 1967–79, to below 1,100, throughout 1985–92. There were fewer demarcation disputes, as the spread of 'single-union agreements' eased industrial tension. They became a prerequisite of any decision by a multinational corporation to establish a British-based operation. Labour practices also became more flexible.

Blair kept the unions at arm's length after he gained power in 1997 and, in launching Labour's manifesto for the 2001 election, declared that 'no barriers, no dogma, no vested interests' should thwart reform of the public services, in which the unions were powerful. He pushed through a private finance initiative to encourage the financing of new public service provision by private finance, but in 2003 the unions were able to thwart the attempt to use this to permit flexibility in labour conditions, while, more generally, reform of the public services was limited.

Labour productivity was a major problem for the economy, and it continues to be so, but there are also other issues. It has been claimed that, on the whole, managers lacked the necessary calibre and vision, not least compared with their American counterparts. Poor management ensured that the return on capital was too low, discouraging investment. Management failure has also been linked to mistaken investment strategies, both within companies and more generally in the economy. As far as the latter is concerned, it has been suggested that there was a preference for investing in well-established companies, rather than in developing sectors. Risk or venture capital was thus insufficient and too expensive: interest rates were too high. Furthermore, there was also a preference for non-industrial investment, both on the money markets and in housing. In addition, much investment was short-term.

Investment choices were linked to politics and to socio-cultural assumptions (for example, with state encouragement, through mortgage-tax relief, for home ownership). The political emphasis in fiscal policy making was more on the City of London than on industrial concerns and influences. This emphasis has been blamed for deflationary policies, and for repeatedly keeping sterling too high, a policy that reduced the cost of imports to the benefit of consumers, and thus limited inflation, but that also helped make exports uncompetitive and thus encouraged company failures.

CRIME

While labour relations in part responded to government policies, crime was seen as an aspect of the human environment that was increasingly not under control. It proved a telling challenge not just to government but to established social practices and, more generally, to the social fabric. The widespread perception that crime had increased, and the contrast of recent decades with a more peaceful earlier period, generally located to include the 1950s, was important to the sense many held that their world was deteriorating and also contributed to the media nostalgia discussed in chapter Two. Statistics were employed to support or challenge this view. The number of recorded offences in Britain rose from about 1.7 million in 1972 to 3 million in 1981, 5 million in 1996 and 5.8 million in 2002; in Scotland alone, they had nearly doubled between 1977 and 1992.

Even so, Home Office statistics were frequently at variance with the British Crime Survey, which generally, based on respondents' experiences, painted an even more pessimistic picture; this was even more the case if the perceptions of respondents, fuelled in part by the media with programmes such as *Crimewatch*, were considered. These perceptions were manifested in public opinion polls, letters to MPs and contributions to radio talk-shows. An increase in non-reporting affected Home Office statistics, and this was linked to shifts in police policy. Thus, the 'tough on crime' approach shared by all major political parties, and the jabs at policies of 'zero tolerance' under the second Blair government, mask a near abandonment of police attempts to deal with petty crime in some areas. Public disquiet was exacerbated by a lack of clarity over the right of individuals to protect themselves against criminals, an issue that again came to prominence in 2003 with reports of projected legislation that was presented as increasing the rights of criminals.

Lawlessness was particularly noted among young males, far more so than elsewhere in Western Europe. Furthermore, the situation deteriorated in the 1990s: by 2000 a third of the 30-year-old male population had criminal records. The Blair government linked this lawlessness to a more widespread pattern of anti-social behaviour. In 2000, in one of his characteristic 'soundbites', Blair announced to the Labour Party conference that 'It is time to end yob culture'.

Anti-social behaviour was linked to a brutalization of society. This had a number of facets, including the triumph of skinhead/football supporter culture, the glorification of the stupid, tattoos, body piercing, and the extent to which pornography and sado-masochism became more prominent in popular culture. Anti-social behaviour combined with the decline of deference, in the rise in attacks on doctors, nurses, teachers and other public sector workers. In 2003, for example, the teachers' union NASUWT claimed that a teacher was attacked every seven minutes.

The pattern of anti-social behaviour was related to the difficulty of integrating the young with the official economy. In the late 1990s the peak age for male offending was 18. The failure of many to remain in education was seen as particularly instructive, although for those at school there was controversy about bad behaviour and the right of schools to expel the troublesome: over 12,000 were excluded each year in 1996–8. Furthermore, in 2002, a quarter of British pupils left school before the age of 17, a high drop-out rate by European standards. The relationship between poor educational standards and a failure to achieve productivity growth in the economy was important but indirect, since much may also be due to the limited vocational character of education and to governmental policies toward training: the training levies of the 1960s were abandoned and responsibility was placed on employers, who were reluctant to spend on training. Nevertheless, skilled labour is required to make best use of new technologies, and such skill appears to be insufficiently spread.

The young complained of not enough to do in most communities. Drug-taking and sex became more common activities. Whereas surveys suggest that at the close of the 1950s the average age at which people began having sex was 20 for men and 21 for women, by the close of the 1990s it was 17. Despite the ready availability of contraception and abortion, there were nearly 90,000 teenage conceptions a year, the highest rate in Western Europe at the end of the century, and one that placed a heavy burden on the state.

Drug use among the young was widespread. According to a Police Federation report of 2000, which proposed the decriminalization of cannabis, a third of those under 30 took it. Clubbing, a prime activity among the young, was frequently accompanied with drug taking. By 2002 it was suggested that about half a million people, most of whom were young, were regular consumers of the drug Ecstasy. Aside from short-term problems that arose from taking the drug, there were suggestions that it would have long-term effects on mental health. More dangerous drugs were also readily obtainable, and the drug statistics were the worst in Western Europe. It was estimated that, by 2001, Scotland alone had 60,000 heroin users, and that the total cost of drugs to the Scottish economy was about 3 per cent of national income.

Changing public attitudes were at stake in the reporting and perception of crime, as well as contributing to the spread of criminal behaviour. A substantial, and increasing, number of people no longer viewed certain activities as criminal, such as buying and using scheduled drugs and buying stolen goods. The ban on dangerous drugs failed to control drug use, and this critically undermined respect for the rule of law. In turn, those taking drugs were more likely to be criminals, resorting to mugging, break-ins or car theft in order to finance their dependency.

Failure in policing was indicated by major falls in the price of drugs. According to the National Criminal Intelligence Service, from November 1990 to December 2001 the price of Ecstasy fell by over 60 per cent and that of cocaine and heroin by about 30 per cent. This helped to make drugs a viable alternative to alcohol and cigarettes. This failure led to increased police and political interest in the early 2000s in the legalization of the use of 'soft' drugs, especially cannabis, although they posed a risk to health. There was also interest in making it permissible for doctors to prescribe heroin to addicts.

Drug crime massively capitalized Britain's formerly modest organized criminal syndicates, as well as attracting new ones from abroad. These profits were reinvested in other forms of crime, such as people smuggling, computer fraud and trade in mobile phones. By 2003 the National Criminal Intelligence Service could estimate that £18 billion worth of assets had been gained through criminal activity. This was both evidence of profit and the source for fresh criminal activity.

Drug crime also helped cause and finance a major expansion in the use of guns, and in gun crime. This in turn helped to foster the public sense that crime as a whole was out of control, and led to concern about the safety of inner-city life, especially in London and Manchester.

In response to rising crime, which increased by 2 per cent in 2001–2 alone, the prison population in England and Wales grew from 45,000 in 1991 to 73,000 in 2003; 6 per cent of the latter were women. The percentage of the population in prison was matched in Western Europe only by Portugal. The ability and willingness of the police and courts to arrest, convict and imprison, or fine, large numbers of those who broke the law were important aspects of the system of government, and police powers were expanded, for example with the Criminal Justice and Public Order Act, which came into force in 1995.

At the same time, the prevalence of anti-social behaviour was seen, in part, especially by lawyers, as a product of inadequate policing. In October 1995 the Lord Chief Justice responded to the Home Secretary's call for tougher sentencing by stating, 'What deters is the likelihood of being caught, which at the moment is small'. Indeed, by the early 2000s only 23 out of every 100 recorded crimes were cleared up, while only 6 out of every 100 led to a conviction. Hit by a rising number of crimes per police officer, the police also complained of bureaucracy and many of them took sick leave.

Drug use was not the sole area in which respect for the rule of law was undermined. A combination of the collapse of Britain's old industrial base with the rise of consumerism and the decline in respect for the law has seen a ballooning of the 'hidden economy'. The Tobacco Manufacturers' Association estimated in 2001 that 80 per cent of hand-rolling tobacco was smuggled, part of the possibly £1.6 billion worth of goods smuggled into Britain across the Channel. The Customs Service estimates that up to one third of cigarettes sold in the UK are sold illegally, in pubs, clubs, markets and openly in the streets. The 'black market' of the wartime rationing years was a precedent, but it was less blatant than the present situation.

The 'hidden economy' is a major problem for tax policy, suggesting that any increase in taxes will not produce the appropriate yield. It also reflects a widespread willingness to ignore government. This takes the form of a range of practices, including paying workmen, such as plumbers, money that will not be entered for income tax and VAT purposes. More generally, the related ethos indicates an alienation of much of the public from government. This was particularly seen in some areas, although it is largely locals who are the victims of criminals and others engaged in anti-social behaviour. Alienation from the government is part of the problem in dealing with crime, as the difficulty of obtaining witness statements shows, but it does not always mean support for criminals.

Another aspect of alienation was provided by evasion of the census, especially by recent immigrants. The worst responses to the 2001 census occurred in inner London. The census returned a figure a million less than anticipated. Illegal immigration itself attracted criminals who got people into the country and then exploited them. This was particularly linked to prostitution, which in 2002 was estimated as employing 90,000; an interesting comment on earlier claims that sexual liberalization from the 1960s would lead to the demise of prostitution.

In Nationalist and 'Loyalist' communities in Northern Ireland, widespread evasion of government was linked to the role of paramilitaries in using means, such as cigarette and petrol smuggling, to raise revenue. In terms of ungovernability in the UK, it is impossible to surpass Northern Ireland. Yet large-scale lawlessness, in the shape of ignoring the fiscal arm of the state, was not restricted to Northern Ireland. Instead, it was an aspect of communities where deference had broken down, leading, for example, to the Merseyside joke: 'What do you call a man in a suit?' 'The defendant.' The passage of legislation failed to alleviate anti-social behaviour and crime. For example, the child curfew and anti-social behaviour orders introduced in the Crime and

Disorder Act of 1998 proved difficult to enforce. With developments such as drink-fuelled football hooliganism, which gave the English a very unwelcome reputation abroad, it is unclear that being caught was in fact a major deterrent.

RELIGION

The rapid decline in deference was not restricted to government or class but extended to all professionals, as well as trade unionists and politicians of all parties. An important aspect, which certainly contrasted with the situation in the USA, was the decline in religion. From the 1960s the Established Churches were hit by the general social currents of the period, particularly the decline of deference, patriarchal authority, social paternalism, the nuclear family and respect for age. The permissive 'social' legislation of the 1960s and later, such as the decriminalization of homosexual acts between consenting adults in England and Wales with the Sexual Offences Act of 1967, changes in divorce legislation, and the granting of equal rights to illegitimate children, flew in the face of Church teachings, and left the Church confused and apparently lacking in 'relevance'. This was especially serious for an age that placed more of an emphasis on present-mindedness than on continuity with historical roots and teachings. Belief in orthodox Christian theology, especially on the nature of Jesus, and in the after-life, the Last Judgement and the existence of hell, lessened. Absolute and relative numbers of believers fell rapidly, especially for the Church of England, the Church of Scotland and the Methodists.

The Church of England sought to respond. Cranmer's Prayerbook English was criticized as antiquated, and was replaced by a series of new liturgies. The Church also sought in the 1980s to reassert its moral authority and its continued allegiance to some sort of social gospel. The report it published in 1985 on the problems facing the inner cities, *Faith in the City*, made a considerable impact. Government policies were lambasted for laying waste to the cities. However, the hostile response of the Thatcher government to the report, dismissing its supposed 'Marxist' leanings, highlighted the difficulties that the Established

Churches had in finding a role in an increasingly secular society. The roots of Thatcherism in part lay in a Nonconformity that was hostile to an Anglicanism perceived as too strongly connected to 'consensus politics'. Thatcher saw the Church of England as wedded to consensus and conciliation. Her call for 'Victorian values' did not extend to a leading role for clerics, many of whom, in turn, were disenchanted by what they saw as an excessive stress in Thatcherism on individualism and economic gain.

This gap between Church and State was not restricted to the Conservatives, but was found across the political spectrum and reflected general social values. The public perception of the Church, as captured on television or in plays such as David Hare's *Racing Demon* (1990), was frequently critical. The Church of England could not readily generate respect; it appeared divided and unsure of itself. Christianity was also satirized, as in the film *Monty Python's Life of Brian* (1979).

The decision in 1992 to ordain women to the priesthood in the Church of England (implemented in 1994) led some traditionalist Anglicans to join the Roman Catholic Church, which rejected female ordination. The attitude of the traditionalists reflected longstanding tensions within the Church of England, and the difficulty of accommodating differences in a society increasingly ready to reject such accommodation. Liberal Anglican theologians fell foul both of Evangelical and of High-Church Anglicans. In 1984 one such theologian, David Jenkins, became Bishop of Durham. His unorthodox views on the Virgin birth and the bodily resurrection of Jesus caused great controversy. When, that year, York Minster, where he had been consecrated, was struck by lightning, this was seen by some Evangelical critics as divine judgement.

The Established Churches also had to confront challenges from within the world of religion. They were affected by other Christian churches, by traditional non-Christian faiths and by new cults. Although the Roman Catholic Church was more successful than the Church of England in retaining the loyalty of its flock, at least as measured by church attendance, its hold over many of its communicants was lessened by widespread hostility towards the ban on artificial methods of contraception in the 1968 papal encyclical *Humanae vitae*.

The Catholic population of England and Wales fell from a peak of 4,257,000 in 1981 to 4,155,000 in 1999, while weekly Mass attendance fell to 1,041,000: Catholic churches in London suffered a decline in congregations in 1989-98 of 19 per cent. In 2003 the Catholic Cardinal-Archbishop of Westminster, Cormac Murphy O'Connor, was put under public media pressure over the issue of the abuse of children by priests, a subject that had been generally hushed up in the past, and in 2002 the Archbishop of Cardiff was forced to retire over the same issue. The ready willingness of the laity to express discontent was a sign of change.

The Nonconformist churches were also affected by a decline in faith. The number of Baptists, for example, fell from 300,000 in 1970 to 230,000 in 1992, and the number of young believers was particularly hit, although in 1989-98 the Baptists reversed an earlier fall in congregations in London, instead seeing a 11 per cent increase. Across all the Christian denominations, however, adult attendance at church fell from 10.2 per cent in 1980 to 7.7 per cent in 1998.

The decline in religious commitment was linked to a decline in sectarian animosity, although the latter also served, in both Northern Ireland and Glasgow, to express group tensions that remained powerful. In both Northern Ireland and Glasgow these group tensions helped to define personal, local and collective senses of identity, and were also divisive. In Glasgow, they were in part expressed in football violence, with the rivalry between Celtic and Rangers.

The Established Churches were also challenged by the rise of 'fundamentalist' Christianity, much of it inspired from America. Far from being hierarchical, this focused on a direct relationship between God and worshipper, without any necessary intervention by clerics and without much, if any, role for the sacraments. Certain aspects of this Christianity, especially its charismatic quality, appealed to some Anglicans, creating tensions within the Church of England. The Christian tradition also became more diverse, as a consequence of the participatory character of worship introduced by immigrants from the West Indies. In addition, non-Trinitarian religions (that do not regard Jesus as the Son of God), such as the Christadelphians and Jehovah's Witnesses, grew in popularity in the 1980s and '90s. The long-established Mormons had 90,000 members in Britain in 1970 and 150,000 in 1992.

Traditional non-Christian faiths had less of an appeal to Christians. Instead, they essentially catered for immigrant groups and their descendants: their logic was ethnic and exclusive. This was true of Jews, Muslims and Sikhs, particularly the first and the last. All three were also affected by the increasingly sceptical and secular nature of society. Islam, however, benefited greatly from its strong presence in large communities of immigrants and from fresh currents of immigration. Although these faiths converted very few Christians, and, apart from Islam, did not seek to do so, they greatly challenged the Christian Churches, because they claimed that Britain was a multi-cultural society, and that Christianity, therefore, should not enjoy what were presented as special privileges: for example, the overwhelming majority of state-aided denominational schools were Christian.

This argument was pushed actively from the 1980s, especially on behalf of Islam. The alleged blasphemy of Salman Rushdie's novel *The Satanic Verses* (1988) created an important controversy in 1989, because Islamic figures were outraged that Christianity, but not Islam, enjoyed protection under the blasphemy laws; not, though, that the Churches had much recourse to them. There were numerous demonstrations against the book and, in 1992, the controversy led to the first meeting of the Muslim Parliament of Great Britain.

Having been 25,000 strong in 1970 and 400,000 in 1975, the number of Muslims in the country doubled between 1980 and 1995, rising to 1.2 million. The number of Hindus rose from 50,000 in 1972 to 320,000 in 1993, and that of Sikhs from 75,000 to 300,000. The first Hindu temple outside India was opened as late as 1962; a quarter-century later, at Neasden in north London, the Mandir Temple, the largest Hindu temple outside India, opened. Thus, whereas in 1970 Jews had outnumbered Hindus, Muslims and Sikhs combined by about 450,000 to 375,000, by 1993 the figures were closer to 300,000 to 1,620,000. This shift altered the content and perception of the non-Christian religious life of Britain.

Christianity also came under challenge from the 1960s from 'new age' religions and Buddhism, which appealed to many who would otherwise have been active Christians. They proved better able than the Churches to capture the enthusiasm of those who wished to believe amidst a material world where faith had become just another commodity. The popularity of cults was also a reflection of the atomization of a society that now placed a premium on individualism and on personal responses. Such a society was peculiarly unsuited to the coherence and historical basis of doctrine, liturgy, practice and organization that was characteristic of the Churches. In addition, astrology, with its very different values, was popular, while there was a revival of interest in Druidism.

By the 1990s only one in seven Britons was an active member of a Christian Church, although more claimed to be believers: generally over two-thirds. Both for most believers and for the less or non-religious, faith became less important, not only to the fabric of life but also to many of the turning points of individual lives, especially dying and death. Events such as marriage ceremonies and baptisms became less important as occasions for displays of family and social cohesion. This in part reflected the extent to which couples were choosing to live together while more parents were choosing not to have their children baptized. A disproportionately high percentage of those who attended church were women, middle-aged and middle class. In England, by 1998, only 2 per cent of the adult population regularly attended Church of England services.

This was a shift that was widespread in Western Europe, but the decline was stronger in England than in Northern Ireland, Eire or Scotland. In the late 1990s only 10 per cent of the English population had been in a church in the previous month, but the percentages for Scotland and Northern Ireland were 16 and 52 respectively. Whereas in Northern Ireland, where communities are tight-knit, religion is a crucial expression of community identity, this was far less true of England. In Wales, adult Sunday church attendance figures for 1979–84 revealed that no county had a rate of 20 per cent or more. Church membership figures also fell.

The failure in the 1990s of the 'Keep Sunday Special' campaign, heavily backed by the Established Churches, to prevent shops from opening on the Sabbath, confirmed the general trend. As another instance of the Churches' inability to sustain their definitions of time or space as sacred, or at least special, noise-abatement orders are now served on some churches by local authorities at the behest of people no longer happy to listen to church bells. In 2003 the Pope complained about a lack of religiosity in Scotland, while Rowan Williams, the new Archbishop of Canterbury, was ready to consider the disestablishment of the Church of England. At the same time, the popularity of the Alpha course, an evangelical introductory Church of England course, indicated the willingness of many to commit.

SOCIAL MORES

The decline of the authority of the Churches was related to the current of social change associated with the 1960s, although it was not confined to them. The hedonism and self-centredness of the permissive society was attacked by some critics, for example Malcolm Bradbury in his satirical novel *The History Man* (1975), but their impact was limited. Indeed the book itself, and its subsequent appearance in a television version, contributed to a sense of social fluidity. Campaigners against pornography and changing public standards, for example Lord Longford and Mary Whitehouse, were cold-shouldered or lampooned by the media, and did not succeed in winning government support.

In the 1980s and early '90s there were attempts to reverse the libertarian trend, with talk of 'family values' and 'back to basics', but the movement had scant success and even its political sponsors, the Conservative government, made only a limited effort. Thatcher attacked what she called the 'progressive consensus', and told *The Times* on 10 October 1987 that children 'needed to be taught to respect traditional moral values', but the liberal legislation of the 1960s was not reversed. Instead, under Labour, after it returned to power in 1997, there was further libertarianism in sexual matters. In 2000 the British Board of Film Classification passed 'hardcore' films for R18 classification.

A sense of social fluidity was captured by the media. Television was more successful in setting the tone of British society than more historic institutions, such as the Established Churches. The latter, nevertheless, responded. In 1995 the General Synod of the Church of England abandoned the phrase 'living in sin'. Television encouraged a permissiveness in language and behaviour by making such conduct appear normal. By the mid-1990s most television and radio 'soaps' supposedly depicting normal life seemed to have their quota of one-parent families, abused children and sympathetically presented homosexuals.

The cartoonists captured the same shifts. One of the best, Mark Boxer, had a braying upper-class woman declare, in the *Guardian* on 1 June 1983, 'Nonsense, nanny, We're *thrilled* Emma's fiancé is self-made', and another, on 3 October 1983, 'We couldn't afford to give Fiona a season; but luckily she is in a soft porn movie' (a reference to the one-time activity of Koo Stark, an actress linked with Prince Andrew). On 27 July 1983 a woman in bed in a Boxer cartoon addressed her partner: 'Will you get out of bed; I want you to be one of the 8 per cent who propose on their knees', an ironic comment on the prevalence of pre-marital cohabitation.

Divorce became more common and the rate was well above that of the European Union as a whole. It was an expression of a greater variety, indeed consumption, of lifestyles, and was central to the growth in single parenting that concerned many commentators. This growth was an important aspect of the extent to which, outside the control of government, there was a whole series of social changes that affected public policies.

GENDER

The most important social changes related to women. What was termed 'consciousness raising' was a feature of the diverse 'women's liberation' movement. Conventional assumptions were widely attacked. Thus, nuclear families, the authoritarian role of men within households, and sexual subservience were all criticized. Demands for the recognition of an independent sexuality included an assertion of women's rights to enjoy sex; to have it before marriage without incurring criticism;

and to control contraception and, thus, their own fertility. There was also pressure for more radical options. The 1970 national conference of the Women's Liberation Movement agreed four main demands: equal education and opportunity, equal pay, free and automatically available contraception and abortion, and widespread nursery provision. An end to discrimination against lesbians followed in 1974, as did legal and financial independence for women.

There was powerful pressure for legal change, leading to a range of results. The Abortion Act of 1967 was followed by a situation close to abortion on demand. Although strictly the Act gave doctors control over abortion, they sought not to exercise it. The Sex Discrimination Act of 1976 had considerable impact on the treatment and employment of women. The police were encouraged to take a firmer line against wife-beating and child abuse. When Labour came to power in 1997, it established a Women's Unit in order to improve their position, and a Minister for Women was appointed.

Aside from demands for legal changes, feminism also led to pressure for changes in lifestyles and for social arrangements that put women's needs and expectations in a more central position. Jobs and lifestyle became more important as aspirations for women, complementing, rather than replacing, home and family. The number of married women entering the job market escalated from the 1960s, and more women returned to work after having children. Women's support groups played a vocal role in the 1984–5 miners' strike.

Women ceased to be seen largely in terms of family units – as daughters, spinsters, wives, mothers and widows – and, instead, benefited greatly from a major increase in opportunities and rights, and from a wholesale shift in social attitudes and expectations. The nuclear family as the normative basis for the household became less common.

Gender was, and is, an issue for men as well as women. The loss of Empire and the end of conscription affected notions of masculinity and also gendered constructions of citizenship. Less emphasis was placed on what had been seen as masculine values, and some of these values were questioned, indeed mocked. This was part of a process of change in the images of masculinity. The decline of manual work, the growing importance of women workers, and the rise of feminism also contributed to the same sense of changing, indeed, in some contexts, imperilled, masculinity. Masculinity became a more urgent social issue, because there was concern about anti-social behaviour among young men and about their readiness to neglect the obligations of parenthood.

For some, different attitudes to homosexuality contributed powerfully to a sense of imperilled masculinity. They also accentuated divisions within both the Conservative Party and the Church of England. The extent to which homosexuality became publicly avowed and respectable would have surprised earlier generations. In 1997 the General Synod of the Church of England asserted the right of cohabiting couples, including homosexuals, to receive fertility treatment. A Gallup poll indicated that over half the population saw heterosexual and homosexual relationships as of equal value.

Nevertheless, there was resistance. Section 28 of the 1988 Local Government Act, a Conservative measure, forbade local authorities from 'promoting homosexuality' or teaching 'its acceptability. . . as a pretended family relationship'. A bill to allow homosexual sex from the age of 16 (giving them the same age of consent as heterosexuals) was defeated in the Conservative-dominated House of Lords in 1998. Two years later, the proposal by the Scottish Executive to repeal the law banning the 'promotion' of homosexuality in schools led to a campaign to keep the clause that was strongly backed by the Scottish tabloids, as well as by Cardinal Thomas Winning, the head of the Catholic Church in Scotland, and by a privately financed referendum. Winning also offered pregnant women money not to have abortions. In 2003, an attempt, supported by the Archbishop of Canterbury, to appoint a homosexual as the Bishop of Reading was thwarted by widespread opposition within the Church of England.

THE DECLINE OF DEFERENCE

The extent of social fluidity will be considered further in chapter Seven, with discussion of both class and race. Social change itself did not make the country less governable, let alone ungovernable, but it created major issues of adaptation. This was particularly the case because people as a whole were apparently less deferential and more inclined both to mock government and to opt in, or out, of observing laws and regulations as they chose. 'Apparently' is an important qualification, because it would be a mistake to exaggerate the extent of earlier respect for authority and the law.

Nevertheless a shift could be seen, particularly in middle-class and publicly disseminated attitudes. Thus, the satire boom of the early 1960s became even more pointed and pungent in later renditions, for example the *Spitting Image* attacks on the Thatcher government. In the 2001 election campaign Blair was confronted in front of the television cameras by a woman furious at the poor quality of hospital treatment available to her husband, and she was not satisfied by his reassurances. In the same campaign, again in front of the cameras, a farm worker threw an egg that hit John Prescott, the Deputy Prime Minister, receiving a thump in return. The sense of a less deferential public, or one that expressed its lack of deference more clearly, was amply captured in early 2003 as controversy over policy towards Iraq led to bitter satirical attacks on the government on the television and, in the Jeremy Paxman BBC interview with the Prime Minister in Newcastle, to members of the audience answering back and showing little respect for office or man. This is not inherently bad. Government to be democratic needs to be accountable. But this process has made it harder to govern Britain. The political narrative of the last three decades amply shows this.

Chapter 5

From the Three-Day Week to the Fall of Thatcher, 1973–90

For all the talk of 'controlled dispersal' and 'containment formations', the scene now had the appearance of medieval siege warfare. Ancient imperial infantry tactics. The legions against the barbarians.

Fictional account of a 1985 police exercise in crowd control from Jake Arnott's novel *He Kills Coppers* (2001)

In 1974 the Conservative Prime Minister, Edward Heath, asked the question 'Who governs Britain?' when he confronted the National Union of Miners over their unwillingness to accept the constraints of the statutory income policy, a refusal that challenged Heath's ability to manage union relations, public finances and the economy. The union's policy was motivated as much by political considerations as by labour relations. The Communist Vice-President of the union, Mick McGahey, told its policy-making conference that 'we shall speed the day when not only will we establish decent wages and a decent standard of living, we will end this Tory government and create conditions for a rapid advance to Socialism in this country.' Labour relations were to be key to the question of whether Britain was indeed governable until Thatcher defeated the miners' strike of 1984–5.

In December 1973, faced by problems with the miners, who pushed their £138 million pay claim hard, the Heath government put industry on a three-day week to conserve power supplies. Faced by power cuts, people had to check newspapers to find out when they would have electricity. The economy was anyway hard hit by the quadrupling of oil prices that followed the outbreak of the Yom Kippur War between Israel, and Egypt and Syria, as Arab states tried to put pressure on Western governments. This was a stark reminder that, however ungovernable the domestic situation might be, the international one was even less subject to direction by government. By the end of his government, Heath was unable to wield or provide power.

Heath called a general election to bolster his position and try to overawe the miners. Held on 28 February 1974, it left the Conservatives with the biggest percentage of the popular vote (37.9 to 37.1 for Labour), but with fewer MPs (297 to 301), and with the Liberals (19.3 per cent and 14 MPs) holding the balance of power. Since the Liberals under Jeremy Thorpe refused to enter into a coalition with Heath, Labour under Harold Wilson returned to power, swiftly reversing the legislation of the Heath years (1970-74). Heath's had been the first government since MacDonald's second Labour government (1929-31) that lasted for only one term.

Labour was to hold office until 1979, thanks to another general election in October 1974; its overall majority was only three, but the majority over the Conservatives was bigger than the one it had gained that February. Wilson, however, was unable to govern effectively, and in 1974-6 he completed the process begun by Heath. An economy, state and society that had been muddling through for decades, operating far below the level of effectiveness of other countries but, nevertheless, at least avoiding crisis and breakdown, slid into chaos.

Due to the downturn in the global economy, the overall situation was far from propitious. The collapse of the long post-war boom triggered a combination of rapid inflation and rising unemployment. This posed problems for Keynesian economists as an adverse relationship of the two had been assumed. Yet Wilson compounded Heath's inability to control wages by measures that let them rip. In 1974 he repealed the Conservatives' Industrial Relations Act and legal sanctions on pay bargaining; in its place he announced a 'social contract' with the Trades Union Congress (TUC), but that could not contain a massive wage explosion that began with buying off the miners. At the same time, there was large-scale borrowing by the government; controls were placed on prices and dividends; company profits collapsed; there was a massive fall on the stock market; and there was no incentive to invest. As a result of this economic illiteracy, which stemmed from a major lack of understanding of the free market and an exaggeration of the capacity of government, 1974–6 was the closest that Britain had come to the collapse of capitalism.

Inflationary demands were pushed by union leaders, who were themselves under pressure from their members. Industrial earnings, which had increased by an average of nearly 14 per cent yearly in 1971–3, itself a very high figure, went up by 19 per cent in 1974 and 23 per cent in 1975. As prices also rose fast in this inflationary maelstrom, there was pressure for further wage increases. As another instance of ungovernability, agreements reached between employers and union leaderships frequently did not stick at plant level. Wilson, unwilling to take on union leaders who refused to accept wage restraint, was unable to move the economy from recession. At last, in June 1975, the TUC responded to the initiative of Jack Jones, the Transport Workers' leader, and offered a voluntary agreement on wage restraint that the government accepted. However, the union leaders who signed up for an income policy lacked any real support from their members. These, and other, institutional weaknesses made it difficult to make corporatism work as it then did in Germany and Sweden, and provided a troublesome background for the extension of public ownership in the economy, which took place with major nationalizations. The 1975 Industry Act established the National Enterprise Board, while, that year, the government took the majority of the shares in the newly consolidated car manufacturer British Leyland. The British National Oil Corporation was created in 1975, and British Aerospace and British Shipbuilders in 1977.

The Labour government confronted a fall in economic growth, high inflation and deficits both in the balance of payments and in spending.

Lower growth reduced anticipated revenue, while higher unemployment pushed up social-welfare costs and cut tax yields. This situation was confronted by a new Prime Minister. Wilson had surprised commentators by resigning in April 1976. His choice as successor, the Foreign Secretary, James Callaghan, won the ballot of MPs for the Labour leadership, beating, on the second ballot, the candidate of the 'soft left', Michael Foot.

Callaghan was defeated, in 1979, on the sole occasion he faced the electorate as party leader, but he had considerable talents, both as leader and as Prime Minister. He was more popular than his ministerial colleagues, was not an ideologue, and was more honest than Wilson. This, however, could not save Callaghan. In 1976, a sterling crisis, which owed much to the withdrawal of funds by the oil states of the Middle East, forced the government to turn for a loan to the International Monetary Fund (IMF), as if Britain was a bankrupt banana economy. This was the first major Western state to be forced to this expedient. The IMF demanded cuts in government spending and, after a political battle within the Cabinet against left-wing opponents and other critics, they were accepted. Cuts were imposed in December 1976. The Left, in contrast, supported a withdrawal from international capitalism by means of import controls.

Compared to the nadir of 1974–6, government policies led to an improvement in the country's economic fortunes, with sterling rising and unemployment and inflation falling, but the economy remained under strain. The level of industrial disputes remained high, although the Social Contract led to a significant reduction in the rate of inflation, which eventually fell to below 10 per cent in 1978. In 1977 violent mass picketing in support of a union-recognition strike at the Grunwick film processing factory in north London (where the employees felt harshly exploited) raised serious issues about public order. Industrial disputes discouraged investment, while, due to the downward pressure on public expenditure, there was a particular crisis with labour relations in the public sector. The role of the unions was vilified in Anthony Burgess's novel *1985* (1978), in which 'TUCland' is revealed as callous and destructive.

The economic crisis culminated in the 'Winter of Discontent' of 1978–9, when TUCland seemed all too real. Callaghan lacked a message and policy to keep Labour united. The TUC and the Labour Party Conference both rejected the norm of 5 per cent in wage increases proposed by the government, and, unlike under Thatcher, there was no legislation to restrain the unions. Instead, Callaghan, who had played a major role in blocking the union reforms advocated by Barbara Castle in 1969, thought it best to rely on agreement with union leaders. However, their attitude was summed up by Moss Evans, General Secretary of the Transport and General Workers' Union, who declared, in January 1979, 'I'm not bothered by percentages. It is not my responsibility to manage the economy. We are concerned about getting the rate for the job.'

Strikes by petrol-tanker and lorry drivers were followed by attempts by public-sector unions to 'catch up'. Hospital ancillary staff, ambulancemen and dustmen went on strike. Hospitals were picketed and, in Liverpool, the dead were left unburied, and troops were called in to shoot rats swarming round accumulated rubbish. The large number of simultaneous strikes, the violence and mean-mindedness of the picketing (which included the turning away of ambulances and widespread secondary picketing), and the lack of interest by the strikers in the public, greatly disrupted the life of most of the population, discredited the rhetoric and practice of trade unionism for much of the public, and clearly showed that Labour could not handle the unions. This was more specifically a failure for Callaghan's search for the pragmatic deal. Thereafter, the 'Winter of Discontent' was a theme in each Conservative general-election campaign.

Callaghan's failure led to a surge in support for the Conservatives under the largely unknown Margaret Thatcher, who had become Party leader, in 1975, because she was the candidate who most clearly was not the unsuccessful and discredited Heath, and because she was willing to stand against him. Callaghan made a serious error in not risking an election in the autumn of 1978, as many expected him to. The following spring he lost control of the Commons when, following the failure of the devolution referendum in Scotland, the Scottish Nationalists joined the Conservatives and the Liberals in passing a vote of no confidence. In the election of 3 May 1979, the Tory vote went up to 43.9 per cent (compared with 35.8 per cent in October

1974), with Labour falling to 36.9 per cent (compared to 39.2 per cent), and the Conservatives won a working majority of 43 seats. With an average national swing towards the Conservatives of 5.2 per cent, Thatcher had benefited from a marked fall of Liberal votes (from 18.3 to 13.8 per cent), as well as from a widespread sense of despair with Labour and the unions, which extended to her winning the support of about one-third of union votes. Thatcher had also campaigned well, ably taking advantage of the opportunities offered by the press and television. The percentage lead over Labour of 7 per cent was the largest since 1945.

THE THATCHER YEARS

Thatcher held office until 1990, and stamped her personality and policies on what are known as the Thatcher years. Relishing the cult of personality that developed round her, she dominated the Cabinet and the Party. Yet, at the same time, Thatcher faced, throughout her period in office, sustained opposition within her own party that contributed to a situation in which she was only imperfectly in control of the political process. Her elevation to the leadership owed more to the fact that Heath had lost three out of four general elections than it did to support for policies that would later become known as 'Thatcherism'. Furthermore, despite three election victories (1979, 1983, 1987), Thatcher was unable to introduce or implement many of the policies she advocated, and, in the end, she fell and was unable to ensure the continuity she sought. Instead, the Conservative governments that remained in office until 1997 became both weak and unpopular; their Labour successors under Blair, although appearing, in some respects, to follow the thrust of her policies, also differed from them in important respects.

Thatcher had a powerful dislike for a tradition, ethos and practice of compromise and consensus that she felt had led to Britain's decline. She was particularly critical of those she called the 'Wets', Conservative one-nation paternalists, whom she thought 'spineless' and who were not 'one of us'. Thatcher blamed the previous Conservative governments, particularly that of Heath, as well as the Labour governments for causing Britain's problems, although, in fact, Callaghan had abandoned Keynesian policies and there was an element of continuity in fiscal policy between him and Thatcher.

Thatcher sought to roll back the state in the interests of free-market participation and competition. She was committed to the view that state intervention in the economy was not a benefit and, instead, that the independence of the free market was constructive. The role of the state in Conservative thinking declined dramatically from the mid-1970s. Like the tariff reformers before the First World War, Thatcher advocated radical prescriptions for conservative purposes, in the sense of maintaining the social system, but she was more disenchanted with the nature and role of the British state than earlier Conservatives. The neo-liberal, anti-corporatist and anti-collectivist rhetoric, attitudes and policies of the Conservative Party under Thatcher ensured that it looked more to the USA than to the Continent for its models and parallels.

Promising strong leadership and pleased to be known as the Iron Lady, Thatcher relished her determination to ensure change and to weather the storm. It endowed her politics with a sense of virtuous struggle. Thatcherism was just as much a moral as an economic creed. This was seen in the formulation of policy. Thatcher had no time for doubt: she sought results, not debate, and her response to criticism was robust and, at times, tribal. I can recall her telling me that she noted that a hospital consultant who complained to her during a visit to Barrow-in-Furness was wearing a red tie, although this was an ironic aside to the contrast she was drawing between investment in new facilities there and in hospital provision in her London constituency.

With her characteristic clarity, Thatcher presented economic factors as crucial to Britain's plight and offered an apparently straightforward solution to Britain's economic problems (control of the money supply) at a time when other politicians seemed lacking in both insight and determination.

In practice, as with other politicians, there was much compromise, especially in her early years. Thatcher was not the most Thatcherite politician: intuition and self-confidence, as much as ideology and doctrine, were central to her leadership. Indeed, there was to be criticism that her rhetoric of 'rolling back the state' was misleading, especially in healthcare where the NHS remained in a dominant position. Furthermore, government expenditure did not fall as anticipated. In part, this was due to a large and predictable rise in unemployment payments in response to a sharp increase in unemployment during her first government (1979–83). Nevertheless, under Thatcher there were also subsequent boosts to public spending, for example that of £5.5 billion agreed in November 1986, while, on 8 November 1990, in the last autumn statement by a Chancellor of the Exchequer (in this case John Major) under a Thatcher government, public expenditure of more than £200 billion was anticipated for the first time, as, aside from inflation, an increase of 4.5 per cent in such expenditure was planned.

Yet, with Thatcher, rhetoric and policies were linked, because there was a clear determination to persist in policies that was different in degree and style to that of her Conservative and Labour predecessors, and led some commentators to compare her to Churchill, whom she referred to as Winston.

Having won power, the Thatcher government rapidly signalled its views with a budget in 1979 that cut direct taxation but also increased Value Added Tax from 8 to 15 per cent, a measure that was criticized as regressive. The budget also announced a dramatic cut in public expenditure, by £4,000 million (i.e., £4 billion), a figure that signified Thatcher's undying concern with costs. Thatcherite economics led to an uneasy co-existence of private wealth and the public poverty of a state sector unable to invest sufficiently in infrastructure, such as school buildings. In the 1979 budget, the basic rate of income tax fell from 33 to 30 per cent, and the top rate on earned income from 83 to 80 per cent, while the top rate on 'unearned' income – interest from savings and other investments – was cut from 98 to 75 per cent. This strategy was pursued in March 1980 with another major cut in public expenditure, by £1,275 million, and with a restriction of the public sector borrowing requirement (PSBR) to £8,500 million.

Cuts in direct taxation were popular, and helped provide Thatcherite Conservatism with a creed: providing incentives and rewarding effort. Rising prosperity, inflationary wage settlements and more widespread taxation had ensured that 80 per cent of households were paying direct taxation by 1975. As a result, taxation levels became more central in public awareness and debate, and the principal factor in the response of many to government policy.

Lower taxes, however, released purchasing power that pushed up inflation to 18 per cent in 1980, leading to a rise in interest rates. Combined with the impact of North Sea oil, this led to a rise in the value of sterling. The value of North Sea production rose greatly as the outbreak of war between Iran and Iraq (1980–88) sent oil prices up to $40 a barrel. Alongside high interest rates, the rise in sterling hit manufacturing, helping greatly to exacerbate the de-industrialization that was already apparent in sectors of the economy. Company bankruptcies pushed up unemployment, which rose above two million in August 1980. Social security payments thus rose, driving up public expenditure. Inflation, indeed, led to the phasing out of the halfpenny in 1984.

In response, the government ignored Keynesian precepts of investing and spending the way out of the crisis, and, with what critics called a 'sado-monetarist' policy, followed a deflationary policy, cutting spending in order to reduce the budget deficit. In the budget on 10 March 1981 spending was cut by £3,290 million, and some taxes (not income tax) were increased. This was an attempt to cut the budget deficit as a percentage of GDP, specifically the PSBR, which had increased by 130 per cent in 1977–9. 'Cuts' became a term associated with government policies, and indeed was the title of a 1987 novel by Malcolm Bradbury, which charted malaise in the public sector.

Unemployment rose further, to reach 3.3 million in the winter of 1982–3. This rise was completely out of line with recent experience. Many factories that were closed, such as the steelworks at Consett in County Durham, Shotton on Deeside in north-east Wales and Corby in Northamptonshire, were crucial to entire communities. This threw into focus the social costs of the long-term decline in heavy industry. A major steel strike in 1980 was unsuccessful and this facilitated a restructuring of the industry that hit jobs. The shrinking of the economy affected manufacturing industry far more than services. In terms of public perception, these were 'real' jobs. They were predominantly male. The toll was repeatedly driven home because unemployment figures were published monthly and not, as with many other indices, quarterly.

Critics urged a change of policy, but Thatcher's response defined her government. 'The lady's not for turning', she told the 1980 Party conference, and the delegates applauded. This was a marked contrast with Heath's willingness in 1971 to abandon the non-interventionism he professed when he came to office. Thatcher was christened 'Tina': 'There is no alternative'.

Throughout her period as Prime Minister, Thatcher was popular with the Conservative Party conference, more so than in the Cabinet and parliamentary party. Partly as a result, the role of the Cabinet was restricted. Anticipating Blair, Thatcher cut the number of Cabinet committees and their length, and preferred to rely on trusted advisers. Again anticipating Blair, one of these was her Press Secretary, Bernard Ingham. Thatcher led, rather than followed, discussion in the Cabinet. She ignored criticism and got rid of critics.

Thatcher remained adamant about her policies in 1981, despite an outbreak of rioting not seen, outside Northern Ireland, since 1832. These were not industrial disputes involving violent secondary picketing, and thus answerable to some sort of control. Instead, from April 1981, in Brixton and Southall in London, Toxteth in Liverpool, Moss Side in Manchester and, to a lesser extent, other centres, such as Derby, crowds rioted, looted and fought with the police. These were small-scale disturbances, many of which reflected specific local problems, especially relations between black youth and the police, which became the focus of the report from the Scarman Inquiry that was set up after the Brixton riots. At the time, however, it was unclear how far these riots would spread and how they would stop.

Evidence of the strains on social cohesion that were a result of government policy did not lead Thatcher to change direction. Instead, having failed to consult the Cabinet 'Wets' on the 1981 budget, Thatcher dismissed leading ones that September (Sir Ian Gilmour, Christopher Soames and Mark Carlisle), and brought in her supporters, particularly Norman Tebbit, who became Employment Secretary, Cecil Parkinson and Nigel Lawson. The reshuffle made it easier to see out the crisis until the next election, which was not due until 1984, a suitably apocalyptic year for those who remembered George Orwell's bleak novel.

Thatcher was far from alone in her quest to transform British politics, and change elsewhere was encouraged not just by the need to respond to Thatcherism but also by the attraction of determining how to respond to what was anticipated as its likely demise. To Thatcher's left (a very large area), there was a process of adjustment in which efforts were made to remake first the Labour Party and then British politics as a whole. Callaghan's defeat had demoralized the Labour realists and, in opposition, the Party drifted leftwards, an important aspect of the political polarization of the decade as ideas and practices of consensus were put under pressure, and one that worked to help Thatcher. Similarly, the Scottish Nationalists moved considerably to the left.

Michael Foot, a veteran left-winger, defeated Denis Healey for the Labour leadership in November 1980, and Anthony Wedgwood [Tony] Benn and his left-wing allies pushed through a conference programme that was designed to entrench a radical agenda: a future Labour government would seek to extend public ownership in the key sectors of the economy. Protectionism was advocated and Britain was to leave the European Economic Community. The House of Lords would be abolished. Britain would abandon the atomic deterrent whatever other nuclear powers did (unilateral nuclear disarmament). Radical policy prescriptions arose in part from a reading of the 1974–9 Labour governments in terms of a failure arising from insufficient radicalism. In opposition, it was also apparently desirable and certainly easier to advocate organizational changes. The Labour left wanted the Party to become tighter-knit and more responsive to their ideas and to its members (or at least constituency activists). To do so, they sought to make it easier for constituency parties to deselect sitting MPs as official candidates. In future, the Party leader would be elected by an electoral college, consisting of three sections: MPs, unions and constituency associations.

This programme helped to divide Labour. Three former Cabinet ministers – David Owen, William Rodgers and Shirley Williams – sought to resist the left within the Labour Party, and, when they became dissatisfied with their lack of success, joined another former minister, Roy Jenkins, in defecting and forming the Social Democratic Party (SDP) on 26 March 1981. The decision to deprive Labour MPs of the sole power to elect the Party leader proved to be the final straw for Owen, Rodgers and Williams, as it was seen as likely to open the way to further radicalism.

Designed to 'break the mould' of British politics, the SDP was intended to be a third force, and to make the impact that the Liberals had failed to do. In his 1979 Dimbleby lecture, Jenkins had spoken of the need for a revived centre in British politics. In pursuit of this aim, the SDP quickly made overtures to the Liberal Party, which was eager to reciprocate: the two formed the Alliance. In terms of electoral calculation, the Alliance benefited from defections by Labour MPs, by-election and local election successes, and ratings in the public opinion polls that put it above the other parties. As 1981 gave way to 1982, the popularity of the Alliance, the unpopularity of the Conservatives and Labour's lack of credibility seemed to indicate that the mould was indeed about to break. With unemployment rising, it looked as though Thatcher would be a one-term Prime Minister, as Callaghan had been.

Politics, however, is the art of taking advantage of the unexpected. Thatcher was able to regain the initiative, thanks to the total defeat, by a British expeditionary force, of the Argentinian units that had captured the British-ruled Falkland Islands in the South Atlantic in April 1982. The victory raised Britain's international prestige and won the government, and Thatcher, widespread support in Britain. It also increased her already strong sense of purpose and self-confidence, and her disinclination to adapt to the views of others. The gut patriotism released and displayed during the war made many commentators uncomfortable, but Thatcher knew how to respond.

Victory abroad was joined to a measure of success at home. The recession had been so strong that it was easier subsequently to demonstrate growth, whether in output or, to a lesser extent, employment. This sense of relative achievement was crucial. Economic growth in 1982–3 was accompanied by a fall in inflation, while, to some, unemployment (for others) was the acceptable cost necessary to ensure weaker unions and lower inflation. The fall in interest rates, and thus in mortgage payments, greatly contributed to a rise in the living standards of many of those who were in work and owned houses. This was taken further with a pre-election budget on 15

March 1983, in which personal allowances were raised by more than the rate of inflation. The £25,000 ceiling on mortgages for tax relief purposes was raised to £30,000.

Increasingly confident, Thatcher decided to call the election early. Held on 9 June 1983, the Conservatives won 397 seats (339 in 1979), compared to Labour's 209 (269), giving Thatcher the biggest working majority of any government since 1945. This success was particularly strongly marked in London and southern England, neither of which had been savagely hit by the recession. Yet the Conservative percentage of the vote (42.4 per cent) was the lowest of any Conservative government since Bonar Law's short-lived ministry of 1922–3. There was no Thatcherite tide among the electors. They remained wedded to the National Health Service and Thatcher was forced to declare that it was safe in her government's hands. It was impressive to retain so much of the Conservative vote in the face of high unemployment and with the electorate offered the option of the Alliance, but a wider indication of the absence of a Thatcherite tide was provided by the major fall in Conservative Party membership in the 1980s. This was part of the structural weakness in the Party bequeathed by Thatcher.

In 1983 Labour's programme did not appeal to the traditional Labour voter, let alone to swing-voters. Foot did not seem a potential Prime Minister, and the manifesto was regarded as extreme. It was memorably described by Gerald Kaufman, a shadow minister, as 'the longest suicide note in history'. The defence policy, particularly unilateral nuclear disarmament, failed to convince many Labour supporters. Others were put off by calls for the extension of public ownership and for withdrawal from the EEC.

This extremism made Labour unelectable and helped the Alliance to win votes, even though its leader, Jenkins, proved a poor campaigner. The Alliance, however, came second in all too many seats. In southern England, it supplanted Labour as the major opposition party, but the Conservatives won the seats. In northern England, most of the SDP MPs who had defected from Labour lost their seats, and attempts to dislodge sitting Labour MPs failed, even in constituencies, such as the City of Durham, where the MP was unpopular and there was a significant number of non-traditional Labour voters. On 27.6 per cent of the votes across the country, Labour won 209 seats, whereas the Alliance won 25.4 per cent of the vote, a major success for third-party politics, but only 23 seats. Stymied by the electoral system, it had failed to achieve its goal of 'breaking the mould' of British politics.

Thatcher celebrated victory by consolidating her control of the Cabinet, replacing Francis Pym, the 'wet' Foreign Secretary, who had been so imprudent as to suggest that big majorities were bad since they encouraged extremism in government. Nigel Lawson, an ardent Thatcherite, and not a man encumbered by doubt, became Chancellor of the Exchequer.

Thatcher soon had another fight on her hands – with the miners. She was determined to be more successful than Heath in defeating what she saw, with much reason, as a 'political strike' by those she termed 'the enemy within'. A first wave of pit closures had been reversed in 1981, when unofficial stoppages forced the government to restore the subsidies it was seeking to remove. The government was better prepared for the second round, when it was determined to push through the closure of twenty pits as the initial stage of a programme to reduce overall capacity. Thatcher was greatly helped by poor and divisive leadership in the NUM, the willingness of 50,000 miners to remain at work, and the availability of energy, including stockpiled and imported coal, and electricity imported from France.

The long dispute (1984–5) exacerbated divisions within the NUM, the union movement and the Labour Party, rather than among the Conservatives. Uncertain of his members' backing, Arthur Scargill, the militant and uncompromising President of the NUM, had refused to call a national strike, as that would have required a national ballot. Instead, he hoped to ensure a snowball process by which the individual areas of the NUM were balloted and the example of the militant would lead the others. Many did, but, Nottinghamshire, where the strike-breaking Union of Democratic Mineworkers was formed, crucially would not. It was central to the conflict. Intimidatory and violent mass picketing there, directed against working miners, helped alienate public support from the strike, not least because it was widely shown on television. Thatcher focused government resources on defeating the strike, particularly by supporting the stockpiling and import of coal. In addition, by moving coal by road to the power stations, the role of the rail unions was lessened. The police benefited from the establishment of a national system to allocate police resources.

The strike collapsed, without an agreed settlement, when the NUM called it off in March 1985 as poverty and helplessness sapped support. Pit closures were then pushed through. Thatcher's recasting of labour away from the traditional heroisms, and towards greater flexibility, particularly in new industries in which the workforce had different social and political values, had been taken a long way forward.

Politics did not stand still during the miners' strike. At its most anarchic and dramatic, there was nearly a change of premier in October 1984, when an IRA bomb carefully planted in the Grand Hotel in Brighton exploded during the Conservative Party conference. There were five deaths and many injured, some, including Norman Tebbit, seriously, but Thatcher was not killed. Nor, of course, was she deflected from her purposes. The struggle with the NUM took much of the government's attention, but it also pressed on with its legislative programme. Privatization had already been moved forward when the Telecommunications Act (12 April 1984) enabled the sale of British Telecom. The rate-capping of local authorities in July 1984 reflected the government's determination to control local government, particularly the Greater London Council; while the Trade Union Act of 26 July 1984 was designed to restrict union militancy further. The provision that, if no ballot was held before a strike, the union lost its legal immunity was seen as a crucial one to embed unions within the constraints of state-controlled legal responsibility and contract.

Instead of trade unions, nationalized industries and council houses, Thatcher wanted a property-owning democracy in which corporatism was weak and capital supreme. Institutions and opinions that resisted were marginalized. One centre of opposition, the Labour-controlled Greater London Council led by Ken Livingstone, a vocal militant, was removed in July 1986 by the Local Government Act, which abolished all the metropolitan authorities. This was part of a wider process of central-ization that took place under Thatcher: some fifty Acts of Parliament were passed transferring power from local government to Westminster and Whitehall. One of the most significant, the Rate Act of June 1984, allowed the government to put a ceiling on rates and thus to control local authority finances. This was used to thwart the attempt, particularly in Liverpool, to create Socialist city-republics ignoring government policy. The extension of compulsory competitive tendering to a wide range of local government services in 1988 was designed to challenge the role of council workers, and their unions. It led to the entrance of private-sector contractors into public-service work, for example refuse collection. Centralization was taken further in 1988 with the Baker Education Act, which was designed to raise standards by creating a national curriculum. Schoolchildren today wonder what baking has to do with their teachers' absence for training on 'Baker days', which in fact, take their name from Kenneth Baker, the former Secretary of State for Education responsible for the relevant legislation.

The dismantling of the legacy of Labour also led to the Housing Act of August 1980, allowing tenants to buy their homes, a process encouraged by giving purchasers favourable deals, and to a widespread process of de-nationalization/privatization. This included British Aerospace, Cable and Wireless, Britoil, the National Bus Company, British Telecom, British Gas, British Airways, Rolls Royce, British Steel, the electricity-generating industry and the water companies. Assets were undervalued to encourage sales and ensure that the share issues were fully subscribed. These sales subsidized government finances, both by bringing in large sums of money (although as capital, not revenue) and by reducing the need for state subsidies. Privatization also weakened the prospect of government economic management, and was thus very important to the dismantling of the corporatist system.

Privatization, reforms in labour relations and a marked reduction in economic and financial regulation encouraged foreign investment. This markedly changed important economic sectors. In the North of England, for example, manufacturing employment in foreign-owned companies rose between 1979 and 1989 from 11.8 per cent to 17.1 per cent.

Share and home ownership were seen as central to the property-owning democracy. Thatcher was concerned to reward not only her core constituency, but also her vision of British society, those she termed 'our people'. In the 1986 (18 March) and 1987 budgets (17 March), the basic rate of income tax was cut to 27 per cent and personal pension plans were launched, allowing large numbers without company pensions to gain tax relief on retirement savings, a measure intended to increase share ownership. Corporation tax was also cut, while the threshold for inheritance tax was raised.

The government also sought to contain social welfare costs, responding both to the high level of expenditure and to the conviction that the cause of genuine recipients suffered by providing for the needs of those termed scroungers. The Social Security Act of 1986 withdrew benefits from 16- and 17-year-olds, a very controversial step, and sought to systematize benefits for others, replacing Supplementary Benefit with Income Support and Family Income Supplement with Family Credit. With the establishment of the Social Fund, controversial changes were also made in the way in which benefits were provided for substantial one-off costs. For those involved, these were no mere footnote to the narrative of the 1980s. In December 1986 the government followed up by announcing a limit on the Supplementary Benefit paid for mortgage interest. Criticism from Conservative backbenchers was a testimony to the sensitivity of an issue that opposed public expenditure, which they wanted cut, and the desire to widen home-ownership. From 1987 until John Major came into power, child benefit allowances were frozen.

The budgets contributed to a strong 'feel-good' factor among much of the electorate, and, on 11 June 1987, Thatcher held another election, again a year earlier than was necessary. Unemployment had fallen from a peak of 3.4 million in January 1986, leading to a fall in welfare costs; the economy was growing, leading to a rise in tax receipts; and interest rates had fallen. Even so, popular support for Thatcherism was less than total. Benefiting again from divisions among their opponents, the Conservatives gained 376 seats on 42.3 per cent of the vote, a comfortable majority of 101 seats, the second largest since 1945, with Labour winning 229 on 30.8 per cent. Under Neil Kinnock, its leader since Michael Foot had resigned after the debacle of the 1983 election, Labour looked more attractive than it had under Foot, but its policies were still to the left of the bulk of the electorate. The Conservatives had also fanned disquiet about the impact of Labour spending plans, devoting particular attention to costing the manifesto promises. The divided

Alliance, with 22 seats on 22.5 per cent, not only again failed to break through, but actually lost support. It had failed to establish an identity other than as a refuge for disaffected Conservatives and Labourites. Labour was now more clearly the leading opposition party. Despite an election campaign that was less accomplished than the 1983 one, the Conservatives continued to do very well in London and southern England, but Labour was far more successful in Scotland and Wales. It won 50 of the 72 Scottish seats, while the Conservatives won only 10.

The failure of the Alliance to break through was followed by its becoming an irrelevance and by the merger of the major part of the SDP with the Liberals in 1988. David Owen led a rump SDP, but, after poor results in by-elections, that collapsed in 1990. Owen was subsequently to urge his supporters to vote Conservative in the 1992 election.

Having won in 1987, Thatcher characteristically avoided all temptation to consolidate. She was determined to end Socialism and to entrench her changes, and was initially helped by buoyant public finances that rested on economic growth and were helped by receipts from privatizations and council house sales. Income tax was cut further, to 25 pence in the pound, in 1988 (with a top rate of 40 per cent), and, combined with lax credit, demonstrated by the ease with which credit cards could be obtained, this fed through into a consumer boom.

The consumer boom pressed on an economy that had lost much of its 'excess capacity' in the recession of the early 1980s. Domestic production could not rise to match demand. Instead, domestic demand outgrew the economy. As a result, inflation shot up, to 10.9 per cent in September 1990, as did imports, pushing the balance of payments into a record deficit of £20 billion in 1989. The fall in the price of oil – from $30 to $10 in 1986 – had a serious impact on GNP and public finances.

Thatcher had abandoned Heath's limited control of bank lending as part of a general 'bonfire' of financial regulations. She argued that public, not total, borrowing was crucial, and sought to contain inflation through this means. This left only short-term means of control, principally raising interest rates, which strengthened sterling and hit manufacturing: they rose to 15 per cent in October 1989, and remained at that figure until October 1990. Government revenues were also under pressure. The Conservatives lost their reputation for economic competence, and growing economic problems helped to foster division within the Party. Martin Amis's description of the 'phosphorescent prosperity' of the 1980s appears all too apt.

Simultaneously, the government's political position was under acute pressure, again largely self-inflicted. In place of funding local government by rates charged on property owners, the government proposed a 'community charge' from every adult, with all those in a given council area paying the same amount. This was designed to forge a link between expenditure and revenue, for now all inhabitants would bear the consequences of rises in the former. It was hoped that this would lead votes to turn away from Labour councils, which tended to spend more. The policy was also designed to reward the home-owners who were seen as the core of Thatcher's support, by making those who remained in council housing join them in bearing the burden of local government. This was electorally necessary for the Conservatives because they had shifted some of the burden of government expenditure toward local taxation.

Budget day on 20 March 1990 also brought support for an overlapping group, savers, with the creation of Tax Exempt Special Savings Accounts (Tessas): building society savings up to a certain amount that were held for five or more years were to be free from tax. This tax break was to be abolished after Labour returned to power. The budget also showed support for savers with the doubling of the upper limit on savings that could be held before entitlement for community charge rebates was lost. This also testified to the sensitivity of the community charge. The last of the Thatcher budgets also included the abolition of stamp duty on share transactions, a measure intended to encourage investment, and an aspect of the removal of financial regulations.

The introduction of the community charge, which was widely termed the Poll Tax, was poorly handled. A tax that would bear equally on dukes and dustmen was seen as unfair. In part, the level was simply set too high, as the electorate paid, and continues to pay, a tax levied on the same basis, the Television Licence Fee, which goes solely to the BBC (£112 per television-owning-household in 2002). Given the near-total nature of television ownership, it is specious to refer to the Licence Fee as a voluntary tax.

Most people paid the Poll Tax (as they had paid the unpopular Ship Money levied by Charles I in the 1630s), and only a small minority took part in violent demonstrations, although the one in Trafalgar Square on 31 March 1990 that culminated in a riot drew about 200,000 supporters (only a small number of whom rioted). Nevertheless, the furore over the Poll Tax hit the government's popularity, especially in Scotland, where it was introduced in April 1989, a year earlier than in England and Wales. This furore encouraged restless Conservative MPs to feel that Thatcher had lost the ability to respond to popular moods, indeed the popular mood. On 22 March 1990 the Conservatives lost the Mid-Staffordshire by-election on a swing of 22 per cent against them. Many of their MPs were vulnerable to any fall in government support in a future election, and they were worried over by-election results.

Economic problems already ensured that Labour was ahead in the polls. Aside from high inflation (to which the Poll Tax contributed) and interest rates, the international stock market crash of October 1987 had removed the feel-good factor that had accompanied the economic recovery of the mid-1980s. By 1990 the economy was moving into recession: inflation's rise was accompanied by that of unemployment, and industry was hit hard by high interest rates, discouraging investment. Thatcher was now less popular than her government. The Poll Tax exemplified her isolation from much of the Conservative Party and an unwillingness to listen and consult. In the autumn of 1989 a backbench Conservative MP, Sir Anthony Meyer, decided to challenge Thatcher for the Party leadership. It was a challenge that was bound to fail, but Meyer succeeded in securing 33 votes.

The developing crisis spun out of control because the Conservative leadership fell apart over the issue of Europe, an issue on which Thatcher found herself at odds with ministers such as Howe, Lawson and Major who were scarcely on the left of the Party. Speaking in September 1988 at Bruges, Thatcher had declared: 'We have not successfully rolled back the frontiers of the state in Britain, only to see them re-imposed at a European level, with a European super-state exercising a new dominance from Brussels'. Instinctively suspicious of the European Economic Community (EEC), Thatcher fell out with the Foreign Secretary, the pro-European Geoffrey Howe, over British membership of the Exchange Rate Mechanism (ERM), which constituted stage one of a projected economic and monetary union for the EEC. In July 1989 Howe was removed from the Foreign Office and made Deputy Prime Minister and Leader of the House of Commons, but without being given power. This left him very bitter, but was not the full extent of the disruption to government. In October 1989 Nigel Lawson, the Chancellor of the Exchequer, resigned in large part because of disagreement over his support for shadowing the Deutschmark, but also because of Lawson's concern that Thatcher was more interested in advice from her economic adviser, Alan Walters. There were increasing charges that Thatcher was a remote leader unwilling to accept advice from ministerial colleagues.

Many major Conservative figures were now outside government or unsympathetic to Thatcher, and the government no longer seemed so impressive. The replacement in 1989, first of Howe at the Foreign Office and then of Lawson, by the relatively inexperienced John Major, who was certainly not a particularly conspicuous success in his short tenure at the Foreign Office, indicated Thatcher's weak position. John Moore, who had been Secretary of State for Health and Social Security in 1987–8 and was, initially, seen as her favoured successor, had failed to justify her support. The retirement, in January 1988, of Willie Whitelaw, the Deputy Prime Minister, who had been an adroit assessor of opinion in the parliamentary party, had weakened Thatcher, as did the retirement of Lord Young, the Secretary of State for Trade. David Waddington, who became Home Secretary in October 1989, did not bring much strength to the government. Norman Fowler and Peter Walker, both long-serving ministers, resigned in early 1990, and Thatcher's ally Nicholas Ridley followed in July.

Having reluctantly been prevailed on to join the ERM, in part by Major and by his successor as Foreign Secretary, Douglas Hurd, Thatcher made it very clear that she had no intention of accepting further integration within the EEC. That path was clearly laid out by the meeting of EEC leaders in the European Council in Rome that October, which declared: 'The European Community will have a single currency which will be an expression of its unity and identity'. She rejected this conclusion, touching off the immediate crisis that led to her fall. Having resigned on 1 November 1990, in anger at Thatcher's strident opposition to further integration, Howe attacked Thatcher, in a speech in the Commons on 13 November, for being unable to accept debate and for her policy on Europe. He also encouraged a leadership bid by Michael Heseltine, another supporter of the EEC, the candidate of the left of the Party and a critic of the Poll Tax. Heseltine had left the Cabinet in 1986 over the Westland affair when he had clashed with Thatcher over whether the Westland helicopter manufacturer should be taken over by an American company (as she wished) or by a European consortium, the course he preferred.

The first ballot for the leadership, on 20 November 1990, gave Thatcher, whose campaign had been very poorly managed, 204 votes to Heseltine's 152. This was not enough (by four votes) to prevent a second ballot, and raised the prospect of Heseltine gaining sufficient support to win then, as Thatcher herself had done against Heath in 1975. Determined to block him, Thatcher, who had initially declared that she would fight on and stand on the second ballot, but whose support was ebbing, stood down as Prime Minister and leader of the Conservative Party on 22 November.

For her successor, Thatcher backed John Major. On 27 November, in the second ballot, he led convincingly: 185, to 131 for Heseltine and 56 for Hurd. This led the other two candidates to concede. The 1980s were over. Major had benefited from being less encumbered than his rivals by negative impressions. Whereas Heseltine and Hurd were seen both as grand and as leftish, Major was middle-class by temperament, far from grand, and able to appeal both to Thatcherites and to those who sought change. In a telling comment on social change, Hurd was driven to explain that, although he was an Old Etonion, he had been a scholarship boy.

CONCLUSIONS

Responses to Thatcher are indicative not just of wider political differences, but also of generational shifts. She made an impact on contemporaries that is difficult to explain to those who have grown subsequently to political awareness. Indeed, psychiatrists had to note that during her period in office one of their standard questions to establish general awareness – who is Prime Minister? – was answered accurately by a far larger percentage of an average sample, a clear indication of her impact.

Part was novelty: a forthright leader after the apparent fudge of Callaghan, and, even more, a woman. Part was the sense of will, captured in the *Punch* cartoon showing Thatcher on the television and an anxious man saying on the telephone that he had already tried to turn it off. There was also a sense of crisis, both the one that preceded the election and the successive crises of her period at the helm. To face a war in 1982 was particularly traumatic, as Britain fought alone and because there had not been a war for decades. Victory was therefore particularly bracing. To many who had supported Thatcher, there was a sense of shadow and decline after her fall. This was exacerbated by disillusionment with the Major governments, which gave the Thatcher years a reflected appeal, especially from late 1992 when the government no longer seemed competent.

This, however, is an approach that has less meaning to the large section of the population that only joined the electorate after Thatcher's fall. To them, her governments, especially their background and early years, appear distant history. It is also less credible to treat history after 1990 as a mere postscript, since this period has grown steadily longer; while to present the Major and Blair governments as Thatcherism stages two and three was to neglect their distinctive features.

This shift opened the possibility of approaching the Thatcher governments and Thatcherism anew, not as the central period and phenomenon of modern British politics, but as a stage in a number of long-term developments, including the Cold War, the debate over corporatism as the organizing principle in political economy, and the struggle over union powers. If the Thatcher governments were a reaction against the previous administration, their abandonment of Keynesianism had, in fact, been prefigured under Callaghan. Furthermore, the Labour governments of Wilson and Callaghan had been robust in their support of NATO. Nevertheless, the break with corporatism was readily apparent. Thatcher kept union leaders at arm's length. Unlike under Wilson, there were to be no beer and sandwiches sessions in No. 10 in order to sort out crises. Union leaders were not seen as 'my people' by Thatcher, and she sought to remould British society in order to circumvent unions and the collective pressures they represented. She succeeded to a point, although far less so with attitudes towards social welfare.

It does not lessen her achievement or impact to suggest that the general move across the West was against collectivism and similarly that there was a widespread process of de-industrialization. Thatcher's policies made the crisis in heavy industry more severe than it needed to be, but she did not invent the crisis. Furthermore, in Britain, this crisis had savage consequences in the short-term, but, in many cases, less so with time. Corby, for example, was hit hard in 1980 when British Steel closed the works, ending more than 5,000 jobs. By 1981, unemployment there was up to 22 per cent. By 1999, however, it had fallen to less than 3 per cent. In part, this was due to diversification. Corby gained Enterprise Zone status and this helped to lure in a wide range of companies, many also attracted by good road links.

The rift in Labour that led to the formation of the Social Democratic Party indicates that resistance to union power and to left-wing politics was not limited to the Conservatives. To Thatcherites, the SDP, like the Conservative 'Wets', were unsound and part of the problem. The latter two, however, were not given the opportunity to test themselves against Scargill, so it is unclear how crucial Thatcher's resolve was. Certainly, had they been in power, both SDP and 'Wets' would have had to respond, like Thatcher, to the consequences of global economic pressures on the British economy. They would probably have cut public expenditure and taxation less, and maintained more control over the financial system, and the latter might have helped to prevent the financial and economic problems of the late 1980s. It is a lame conclusion to give Thatcher the credit for most of the achievements of her government and for the problems that it left, but it is a testimony to her impact that subsequent governments found it difficult to escape her shadow.

Chapter 6

Changing Directions

John Major, the youngest Prime Minister of the century when he was appointed, proved more and less successful than had been anticipated. More because he was Prime Minister for six and a half years, until defeated by Labour under Tony Blair in the general election held on 1 May 1997. To do so, Major both saw off challenges from within the Conservative Party and, in 1992, won a general election that he had been widely expected to lose. Less successful, because Major's years in office witnessed serious blows to government policy, a disunited ministry that lost public confidence, and a Party whose reputation for competence and probity was increasingly tarnished. The 1997 election saw a widespread rejection of the government.

The root problem was that the pleasant, calm and competent, but uncharismatic, Major was less able to control developments than most Prime Ministers and, crucially, unable to create a sense that he was in control. From this followed many of his problems with colleagues, party and public. Initially, Major was helped by the less than first-rate leadership of Labour by Neil Kinnock, but, after he resigned, following the general election of 1992, and was replaced by John Smith, and then, after Smith's death in 1994, by Tony Blair, the quality of Labour leadership cast a harsh light on Major.

He lacked any distinctive ideas or policies with which to win favour with the electorate. Although the Poll Tax was ditched, Major continued the direction of Thatcherite policies, but without her charisma or, from 1992, parliamentary strength. He failed to strike a distinctive note, leading to the question of what Majorism stood for, other than pragmatism. Although unfair, as Major was committed to opportunity, responsibility and fairness, this captured a weakness in his position and policies. Furthermore, pragmatism in office appeared lacking in competence, while, in contrast, the novel pragmatic adaptability shown by Labour in opposition seemed attractive.

In response both to the Thatcherite conviction that inflation was a serious threat to social cohesion and values, and to the sense that the rise in inflation in the late 1980s revealed a failure of Conservative fiscal strategy that could not be blamed on earlier Labour governments, Major made fighting inflation his leading economic goal. It was central to his commitment to financial prudence. This affected both his European policy and his domestic policies. In the former, Major was willing to see sterling in the European Exchange Rate Mechanism at a high rate against the Deutschmark because he believed that this would squeeze inflation out of Britain and provide stable exchange rates. Sterling had entered the ERM on 8 October 1990, Thatcher being pressed into accepting the policy by political and administrative advice, including that of Major.

Major's economic, fiscal and political inheritance was a difficult one, although Thatcher's departure led public opinion to swing back to the Conservatives in late 1990. The European issue seriously and publicly divided the Conservative Party, inside and outside Parliament, while the economy faced serious problems. Inflation was in double figures, and recession deepened in the early 1990s so that, by January 1993, when there were over three million unemployed, the unemployment rate was 10.6 per cent.

A Labour victory was widely anticipated in the general election held on 9 April 1992, but the electorate was wary of Kinnock. There was a suspicion that taxes would rise sharply if Labour gained power, and this affected an electorate keen to retain the cuts in income tax introduced by Thatcher. The Conservatives misled the electorate about the possibility of avoiding tax increases in the future, part of the process by which both major parties competed to debauch the electorate with false assumptions; but then, as on many other occasions, much of the electorate wished to be misled. The Conservatives were able to focus on the 'tax-and-spend' aspects of Labour policies and to claim that this would lead to a 'tax bombshell'. In the pre-election budget, the government had increased the focus on tax and strengthened the presentation of the Conservatives as the tax-cutting party by introducing a 20 per cent income tax band for the first £2,000 earned in excess of personal allowances, halving the rate of car tax and doubling the value of personal equity plan tax shelters.

In addition, Major was a popular Prime Minister, seen as honest and, crucially, not as abrasive or divisive as Thatcher. Ditching her had enabled the Conservatives to shed some of the unpopular legacy of the 1980s. Despite the recession, the Conservatives were also seen as more competent managers of the economy than Labour; a reputation they were swiftly to lose after the election. In addition, Major's foreign policy was then seen as successful. Aside from displaying leadership and sharing in the success of the 1991 Gulf War with Iraq, he was able to present the agreement reached at the Maastricht summit of EEC leaders as in Britain's interests. More seductive to many electors was Major's willingness to mix with them when campaigning, standing in the street on a packing case and using a loudhailer. The Conservatives also benefited from the fact that Poll-Tax evaders were not on the voting register.

The Conservative majority of 21 was small (disproportionately small in comparison to their share of the vote, which was still 42 per cent), in part because of tactical voting by their opponents: far more than in 1983 and 1987, Labour and Liberal Democrat supporters voted for whichever of their two candidates was most likely to defeat Conservatives, although the division between Labour and the Scottish Nationalists helped the Conservatives in Scotland. Labour, which polled 34 per cent of the vote, compared to 31 per cent in 1987, also benefited from an above-average swing to it in London and the East Midlands, in both of which there were many Conservative marginal seats. London was badly affected by the recession, which was hitting the service sector. The Conservatives won 336 seats, compared to 376 in 1987; Labour 271 (229, 1987). The Liberal Democrats, whom Thatcher had described as a dead parrot in her speech to the Party conference in October 1990, had the same level of electoral support as the Liberals had enjoyed in the 1970s: the SDP had made scant difference.

The small majority that followed the 1992 election weakened the government since it was deprived of a number of able Tories, such as Chris Patten, and hamstrung Major, especially because it made it very difficult to follow a policy on Europe that was not at risk from wrecking opposition from within the Conservative Parliamentary Party. Eurosceptic MPS, who focused on the outcome of the Maastricht summit of EEC leaders in December 1991, were willing to break ranks in order to block the implementation of the agreement, which brought a commitment to greater integration. The struggle to win parliamentary endorsement for Maastricht divided the Conservative Party and badly weakened the government. The Conservative vote against Maastricht eventually encompassed one-fifth of the party's backbench MPS. The Commons ratified the treaty in June 1993, but by a majority of only three. Denmark, France and Ireland all held referenda that year on the treaty, but the Major government refused to do so.

Depriving parliamentary opponents of the Party whip in November 1994 only exacerbated divisions. Euroscepticism also provided a means for disaffected Thatcherites, angry at her fall, to express their fury. A sense that Major was weak over Europe and that Thatcher had been betrayed, contributed to this potent and destabilizing division; and Major lacked the big idea necessary to regain the initiative.

The government's position was gravely weakened on 16 September 1992, 'Black Wednesday', when an overvalued exchange rate, the interest-rate policies of the Bundesbank and speculators forced sterling out of the European Exchange Rate Mechanism in a humiliating defeat for fiscal policy, and one that involved the Bank of England deploying over £15 billion from its reserves and interest rates being raised to 15 per cent. In practice, the exit brought much benefit, enabling Britain to manage its own finances and helping encourage economic growth from the mid-1990s, but, at the time, it created an abiding impression of poor, not to say inept, leadership. As Major later admitted, the public thereafter was never prepared to give his government the benefit of the doubt. Major indeed considered resigning, although at the time not even the Chancellor of the Exchequer, Norman Lamont, did so. The government's position in the public opinion polls collapsed.

Divisions sapped Conservative unity, purpose and popularity, even when the economy recovered from the mid-1990s, a recovery that owed much to the possibilities for independent economic management that followed departure from the Exchange Rate Mechanism. Annual inflation fell to 1.3 per cent in May 1993. The recovery, however, brought less of a 'feel good' factor than that in the mid-1980s, in part because property prices did not rise. Unemployment fell, helping growth, and purchasing power rose, but many of the new jobs were part-time and, anyway, the electorate was not minded to reward the increasingly exhausted Conservative government. Increases in taxation in 1993-4 did not help. They were a response to the economic problems of the early 1990s, which led to a Budget deficit of £46 billion in 1993-4, but broke Major's promises on taxes. The proposal to put VAT on domestic (heating) fuel was particularly unpopular and was rejected by the Commons in December 1994. The opposition of the MPs who had been deprived of the whip the previous month was crucial.

In other respects, there were also important continuities between the Thatcher and Major governments, unsurprisingly so as most ministers had served under Thatcher. In domestic policy, the Thatcherite attack on public expenditure was continued. This led both to cuts in defence expenditure, as part of the benefit stemming from the end of the Cold War, and to pressure on welfare payments. Efforts were also made to encourage internal competition within the public sector, which was seen as likely both to raise efficiency and to 'empower' consumers, a theme seen with the Citizen's Charter in 1991, which was part of Major's agenda for focusing on quality of life issues. To his critics, this represented an absence of political principles, but Major was concerned to humanize the public services as part of his attempt to create a new relationship between state and people. Under the National Health Service and Community Care Act of 1990, which was based on a government review in early 1988, the NHS was extensively reorganized, with a purchaser–provider split and GP fundholding to drive the internal market, and hospitals being given the possibility of becoming more autonomous trusts. In health and elsewhere, performance standards became an adjunct of policy. Attempts were also made, particularly with the Deregulation and Contracting Out Act of 1994, to attract private investment into the public sector. This was

presented as having the same goals of raising efficiency through competition and providing value to taxpayers and consumers.

Thus, the public got used to a vocabulary of internal markets,
contracting-out and private finance initiatives. The success of these
was less clear, understandably so, as all these schemes required time.
In fact, subsequent research suggested that hospital productivity rose
from the introduction of the internal market, only to fall when, once
in office, Labour attacked GP fundholding. However, the net effect in
popular terms was an impression of frenetic change and a challenging
disruption to assumptions, but no notable improvement in services.
The idea of using private finance, rather than taxation, to finance
improvements in education, health, transport and other provisions
was difficult to sell to a public much of which remained suspicious of
the notion of other people's profit and distrustful of businessmen.

This mismatch between popular and government assumptions was
pushed further as, in an important sign of continuity, the privatizations
of the 1980s were continued. Those of the sadly reduced coal industry
(1994), nuclear power (1996) and the government Stationery Office
(1996) did not prove too contentious. The continued decline of the coal
industry was an indicator of continuity with the Thatcher years that was
so obvious, in terms of governmental assumptions, that it scarcely
needed mentioning. Nevertheless, the closure of 31 pits and a major
reduction in the industry's workforce, announced in October 1992, led
to a public storm that extended to serious opposition within the
Conservative Party, and the closure programme was restricted and
delayed.

There was far more concern about the privatization of the railways,
for which the legislation was passed in 1993; the first private trains on
the formerly national network ran in 1996. This seemed to many rail
passengers to be a step too far. There was also opposition to the
manner of the privatization. Instead of transferring the entire industry to private ownership, as had happened with gas, the railway system,
in accordance with Treasury wishes, was separated in a complex
manner between Railtrack, which owned the infrastructure, and the
operating companies. This was, correctly, seen as likely to encourage a
shifting of the buck, and there was a lack of confidence in the govern-

ment's habitual reliance on regulators. Furthermore, the limited franchise granted to the companies led to concern that the basis for large-scale investment had not been created. The controversy threatened the Conservatives' position in many commuter constituencies and contributed to an impression that privatization had ceased to be sensible. Post Office privatization was seriously considered in 1994, but opposition within the Conservative Parliamentary Party led the Cabinet to abandon the project. This helped give Major an appearance of weakness and encouraged hostility to his leadership on the right.

Social policy continued on the same lines as under Thatcher, with an emphasis on law and order leading to the extension of police powers, and with fresh restrictions on immigration. Whereas the 1990 crisis had led many Conservative MPs to feel that a change of tone, if not substance, was necessary over European policy, and there was specific concern about the Poll Tax, there had been no comparable anger or anxiety, within Conservative ranks, over social policy.

A Gallup poll in June 1993 suggested that Major was the least popular Prime Minister since opinion polling began. A strongly hostile media, most of the Conservative section of which sympathized with the Eurosceptics, did not help. In the knowledge that Major scoured the papers and was affected by criticism, the press took great delight in chronicling the misfortunes of the government. These included an atmosphere of sleaze stemming both from 'cash for questions' (Conservative MPs revealed in 1994 to be receiving money from interested parties in order to raise questions in Parliament) and also involving sexual scandals, David Mellor resigning as Heritage Minister due to one in 1992. 'Cash for questions' was an aspect of the rise in lobbying and, in particular, lobbying companies that was the product both of the extensive role of government and of a sense that anything went as money became a key means of influence.

The 'Back to Basics' theme announced by Major at the Conservative Party conference in October 1993 was discredited within four months as a result of scandals involving Conservative MPs, first Tim Yeo, who was dismissed as a minister in January 1994 after it was revealed that he had had a child by his mistress. Scandals contributed badly to a sense of failure and drift. It was not, however, revealed that Major had

had an affair with another minister, Edwina Currie, prior to becoming Prime Minister.

In fact, Major's 'Back to Basics' speech revealed him not to be a puritanical moralist but, instead, to be a Prime Minister seeking to engage with social developments. He pressed for 'the old values, neighbourliness, decency, courtesy', argued for a morality based on teaching by parents, churches, schools and the citizenry, not on government and fashionable nostrums, for example that criminals required treatment, not punishment, and concluded: 'We must go back to basics, we want our children to be taught the best; our public services to give the best; our British industry to beat the best'.

Having lost the initiative in 1992, the government performed terribly in public opinion polls, had major swings against it in by-elections, such as Eastleigh in June 1994 and Dudley West in December 1994, and did very badly in European and council elections: in 1993 it lost control of every county council apart from Buckinghamshire. The following year Labour won 62 seats in the European elections, the Conservatives only 18, compared to 32 in 1989. Although the economy was improving, with unemployment and public borrowing falling, and it was possible, in part thanks to rising revenues from the petroleum revenue tax on North Sea oil, to afford income tax cuts in 1995–6, this did not work to Major's benefit.

In June 1995 Major felt it necessary to resign as leader of the Party and stand for re-election, in order to reassert his authority within the Cabinet and the Parliamentary Party. He defeated John Redwood, a former head of Thatcher's Policy Unit in No. 10, by 218 to 89 votes on 4 July, but that did not end the divisions. It was clear that a large portion of the Parliamentary Party was not prepared to support Major as Prime Minister. He survived in 1995 because the Right was unwilling to give full support to Redwood, while Major, who had been the candidate of the Right in 1990, won the backing of the Left. Their most prominent member, Michael Heseltine, was made Deputy Prime Minister and First Secretary of State after this election, and he and the Chancellor of the Exchequer, Kenneth Clarke, made it difficult for Major to woo the Eurosceptics who were bitterly opposed to the Euro and keen on a commitment not to enter it. Major's hope of uniting the Party was futile, and not even his attitude of 'wait and see' over the Euro could hold the Conservatives together.

These divisions took up far too much of the Prime Minister's time and energy, and badly hit the morale and enthusiasm of Party supporters. They also exacerbated the tendency to plan and plot for Major's succession. Nevertheless, Major was not overthrown by his party as Thatcher had been in 1990.

Major limped on until the 1997 election, held on 1 May, but its result, the worst defeat for the Conservatives since 1906, surprised few. In large part in order to catch the benefit of economic recovery, Major delayed the election until the last possible moment, a sure sign that he expected his government to be defeated. The only real success Major could claim, the beginnings of a peace process in Northern Ireland, was not enough to secure the Conservatives a fifth consecutive term of office, and the government was affected by its continued divisions over Europe, by sleaze and by the disquiet arising from the crisis over BSE (see chapter Three).

The biggest surprise was the scale of the defeat; Major had hoped that Labour's majority could be contained to 80 or 90. However, thanks, again in part, to tactical voting by Labour and Liberal Democrats, the Conservatives, with only 30.7 per cent of the British vote, lost heavily in England, while a collapse of their support cost them all their seats in Scotland and Wales. Labour won 418 seats and a majority of 179. This reflected the absence of proportional representation: Labour took 63.6 per cent of the seats on 43.4 per cent of the votes, while the Conservatives and Liberal Democrats between them took only 32.0 per cent of the seats on 47.5 per cent of the votes. The geography of the results was particularly striking as Labour made major gains in south-ern England, winning seats such as Exeter, Gloucester, Forest of Dean and Stroud. The Conservatives also lost southern seats such as Taunton and Torbay to the Liberal Democrats. Tactical voting for Labour reflected a willingness of voters to trust Blair and his presentation of a reformed Labour. However, although Labour's share of the vote had risen by 10.8 per cent, and was particularly apparent in the middle class, this rise was among a smaller turnout. The Conservatives won more support in 1992 than Labour did in 1997. Indeed, what was notable in 1997 was the readiness of Conservative supporters not to vote.

Whereas, prior to the 1990s, Labour had offered little credible or attractive modernization since the election of 1966, the victorious Blair fought on the platform of 'New Labour'. Once Major had lost direction and it looked as though he would not be re-elected, attention had shifted to Labour, increasingly seen as a government in waiting and one that was better led and more coherent than the Conservative government. Under Kinnock, Smith and then, from 1994, with more determination and clarity under Blair, Labour moved away from collectivist solutions based on interventionism and state planning, and prepared to embrace aspects of Thatcherism, not least the marketplace and modest rates of taxation.

Already under Kinnock, the Labour Party policy review of 1989, *Meet the Challenge, Make the Change*, dropped many recent policies including price and import controls, high income tax, unilateral nuclear disarmament, wealth tax and the restoration of union legal immunities. The review borrowed from Thatcherism in its favourable references to the free market, and it discarded much of the rhetoric and substance of Socialism. It was a key document in the conversion of Labour to the marketplace. Blair, who was Labour's shadow Employment Secretary in 1989-92, moved the party toward Conservative views on trade union rights. In the 1992 campaign, Labour committed itself to continued membership of the Exchange Rate Mechanism, to multilateral, rather than unilateral, nuclear disarmament, and to the market economy.

Changes in organization were also important. The exclusion of the left-wing Militant Tendency continued with Dave Nellist, MP for Coventry North East, expelled from the Labour Party in 1992. Smith moved away from the block vote of trade unions at Party conferences and in constituency parties, and, instead, favoured a one member, one vote approach. It was designed to democratize the party, and also both symbolize and make effective the growing breach between Labour and the unions. The symbolic importance of this issue was heightened by its major role in the internal Labour feuds in the early 1980s. Under Blair's leadership, the Labour Party became a more disciplined entity whose organizational structures and internal culture were geared towards electoral victory. There was an emphasis on discipline. From the Party's new base, Millbank Tower in London, its instant rebuttal system gave Labour the campaigning edge in 1997.

In 1994 Blair, the new leader, spoke to the Party conference about his goals: a society 'rich in economic prosperity, secure in social justice, confident in political change' and the linkage of 'New Labour, New Britain'. As shadow Home Secretary in 1992–4, he had promised toughness on crime, a policy not hitherto associated with Labour, and one that helped regain the initiative for the Party. This was an aspect of his stress on responsibilities as an aspect of community life, something that Blair had in common with Major. Both sought to temper individualism and permissiveness.

This was not the limit of Blair's revision of Labour attitudes. His victory for the leadership over John Prescott and Margaret Beckett, a victory based on the vote of individual Party members, not on block votes cast by trade union leaders, gave him a mandate for further change. In 1995, 'Clause IV' of the Party's 1918 constitution – its commitment to public ownership of the means of production, distribution and exchange – was abandoned at Blair's instigation after a ballot of Party members. This was seen as the end of an era. Hugh Gaitskell had singularly failed to achieve the same goal when he tried to push it through in 1959. The new objective was a country, 'in which power, wealth and opportunity are in the hands of the many not the few, where the rights we enjoy reflect the duties we owe, and where we live together, freely, in a spirit of solidarity, tolerance and respect'.

Rejecting Keynesian demand management, Blair wooed the City and was careful to limit spending pledges and to avoid talk of higher taxes; he indeed shared the Conservatives' commitment to low taxation. In the 1997 campaign Blair undertook to keep to the spending plans of the Conservative government and to retain their income tax rates. The reconfiguration of the left extended to the Communist Party of Great Britain. Discredited by the collapse of Communism in Eastern Europe, the Party was wound up at its congress in 1991, and became the Democratic Left, although a minority that refused to accept this split off and kept the original name.

Blair's theme was 'New Labour', a different Labour Party eager for modernization, although he ignored the extent to which his attitudes had been prefigured by Harold Wilson in the 1960s. Blair appeared to offer a more appealing vision of life in post-Thatcherite Britain, by championing a society in which the dominance of the marketplace was not to be allowed to undermine social cohesion. Instead, business and government were to be encouraged to work together in a New Deal launched in 1998 to get young unemployed people to work. Blair presented a different Labour Party eager for modernization. This entailed what he termed a 'Third Way' between Socialism and Conservatism, as well as the 'Cool Britannia' of a modishly new set of cultural values, which led to what was called a 'young country'. Honours lists were used to signal these preferences, with awards in plenty for sports celebrities and popular entertainers. On 27 October 1997 the cover of *Time* magazine proclaimed, 'Renewed Britannia'. Blair presented himself as an 'ordinary bloke' and deliberately dressed in an informal fashion. Although correctly mocked by critics as superficial, and criticized more searchingly as authoritarian, Blair had the advantage over Major of having clearly expressed ideas and plans, and being willing to propose an ideology. He had actively used his period of preparing for office, one that Major had lacked. Also unlike Major, Blair for long benefited from having little intrigue against him within the Cabinet and the parliamentary Party.

'Modernization' of the country became a focus of government activity, and this necessitated a protracted period of constitutional change in order, it was claimed, to bring power close to the people. Blair presented himself as embattled with the 'forces of conservatism'. The 1997 joke 'Did you know that Tony Blair MP is an anagram of "I'm Tory Plan B"?', was a reference to alleged continuity between Conservatism and New Labour. In fact, the charge of being Thatcherite brought against Blair indicated more about longstanding and powerful tensions within the Labour Party than about Blair's ethos and policies. As with 'Butskellism' in the 1950s and, although less clearly, the absence of Socialism from the minority Labour governments of the 1920s, differences and similarities between Conservatives and Labour were both striking, but the joke above certainly made little sense in Scotland or Wales, where Blair inherited from John Smith a commitment to constitutional reform, one, ironically, that many commentators saw as sitting uncomfortably with Blair's centralist tendencies.

A large majority in a referendum in Scotland in September 1997 (74.9 per cent of those who voted), and a tiny one in Wales (50.3 per cent), provided the basis for the creation of assemblies with legislative powers. They first met in 1999, with the Scottish Parliament, but not the Welsh Assembly, enjoying tax-varying powers, and the House of Lords losing its power over Scottish laws.

Having promised in its manifestos of 1997 and 2001 to make the House of Lords more 'democratic and representative', the government in 1999 removed most of the hereditary peerage as part of its policy of, at once, 'rebranding' Britain and securing Labour hegemony. Only 92 hereditary peers were left, with another 17 being made life peers. A Royal Commission subsequently proposed the addition of an elected element into the second chamber, and this was outlined in the White Paper *Completing the Reform* (November 2001). However, when Blair's ally and one-time patron Lord Irvine, the Lord Chancellor, declared in January 2003 that a part-elected chamber was unworkable, Blair followed in opposing the measure and, in February 2003, all the options for reform were rejected by the Commons. The creation of new peers remained a matter of Prime Ministerial patronage and was ruthlessly managed in order to build up the Labour position. Blair was more systematic in this than his Conservative predecessors, but then, due to Conservative strength in the Lords, the position he faced there was more difficult.

In part, however, there was also a habit on Blair's part of what was called control-freakery, although the independence given to the Bank of England to set interest rates was an important exception. Nevertheless, a drive to control situations characterized Blair's use of government patronage to reward friends (cronies to critics) and his determination to prevent the advance of others, particularly those who were 'off-message'. This practice extended to supposedly independent polities. Thus, in 1999 Blair used an electoral college (rather than a system of direct democracy) to block Rhodri Morgan from headship of the Welsh local Party, instead selecting an ally, Alun Michael. As a result, Labour was punished in the elections that year for the Welsh Assembly, and in 2000 Morgan replaced Michael. Another college was devised in 2000 to choose the Labour candidate for London's first directly elected mayor; this was used to thwart the Labour radical Ken Livingstone and, instead, in February 2000, to deliver the choice to the less popular Frank Dobson. In the election held three months later, Livingstone stood as an independent and won. Labour supporters were made Director-General of the BBC (Greg Dyke, 2000) and its Chairman (Gavyn Davies, 2001). In some respects this was bringing Britain into line with the politicization of official bodies widely seen in the USA and Europe, but it was alien to the tradition of civil service impartiality and overly linked to a government stronger on conviction than competence or debate.

In some respects, there was an obvious continuity between Conservative and Labour governments. Public expenditure was contained in the 1997 and 1998 budgets, helping to ensure that there was a basis subsequently for increasing public expenditure without at once causing a major debt burden. In addition, income tax levels were not raised. In 1999 a 10p in the £ starting rate of income tax was introduced, and in 2000 the basic rate of income tax was cut from 23p to 22p. Other taxes rose, however, not least with the end of the married couple's allowance and of mortgage-interest tax relief, and with increases in petrol duty above the rate of inflation. The Office for National Statistics reported that the tax burden rose from 35.5 per cent of GDP in 1996–7 to 37.5 per cent in 1999–2000. Labour maintained the Conservative position on pensions, linking pensions to prices, not earnings. The latter link had been abolished under Thatcher. This caused a major controversy in 2000, when the index-linked increase on the basic state pension was only 75p.

The Labour government was closer to the unions than the Conservatives, but took great pains to keep them at a distance, and, in 2002–3, was willing to use troops to thwart a strike by the militant firemen's union. As under the Conservatives, a robust pro-Americanism characterized British foreign policy. This was seen most clearly in policy towards Afghanistan and Iraq in 2001–3. The Blair government was also very much middle-class in composition. Many Conservatives were ready to find Blair an acceptable Prime Minister, and in the 2001 election campaign the Conservative Party was unsuccessful in energizing opposition.

Yet there were also important differences, particularly in attitudes to social welfare and in business policy. The Blair government made a major effort to deal with poverty, by ensuring a minimum wage and offering income credits to an extent that critics spoke of a dependency culture. Family Credit was replaced by the more generous Working Families Tax Credit, introduced in October 1999, and much effort was devoted to trying to ensure the take-up of benefits. There was a particular emphasis on countering child poverty, which the government promised to halve by 2010. This could be seen as a way of sugar-coating redistribution of wealth via taxation, although child poverty was presented as the root of social problems including limited educational attainment and crime. The government made the abolition of what was termed social exclusion its prime domestic policy objective. One of Blair's first acts as Prime Minister was to visit the Aylesbury housing estate in Southwark, south London, on 2 June 1997. A new, Cabinet Office-based, Social Exclusion Unit was established. Both the Major and the Blair governments sought to deal with the problem of young people sleeping rough.

However, by defining citizenship in terms of participation in the labour market, for example through its 'welfare to work' scheme, it was unclear whether the Blair government would be able to find an answer to the age-old problem of poverty. Rather, the problem was posed, and answered (or possibly marginalized) in a different form. The attack on begging in 2003 was a reminder of the authoritarian character of New Labour's social policies, although to its supporters this was a matter of emphasizing personal responsibility, communal policies and public morality. This authoritarianism, seen in aspects of the policies of Jack Straw and David Blunkett, the two Labour Home Secretaries so far, was popular with the *Daily Mail*, the newspaper of Conservative populism.

Blair might share authoritarianism with the Conservatives, but the attitude of their governments to public housing was very different. Thus, in 2002, the Labour government tried to expand 'social', in other words publicly supported, housing. This, however, was by no means a return to building large council estates. Instead, the Conservative government's reliance on local housing associations, a successful instance of public–private partnership, was maintained and expanded, with not only greater expenditure but also an attempt to offer affordable housing to public-sector workers. This ensured that the government did not have to address the more serious problem of inflexible national pay scales arising from overly centralized public provision.

Business policy was also different to that of the Conservatives. There was a greater emphasis on regulation, which, to its critics, was red tape. European and national regulations over working hours, health and safety, environmental standards and taxation imposed many burdens on business. Under Blair, there was also more political interference in the work of the regulators. Increases in taxation, especially that of dividends, with the abolition in 1997 of dividend tax credits for pension funds, which brought the government £5.5 billion a year, was seen as threatening the appeal of investing in business, as, to a lesser extent, was a one-off windfall tax on privatized utilities. This bore some responsibility for the stock–market crisis in 2002–3 that hit pension provision particularly hard, although this was also part of a more widespread international crisis in economic confidence. Since the extent of private pension assets distinguished Britain from the rest of Europe (with the exception of the Netherlands), this was a slackening of distinctiveness.

Compared with what a traditional Labour government would have offered, Blair's first government was still a business-friendly ministry, and it was initially criticized in these terms by the unions. Focusing on supply-side factors, Labour sought to tackle serious productivity problems by raising the skill level of the labour force through education. The American economy, which boomed in the 1990s, was held up as a model, a course that Blair's respect for Bill Clinton's success encouraged. This route was presented as a contrast to the more regulated, corporatist policies of continental Europe, and Blair, in particular, distanced himself from the more traditional Socialist policies of the Jospin government in France. However, in a speech in autumn 1998 to the annual conference of the Confederation of British Industry (CBI), its Director-General, Adair Turner, warned: 'The Government's rhetoric has not been delivered. In a few years the country will be back either on a path of a steadily rising tax burden or will be unable to invest in public services'.

Compared to Thatcher, Major and previous Labour governments, Blair had singularly few problems with dissidence within the Party during his first government (1997–2001). There were claims, from the Left, of a betrayal of principles, but they had no political impact in Parliament, although they helped to accentuate a feeling of alienation on the part of union activists. With terms such as 'big tent', Blair stressed the inclusive nature of his ambitions for nation, party and government, and this encouraged him to maintain his rejection of traditional Labour policies and assumptions. Despite pressure, the government refused to renationalize the railways and, instead, against opposition, part-privatized the air-traffic control system; the establishment of a minimum wage, however, and the passage of employment legislation forcing companies to recognize unions if the majority of their workers wished them to do so met important union demands.

As part of his inclusiveness, Blair was keen to encourage defectors from other parties, while he also sought to woo business, not least the CBI. The Liberal Democrats were tempted with talk of constitutional change, although Blair shied away from their central demand, proportional representation, and the Liberal Democratic leader, Paddy Ashdown, became disillusioned. His successor, Charles Kennedy, had fewer illusions from the outset.

In control of both Cabinet and Parliament, and making obsessive efforts at news management, Blair was castigated for being presidential. The notion of an 'elective dictatorship' advanced as a criticism of Thatcher appeared to be adopted as a means of government by the autocratic Blair. Cabinet meetings were frequently short and Blair limited the number of occasions on which he appeared, spoke or voted in Parliament. Soon after he gained power, Blair increased the role of 10 Downing Street in co-ordinating and presenting government policy, expanded the number of staff who worked there, and allowed political advisers more power in ministries. He also took an important role in senior Civil Service appointments.

Thanks to the continued unpopularity of the Conservatives, Blair easily won the general election held on 7 June 2001; standing on a manifesto similar to that of 1997, he benefited from the reputation for economic prudence enjoyed (without much cause, or perhaps largely because he continued the policies of his Conservative predecessor, Kenneth Clarke) by the Chancellor of the Exchequer, Gordon Brown, and from his continuation of the Conservative policy on income tax. More generally, the economic growth of the late 1990s, which reflected a more widespread boom (especially in the USA), as well as the fiscal policies of the Conservatives, and Britain's financial independence from the European Union, helped to encourage a 'feel good' factor. These were the best of times for an election: inflation, interest rates and unemployment were all low.

The Conservatives had, in Major's successor, William Hague, a brighter leader and a better Commons' performer than Blair (although Hague was poorer in media image), but they suffered from an uncertainty over whether to advocate policies that appealed to core supporters or to back a 'modernization' approach aimed at winning over uncommitted voters. Having started in 1997 with the latter strategy, Hague moved to the former one, promising, for example, to incarcerate all asylum seekers in reception centres. Attitudes to asylum seekers and crime were points of tension over Conservative modernization, but the most significant symbolic issue was the repeal of an earlier Conservative step, one of the few legislative moves aimed at stopping institutions adapting to social trends. Section 28 of the 1988 Local Government Act had forbidden local authorities from 'promoting homosexuality' or teaching 'its acceptability – as a pretended family relationship'. There were no prosecutions under the Act, but traditionalists resisted its repeal.

The Conservatives found it difficult to gain a favourable public image. Their divisions helped Labour to paint them, and Hague in particular, as far more extreme than was in fact the case. Blair told his Party conference in 1999 that the Conservatives were 'weird'. This was untrue, but they were certainly maladroit, and it was easy for Labour to present itself as more moderate. Hague's election call to 'save the pound' did not excite the country, although it captured the extent to which Blair's willingness to enter the Eurozone threatened national sovereignty.

Despite Conservative weaknesses, the 2001 campaign indicated that the government was under embarrassing pressure from a variety of sources. Thus, the seat of Wyre Forest was won by a doctor protesting at the closure of the accident and emergency unit in the local hospital. The furore over pensions the previous year still echoed, but did not lead to large numbers of pensioners switching over to support the Conservatives.

The election left Labour with a commanding majority of 167, even though there had been a 1.8 per cent swing against it in votes as the Conservative share of the vote rose. Labour success owed much to support from Liberal Democrats in marginal seats. Furthermore, the swing to the Conservatives was greatest in Wales (3.8 per cent) and the North-East (3.1 per cent), areas where Labour was strongest, and, aside from in Scotland (-0.1 per cent), weakest in the South-East (0.4 per cent), London (0.7 per cent) and the South-West (1.0 per cent), all regions where the Conservatives hoped to make major gains. Thus, the southern, middle-class constituencies wooed by New Labour remained loyal. In contrast, loyalty fell among the working class, partly because of disillusionment and partly because the Conservatives had little prospect of winning those seats.

The Liberal Democrats took seats from the Conservatives, for example Teignbridge, but their attempt to win an electoral breakthrough failed and they lost a few seats, including Taunton, to the Conservatives. Despite the increase in Liberal Democratic representation in the 1997 and 2001 elections, the Party had been unable to gain benefit from Conservative weakness that in any way approached that seized by Labour. This reflected structural weaknesses in the Party and in its appeal.

Despite Blair's victory in 2001, confidence in Labour's intentions, integrity and competence had been hit by its years in office. Controversies linked to political donations, especially those from Bernie Ecclestone and Lakshmi Mittal, and the questionable practices of a number of ministers, including Blair's close ally Peter Mandelson, as well as Geoffrey Robinson and Keith Vaz, affected the government's reputation. In addition, image was seen as overly all-important, as the name New Labour suggests. There was much criticism of the attempts to manage news, which led to attacks on 'spin doctors', while the role of focus groups in helping determine policy choices aroused disquiet.

More serious was the extent to which, despite the promise in the 2001 election to improve the quality of public services, as well as much subsequent expenditure, rising to an anticipated £455.7 billion in the 2003–4 tax year, there was only a limited improvement in key areas of the public services, especially health. By 2002 increased concern about the state of education, health, crime and transport led to a growing sense that government could not solve these problems. This is a major issue for the political process, since opposition to Labour also lacks credibility.

The fall in turnout in the 2001 election to 59 per cent (and less than 40 per cent for those aged 18–24) was a reflection of a sense that there was little difference between Labour and the Conservatives, limited support for change in favour of the latter, and widespread dissatisfaction with politicians; it was not a testimony to confidence in the government. The sense of alienation felt by 'old' Labour supporters was important, as was dissatisfaction with the Conservatives. Nevertheless, victory meant that Labour did not need to continue to attract Liberal Democratic support by holding out the prospect of proportional representation. Furthermore, the Left had failed to mount a serious challenge. The Socialist Labour Party promised full employment, the re-nationalization of privatized industries, a four-day working week, withdrawal from the European Union and the abolition of the monarchy, but it failed to win a single seat, not even Hartlepool where its General Secretary, Arthur Scargill, still President of the NUM, took on Peter Mandelson, the classic Blairite.

Disillusionment with the government was also seen in the council elections held on 1 May 2003, in which Labour lost 793 seats, the Conservatives gained 652 and the Liberal Democrats 138. With a swing from Labour to the Conservatives since the 2001 election of 7 per cent, this gave the Conservatives a share of 35 per cent on a national equivalent vote, Labour 30 per cent and the Liberal Democrats 27 per cent. It is unclear how far these results were indicative for the next general election: Conservative successes in the previous council elections had been followed by Labour's sweeping victory in 2001.

Concern about the public services led Blair in his second term to shift the emphasis in his government towards social democracy and to support heavy expenditure on them. Despite Blair's attack, in February 2002, on the 'wreckers' who opposed his plans for reform, this expenditure was not linked to the structural reforms that were necessary in order to ensure flexibility and the best use of investment. The government was unwilling to confront the unions, despite its willingness to resist the firemen's strike. By committing itself so heavily to the public services, especially the NHS, the government ensured that it would be difficult for it to do anything other than raise taxation. This was an important aspect of the redistributive character of Labour policies. Without any rise in taxation, government revenues for the 2003–4 tax year were still estimated in the April 2003 Budget as likely to be 38.6 percent of national income.

In practice, the rhetoric of the first term, of thinking the unthinkable in social policy, and also of encouraging individuals to rely on their own savings, rather than the state, for pensions, had been crowded out by a conservative unwillingness to challenge the established paradigms in social policies combined by the reluctance to temper taxation that was characteristic of Socialists. It was symptomatic of a more general caution that, on 18 December 2002, in a House of Lords' debate on constitutional change, Blair's ally, Lord Irvine, declared that the government was motivated by a 'pragmatism based on principle, without the need for an all-embracing theory'.

The allegations, made in the late 1990s, that Blair was Thatcherite or the 'son of Thatcher' seemed less credible for domestic policy in 2002–3. Instead, it is more appropriate to discern a post-Thatcherite social democracy that was wary of individualism and, instead, presented a new corporatism, more open to market pressures at the margins but with no root-and-branch reform. Frank Field, who had been instructed to provide radical solutions in Social Security, was removed from office in Blair's first Cabinet reshuffle in 1998. The commitment to a cultural, if not quasi-mystical, approach to public services was captured by the speech by Gordon Brown, the Chancellor of the Exchequer, to the Labour Party conference in 2002:

What we say and do about the NHS is not just about the future of our public services, but about the character of our country. It is an affirmation that duty, obligation, service, and not just markets and self-interest, are at the very heart of what it means to be a citizen of Britain.

Less attention was devoted to securing the economic growth able to pay for this inefficient and centralist system, although, helped by adroit management by the Bank of England (rather than a need to rely on the European Central Bank had Britain entered the Eurozone), Britain benefited from growth figures that were better than those of Germany, while inflation remained low, as did unemployment. Nevertheless, the failure to bring cuts and reforms to public expenditure left it pressing hard on the rest of the economy, affecting Britain's economic performance. This was further demonstrated in April 2003 when employers' National Insurance contributions rose, adding an annual burden of £4 billion. The contrast between Britain and the high-tax economies of much of Europe, such as France, was eroded. Growing labour militancy was also apparent from 2002 as unions, which were most strongly represented in the public sector, sought to justify their existence by demanding a large share of higher public expenditure. A marked decline in private sector investment in 2002 indicated widespread domestic and international concerns about the future of the British economy. Since investment is crucial to the applied technology, especially information technology, necessary to raise labour productivity, its loss was serious. As in the late 1980s, domestic demand outgrew the economy, fuelling imports.

The failure of much of the population to make due provision for the future, especially through pensions, was another indication of malaise. Household savings as a percentage of disposable income fell by nearly half between 1992 and 2002. Instead, people borrowed to spend, not least by remortgaging to release capital from home equity, helping to support the economy on debt-fuelled demand. In April 2003 an average rise in council tax bills of 12.9 per cent and an increase in National Insurance contributions combined to squeeze consumers.

UNGOVERNABLE?

A political narrative does not address the issue raised in chapter Four of whether Britain was increasingly ungovernable. Looked at differently, the extent of this ungovernability was a comment on discussing politics in terms of such a narrative. The rise in criminality was certainly a major comment. It was related to a widespread breakdown in the socialization of the young, especially of young males. The percentage with criminal records rose. Crime hit most in run-down neighbourhoods, further de-socializing life there. Although blamed by many commentators on Conservative government between 1979 and 1997, crime had, in fact, increased from the 1950s and, for much of this period, unemployment rates were low and the standard of living of the poor rose. Robberies in London rose by 105 per cent between 1991 and 2002, a period of falling unemployment. Thus, an economic explanation of rising crime appears less pertinent than one that focuses on social dislocation, especially family breakdown, while detailed variations owed much to changing age profiles, in the shape of the number of adolescent males. Recorded crimes per capita rose particularly steeply in the 1980s, passing German and American rates, and they continued to rise in the 1990s when those in the USA fell. The social problems that contributed to crime varied greatly by area. 'Sink housing' areas tended to have higher rates of crime and drug addiction. The 'Schemies', who lived in public housing schemes in Scotland, were greatly affected by the spread of hard drugs in the 1980s. In desperation, local authorities increasingly demolished such housing from the mid-1990s, a ready testimony to the problems they posed.

Alongside social problems, there were serious deficiencies in the criminal justice system. It was difficult to get convictions, and this con-tributed to public scepticism about the operation of the law, scepticism that lawyers, the most self-regarding and effective producer-lobby, were unable to address. Thus, measures such as limiting the right to trial by jury, or to remove the double jeopardy law, were met by an-guished complaints by lawyers and civil liberties' pressure groups. Distrustful of the police, many juries proved willing to acquit criminals against whom good cases had been presented.

Ungovernability is a relative concept. It cannot be assumed that the ends of government are necessarily a good, and debate is integral to public life; but, in a democratic society, it is troubling if legislation cannot be implemented and laws enforced. In 2000 John Prescott, the Deputy Prime Minister, declared that the government could not retreat in the face of the fuel protests, renegotiating taxes 'at a refinery gate, under threat of 60 days notice', while Blair, characteristically in a newspaper interview, declared 'No government can act on the basis of people threatening to bring the country to a halt.' In fact, the government abandoned the policy of raising fuel duties by more than inflation, and was very careful thereafter to limit increases.

Problems with the implementation of legislation were far more widespread than the public rejection of the state seen in major episodes of lawlessness, such as the Poll Tax riots or in urban riots, such as those in Tottenham in London and Handsworth in 1985, Brixton in 1995, and Bradford, Burnley and Oldham in 2002. Similarly, the limited nature of the electoral success enjoyed by extremist political movements, while notable, was not a measure of total disaffection, in part because of radical 'entryism' into the Labour Party, especially in the 1970s, and because of the major role of such radicals in many trade unions. In October 1974 the Communist Party polled only 11,606 votes. The hardcore who refused in 1991 to accept the reconfiguration of the Party into Democratic Left put up four candidates in 1992, only for them to win an average of 150 votes. The Workers' Revolutionary Party put up 101 candidates for parliamentary elections in 1974–83; all lost their deposits. The Socialist Workers' Party, formed in 1976, had about 3,000 members at its height, but had no impact on the mainstream. On the other extreme, the National Front had an average vote of 3.3 per cent for the 54 constituencies it contested in February 1974. By 1983 this had dropped to just over 1 per cent for 58 constituencies: the party did not take part in the 1987 general election. Its successor, the British National Party, however, made a strong local impact in Burnley in the 2003 council elections, and won sixteen crucial seats across the country.

Ungovernability was not restricted to relations with the public. It was also increasingly a problem that confronted the government in relations with the judiciary, as the latter sought to enforce their notions of international human rights against the wishes of Conservative and Labour governments, for example over asylum. This reflected issues of identity to which we turn in the next chapter.

Chapter 7

Identities and Roles

My mother has got an interview for a job. She is practising her typing and not doing any cooking. So what will it be like if she *gets* the job?

The Secret Diary of Adrian Mole aged 13 ³/₄ (1982) by Sue Townsend

SOCIAL STRUCTURES

Standing for the leadership of the Conservative Party, and to be thus Prime Minister, in 1990 John Major promised to create by 2000 a 'classless society', meaning a society where birth no longer automatically constrained opportunities. But the persistence of social divisions was one of the features of the period, however much politicians sought to ignore them. It is not easy to define these divisions. There has not yet emerged a comprehensible way of talking about social and economic class in post-corporatist, 'post-industrial' (in the sense of industry's more marginal position in the economy) Britain. Occupational classification, centred on a difference between the 'middle' class, 'white-collar' (non-manual), workers, and the 'working' class, 'blue-collar' (manual) workers, was further refined, by consumer analysts concerned to dissect society for marketing purposes and by government surveys, to produce a system in which society is divided between professionals (class A), managers (B), clerical workers (C1), skilled manual workers (C2), semi-skilled and unskilled workers (D), and those who are unemployed or unable to work (E). This classification gained considerable public attention in the last quarter of the century, sufficiently so for people to understand what was meant by saying that support from C2s was crucial to Thatcher's electoral successes in 1979, 1983 and 1987. Occupational classification, however, is weakened by a focus on male, not female, occupations, while it is also necessary to consider the particular characteristics of youth society. More generally, to be 'working' or 'middle' class meant very different things at different stages of life, and this undermined any notion of class coherence, let alone unity.

The period covered by this book saw the continuation of powerful inegalitarian tendencies, not simply in terms of wealth, both capital and income, but also with regard to assumptions. This was, and is, true not only of assumptions of particular groups about themselves, but also of their assumptions about others. Yet, there have also been important changes, particularly a decline in the traditional upper class and a broadening of the middle class. The expanding nature of the middle class was shown by the rise in those who had to pay higher-rate income tax. In the first five years of Blair's governments, the figure rose by nearly three million. The structure of society is increasingly one in which a large portion is comfortably off, and the essential divide is between this broader middle class and those who are poor, sufficiently so for them to be eligible for regular social welfare payments. This social distinction has a major impact. Longitudinal surveys of babies born in 1946 and 1958 showed how social class was linked to life chances, and the same was seen in the 7UP series of television documentaries that followed a group of fourteen English children at seven-year breaks.

The broadening of the middle class affected social practices and sites. Thus wine bars became popular from the 1970s, and this forced the traditional pub to win back customers. Pubs ceased to be male-orientated, domino-playing, crisp-eating places. Instead, the need to attract younger people led to the emergence of the 'theme pub' serving a wide range of beers and spirits, to the sound of the latest chart hits. In addition, it became easier from the 1980s to buy wine in pubs, while they also increasingly served food in order to make them more family-friendly. The advent of beer gardens also allowed children to accompany their parents to the pub.

Society is far more complex in its dynamics than a structural account might suggest. Alongside definitions in terms of class, it is necessary to emphasize the role of human agency, and thus of concepts and ideologies, leading to a less clear-cut and more complex, not to say indistinct, situation, especially if the individual rather than the collective is seen as the basic unit of decision-making. This can be seen in voting preferences: many electors did not vote as their class interests might seem to dictate. The willingness of part of the middle class to abandon the Conservatives in the 1997 election was a clear aspect of the changing nature of class identities and also of the role of ideology, at least as mediated by the creation of attractive images.

At the 'micro' level, families after the mid-twentieth century increasingly contained individuals who were in different social groups. This variety was accentuated, at the structural level, by the general characteristics of different generations. Thus, whereas, in 2001, nearly 40 per cent of all employees aged 40–49 were members of unions, for those aged 23–9 the percentage was about 20. The average worker in the more unionized public sector was older than his or her private-sector counterparts. In addition, the development of more single-issue interest groups, for example the disability movement, which campaigned for rights, rather than charity, increased the complexity of social categorization.

Furthermore, the growing emphasis on self-identification as a major source of social location necessarily limited both broad-brush approaches and 'realist' analyses based on measurable criteria, whether related to the means of production, income or other factors. Social location through self-identification involved a number of factors, including not only age, religion and ethnicity, but also lifestyle. Thus, there has been important work on leisure activities that has traced the social configurations of organized sport, and their importance for individual and collective senses of identity. This has to be handled carefully. For example, football may have emerged as a working-class game, but its following is far from socially limited, and this has become more apparent as seating has replaced standing. In addition, there is a regional dimension. Golf in England tends to be more exclusive than in Scotland. Nevertheless, sport and related activities reflect and, in part, create social differences, and thus a sense of social location.

Another factor stressed in the 1990s relates to the idea of 'sectoral cleavages'. From this perspective, it is the sector of the economy in which an individual works, private or public, that is the key criterion of self-identification. The private and public sectors were seen as having different cultures and contrasting attitudes. Sectoral cleavages also emerge from patterns of consumption. Despite efforts to lessen these cleavages, for example by introducing the pressures and, to a lesser extent, opportunities of the free market into the public sector, they remained potent. Thus, in recessions, public-sector workers did better, while, in periods of growth, their private-sector counterparts were more successful. The recession of the early 2000s challenged the pension provision provided by the private sector, while leaving the public-sector pension liabilities – £350 billion in March 2001 – as an unrestricted burden on the taxpayer. These cleavages correlate with electoral preference (private sector: Conservatives; public sector: Labour) and help to explain political trends. For example, the privatization policies of Thatcher challenged Labour's support base in the public sector.

A different typology was offered by Will Hutton in his influential left-wing critique of Conservative Britain, *The State We're In* (1995). Hutton saw Britain as a 20:40:40 society: 20 per cent of the population were rich and without fears; but, at the other extreme, 40 per cent had enjoyed none or little of the economic growth of the 1980s – they were casual or poorly paid workers, single mothers and the long-term unemployed; the other 40 per cent, although relatively affluent when in work, lived in fear of unemployment and house forfeitures. Indeed, many of the middle class experienced periods of unemployment and hardship, including house repossessions, in the recessions of the early 1980s and early '90s. In the early 2000s their fears focused on declining pension prospects. The theme of social insecurity was probed by writers including the playwrights Alan Ayckbourn in *Absurd Person Singular* (1972) and Steven Berkoff in *Kvetch* (1986). This insecurity contributed both to the popularity of Thatcherite policies, and to disillusionment with the Conservatives in the 1990s and 2000s.

Economic shifts and government policy greatly contributed to social volatility. Until the 1970s there was a strong labour market for skilled and semi-skilled workers and many jobs for the unskilled, but extensive de-industrialization since has reduced opportunities for unskilled labour. The end of the prolonged boom in the Western economy that had powered growth between 1945 and 1973 undermined the policies of full employment that had kept unemployment relatively low. This also accentuated regional and local differences in prosperity and employment.

In some spheres, there were major falls in employment. For example, on the South Wales coalfield, where there had been 28 pits in 1984, there were fewer than 1,000 miners by 1992. The near-wholesale disappearance of the coal industry was a major transformation not only in the economy of South Wales, but also in the life of many Welsh localities. The decline of the national coal industry, from 200,000 miners in 1975 to 10,000 in 2002, owed much to its uncompetitiveness, but government policies were also important, not least in investment and pricing decisions. The lack of sympathy of the Thatcher government for the miners was significant in the fate of the coal industry.

The miners were not alone. Long-established heavy industries also suffered serious decline, contributing to the sense of identities under strain. In 2003 the last train-manufacturing plant in Britain looked set to close. From the late 1950s shipbuilding had been losing orders to the lower charges of foreign yards. In addition, the latter were able to promise earlier and more reliable delivery dates, a consequence of the absence in Britain of modern yards able to offer flow-line production and the consequent higher productivity. This absence reflected a lack of investment, born of short-term attitudes and of limited planning for the long term. Government intervention took the form of structural change, especially the creation of larger groupings, rather than the reform of practices. Structural change led, in 1971, to the occupation, by their workers, of yards on the Upper Clyde threatened by closure. The Heath government backed down in 1972, subsequently claiming that it feared large-scale civil violence, although this was probably not the sole major factor. Subsequently, the economic crisis caused by the quadrupling of oil prices in 1973 hit British shipbuilding as tanker orders fell dramatically. A major collapse in order books affected Britain alongside the rest of the world. The Labour government responded by nationalizing the Belfast yard of Harland and Wolff in 1975, in order to prevent bankruptcy, following, in 1977, with the rest of the industry, which was nationalized to create British Shipbuilders.

The auguries were not auspicious for successful reorganization. Orders remained low. In response, the number of shipbuilding sites was cut: by the close of 1981, from 27 to 15, and employment from 87,000 to 66,000. The recession of the early 1980s inflicted further damage. Trading losses continued to be heavy, £117 million alone in the financial year 1982-3, and the gross registered tonnage launched fell from 1,281,000 in 1974 to 191,000 in 1984 and 46,000 in 1987.

British Shipbuilders was also under great pressure from the Thatcher government, which was opposed to state ownership and public subsidy, and psychologically out of sympathy with heavy indus-try and what was seen as a world dominated by militant trade unionism and inadequate management. These hostile views, in fact, were no longer appropriate. Design was now informed by computers, and restrictive working practices had been greatly reduced, but, on the part of ministers, there was a preference for doctrinal objective over practical consequences, and a lack of interest in ensuring that privati-zation led to the creation of an effective industry.

Instead, shipbuilding was described, in the indicative vocabulary of the period, as a 'sunset' and 'smokestake' industry. In 1984 privatization was formally announced as a policy. This was completed by the end of 1988, but at the cost of the loss of volume shipbuilding in the United Kingdom: the closures of yards on the Tees and at Troon, and of the Wallsend engine works were announced in 1986, and the Sunderland-based North-East Shipbuilders Ltd followed two years later. The combination of a European Union policy of limiting subsidies in order to reduce capacity, and of a maladroit handling of the situation by the government, was fatal. By 2002 the only remaining merchant yards were in Belfast, Appledore in Devon and on the Clyde, and in early 2003 there were job losses at Appledore and warnings of possible closure. There had also been serious redundancies in the oil platform yards at Ardersier and Nigg in 1999–2000.

The effect of de-industrialization in the form of the closure of shipyards on towns such as Birkenhead and Sunderland was very serious. Aside from high unemployment, there was the knock-on impact on suppliers and on other local activities. These combined to ensure a decline in the local urban fabric, as well as in local tax revenues, and a shift towards the expedients of re-training and welfare.

It was not only 'smokestake' industries that faced severe difficulties, with attendant social problems for particular communities. The growth industries of the inter-war and post-war years were also badly hit. This was particularly clear in one of the leading industries, car manufacture. It was easy in the 1970s and early '80s, when strikes were frequent in the industry, for commentators to blame the unions for decline, but the problems were long-term. A fragmented industrial structure, leading to too many models, was highlighted in successive reports, for example that of the Central Policy Review Staff in 1975, alongside low productivity and a lack of investment. The long-term consequences of government pressure to locate in areas of industrial decline, such as Merseyside (with plants at Speke, Halewood and Ellesmere Port) and Central Scotland (Bathgate and Linwood), were also serious, not least because it contributed to the continued fragmentation of the industry.

The Labour governments of 1964–70 sought to reform the industry through consolidation, encouraging the formation, in 1968, of the British Leyland Motor Company (BLMC), which was renamed British Leyland (BL) in 1975. However, the new company hit many problems. Its inheritance was unwieldy. Across its 48 factories, BLMC produced the full range of cars and goods vehicles, to the detriment of volume production. Outdated and poorly maintained plant and machinery was a major problem that reflected insufficient investment. The failure of unions to enforce collective agreements led to numerous unofficial strikes, while the frequent laying-off of production workers and changes in overtime, in response to shifts in demand, helped to exacerbate labour relations.

By 1975 imported cars accounted for 33 per cent of new registrations, while BLMC's share was only 31 per cent of the market; the

American-owned manufacturers in Britain, Ford and Vauxhall, were more successful. BLMC lost £76 million in 1975, a considerable sum on each car sold. The Labour government, however, could not let such a major employer go bankrupt and, in the mid-1970s, government interventionism was at its height. Large sums of public money were invested, especially in 1975 and 1977; and the workforce was heavily cut from 1977 in an attempt to improve productivity by cutting excess capacity. Speke was shut in 1978, Abingdon and Canley in 1980, and Solihull in 1982; 36,400 jobs were lost between 1976 and 1981.

These changes were unsuccessful. BL could not respond sufficiently fast to match developments in domestic and international markets. It was poor both as a manufacturing company and as a competitive enterprise. By 1978 BL had a smaller market share in Britain than Ford; by 1988 than Vauxhall. By 1987 the car division held only 15 per cent of the home market. BL was broken up and sold: the Rover Group to British Aerospace in 1988 and then to BMW in 1994, and Jaguar/Daimler to Ford in 1989. In 1987 Leyland Trucks was sold to DAF, a Dutch company, and the buses division went to Volvo.

In contrast, Nissan, a Japanese car-maker that established a new plant near Sunderland, was far more successful. Benefiting from the newness of its plant and continued investment, Nissan's factory built 98 cars per assembly-line worker in 1997, compared with 62 at Honda's plant in Swindon, 62 at Ford's plant at Dagenham and 33 at Rover's plant at Longbridge. A relative lack of competitiveness across much of the industry was exacerbated in the early 2000s by the strength of sterling against the Euro, leading to threats to close Dagenham and Longbridge and to cut investment at Swindon and Sunderland. These threats served as a reminder of the problems posed by foreign control, although the investment and manufacturing and managerial expertise it brought were also crucial.

De-industrialization also affected newer light industries. In Northern Ireland, synthetic-fibre plants established in the 1960s closed in the early 1980s, and, in the late 1990s and early 2000s, computer-chip and other IT factories in Tyneside, Scotland's 'Silicon Glen' and south Devon were all hit. The mothballing of the Hyundai factory at Dunfermline in 1998 before it could open was a vivid demonstration of the change for the worse, and one driven home by the fact that the Chancellor of the Exchequer, Gordon Brown, was a local MP. Furthermore, in the early 2000s major British manufacturing companies hit terminal or, at the very least, extremely serious problems, spectacularly so in the case of Marconi, and badly so in that of ICI.

By the mid-1980s Britain was importing more manufactured goods than it exported. This reflected not only the crisis in British industry, but also the changing balance of priorities within the economy that was responsive both to the sectors in which Britain enjoyed competitive advantages, and to investment opportunities. In 1998 the numbers employed in manufacturing fell, both below 4.05 million and below those employed in wholesale and retail. By 2003 investment in service industries accounted for about three-quarters of British business investment.

SOCIAL ACCESS

These changes in the world of work had important consequences for social structure and attitudes. The percentage of the labour force classified as manual workers fell from 47 in 1974 to 36 in 1991. Furthermore, the nature of much manufacturing work changed. Different skills were emphasized, especially in Information Technology, and physical strength became far less important than in the past. Women became more important in the labour market. They outnumbered men in the service sector, especially in health work, shops and catering. Female employment in traditional manufacturing sectors, such as textiles, declined however, while for both men and women poverty and despair were present in run-down industrial areas, for example Sheffield as captured in the film *The Full Monty* (1997). By the late 1970s the largest employers in Newcastle, earlier a major centre of industry, were the City Council, the Department of Health and Social Security, the Area Health Authority and the University. Across the country, 'white blouse' jobs, such as banking, teaching and office work, grew in importance for women.

The problems of the traditional employment base in Clydeside, South Wales and north-east England ensured that unemployment figures were higher there in the recessions of the early 1980s and early '90s than they were across much of southern England. In October 1984 every county in Wales had an unemployment rate above 10 per cent, and for all bar Powys and South Glamorgan it was over 15 per cent. Despite the cushioning of Social Security, such figures brought with them heavy social problems, including depression, alcoholism and family breakdown. Poverty was also linked to poor health.

The differentiation within the workforce linked to skills and income rose greatly. The real income of the bottom 10 per cent of the British population increased by 10 per cent in 1973–91, but the top 10 per cent gained 55 per cent, a reflection of the strong demand for educated labour. The bottom tenth of manual workers earned only 64 per cent of average income in 1991. Differentiation within the workforce was an important aspect of a more widespread divide in resources. The percentage of the population earning, or, at least, receiving, less than half the national average income rose, although this was a measure of relative, not absolute, poverty since average incomes rose markedly. Differences in disposable wealth were related to other financial indices, such as savings and house prices. In 1999 it was claimed that half the adult population had less than £200 in savings. Differences in disposable wealth were also linked to variations in consumption patterns, such as car ownership and tourism. Some of these variations were a matter not only of quality of life, but also of life safety indices. This was true, for example, of the ability to keep homes warm.

The differing rates of access of children from social groups to university became a contentious issue in 2000 when the Chancellor of the Exchequer, Gordon Brown, not fully in command of the facts, responded to a fuss about alleged prejudice at Oxford University by calling the exclusion of a state-school pupil 'an absolute scandal'. The issue became more charged in 2003 as the government sought to tighten up the benchmarks for admissions it had already set universities. The latter were paid a bonus for taking students from postcode areas with low participation ratios. A laudable goal, raising expectations, however, became a policy that combined authoritarianism and social engineering. This was taken further when an Office for Fair Access was created in 2003.

Social indices for the working class were frequently affected by the inclusion of what was, in the 1990s, increasingly termed the under-class. The closure of mental hospitals created problems, since the alternative policy of 'care in the community' proved inadequate, as had been predicted. Cases of tuberculosis among the homeless rose, as did the number of homeless themselves: parts of London rapidly became a 'cardboard city' as the number of inhabitants who slept rough, usually teenagers who had left home to look for work or to escape parental pressure, increased. In November 1986 Michael Meacher, Labour's shadow Health Minister, claimed 'We are seeing the re-emergence of an underclass of the dispossessed on a horrifying scale'. The percentage of 16–17-year-olds neither in work nor in full-time education doubled from 5 to 10 in 1989–96. Over 20 per cent of 18–35-year-olds had not registered to vote at the time of the 1992 election. This was an impor-tant aspect of the extent to which much of the poor lacked a voice that was heard.

Awareness of the extent and nature of poverty varied, although in central London and other metropolitan areas there were increasing numbers of beggars. The *Spitting Image* television series of the 1980s and the 'Alternative' comics of the 1990s and 2000s savaged politicians and government policies, but the social bite of such works was less strong than its political counterpart. Meanwhile, the vast majority of non-documentary television programmes, whether 'sit-coms' or 'soaps', did not challenge, let alone push hard at, such issues as differ-ent social opportunities.

GENDER

Class interacted with other forms of identity such as gender. For example, responding to gender inequalities has not necessarily helped with the more general problems of class differences, as 'posit-ive discrimination' in favour of hiring and promoting women has worked most to the benefit of middle-class women. Rising female opportunities in the world of work were also linked to the increase in school attainment among girls, which rose markedly at GCSE-level from 1987, with the gap between male and female attainment also rising in the same period.

Since men and women tend to marry those of similar background, especially in terms of educational attainment, the net effect of greater opportunities for women may be a strengthening of class differences. Furthermore, because men have usually played a minor role in full-time child care, greater opportunities for middle-class women can be linked directly to an expansion in the number of paid domestic workers, especially child-minders and cleaners. These are overwhelmingly women, and most receive low salaries. More generally, there is a difference between a middle-class feminism focused on the terms of access to the middle-class workplace, and a working-class counterpart concerned about the conditions of work. The bleakness of the lives of many working-class women was captured in Pat Barker's novel *Union Street* (1982).

By 1994 female employment was nearly 53 per cent of the workforce. However, an increasing percentage of female employment was part-time, and much was in low-skill and low-pay jobs. These were particularly vulnerable to new labour-saving office equipment and practices. The banks, which employed many women, shed large numbers of staff in 1989–90 and 1993–5.

ETHNICITY

As well as gender, ethnicity was an increasingly important theme in social identity and issue in politics from the 1960s. Racial tension, and concerns about the impact of immigration on unemployment levels, led to a redefinition of nationality. The British Nationality Act of 1948 had promised freedom of entry from the Commonwealth and colonies, but this was progressively limited by the Commonwealth Immigration Acts of 1962 and 1968, the Immigration Act of 1971, the British Nationality Act of 1981, and the Immigration Act of 1988. After the 1971 Act, there were few differences between the rights of Commonwealth and foreign immigrants.

The rights of those who had (legally) immigrated were, in contrast, strengthened. Race Relations Acts in 1965, 1968 and 1976 prohibited discrimination and established a Commission for Racial Equality to deal with general problems of discrimination as well as individual cases. This legislation failed to convince many immigrants that they were not the victims of a racialist system, but it marked a major advance on the earlier legal situation. These Acts were very different in content and tone from the exclusionist arguments of the racists of the period. More significantly, British society became less racist in the sense that fewer people formally challenged racial diversity. The success of immigrants and their descendants in sport was particularly important in changing attitudes. Thus, in November 1999, Lenox Lewis became world heavyweight boxing champion. Three years later Paul Boateng became Chief Secretary to the Treasury and the first 'black' man in the Cabinet, while the Pakistani-born Michael Nazir-Ali, Bishop of Rochester, was much (although unsuccessfully) touted as a possible Archbishop of Canterbury.

Many immigrants had rapidly showed that they had no intention of being typecast and organized with reference simply to existing divisions within society. Instead, multi-culturalism gave the process of self-identification within contemporary British society another dimension. The existence of ethnic divides also cut across attempts to explain social structure in occupational terms. These divides were a matter of identity and identification, the latter an aspect of the discrimination that helped to account for higher rates of unemployment among young blacks and Asians. This helped fire dissatisfaction seen, for example, with the formation in 1998 of the People's Justice Party by Birmingham's Kashmiri population.

Many immigrant groups strove to retain a distinctive identity, in certain cases linked to a lack of sympathy for generally accepted values. Over some issues, such as the mixed education of Asian Islamic girls, this created administrative and legal problems, and in 2003 the slaughter, without prior stunning, of animals by Jews and Moslems threatened to pose fresh issues. The acceptability of British society to immigrants varied greatly. Whereas Islamic fundamentalists spray-painted advertisements they deemed obscene, other immigrants were far less offended.

Furthermore, alongside multi-culturalism, Britain has a degree of racial tension. Afro-Caribbean hostility to what was seen as a discriminatory police force played a major role in urban riots. In October 1994 the 28,000-strong Metropolitan Police Force contained only 679 ethnic-minority officers; only one of the country's 384 chief superintendents then was from the same group.

The distribution of immigrant communities varied greatly. Immigrants were concentrated in the English cities, especially London and cities in the Midlands, Lancashire and Yorkshire. There were fewer in the cities of the North-East, and far fewer in rural areas, Scotland and Wales. Within individual cities, immigrants concentrated in particular areas, influenced by a mixture of opportunity and self-segregation. Few immigrants re-migrated. The overwhelming majority of the Caribbean immigrants who arrived in the 1950s and early 1960s planned to save money in order to buy land in the West Indies and return, but they seldom earned enough: only a tenth of these immigrants returned in the 1980s.

Growing cultural diversity ensured that multiple cultural identities became more common. Britishness as a result became a container for many nationalities. There was a greater understanding of different types of Britishness: British/Englishness, British/Scottishness etc. were increasingly seen as very different. Britishness (and Englishness) were also seen from the 1990s more like a set of interlocking identities, rather than as an overarching phenomenon. It was possible to be British and Pakistani, Ghanaian, Greek and so on. Public discussion about racism cast in terms of 'black and white' addressed the somewhat nebulous issue of institutional racism, but also tended to posit a non-existent unitary 'black community' and a dubious notion of 'whiteness'. Instead, multi-cultural Britain witnessed a myriad of tensions and alliances, in which place, ethnicity, class, religion and other factors co-exist, producing rifts, such as that between church-going Caribbean and criminous Jamaican Yardies. Income and educational attainment levels varied greatly between, and within, ethnic groups. Thus educational performances by Chinese and Indians were higher than those by African-Caribbean, Pakistanis and Bangladeshis, in part for the last two because of limited aspirations on behalf of many girls.

Divisions within and between ethnic groups were lent added force by the crisis following the terrorist attacks on New York and Washington on 11 September 2001. The extent to which some British Muslims failed to criticize, and even applauded, the attacks not only shocked others but also exposed divisions within Islamic opinion. For some preachers, the crisis was understood in terms of a religious conflict that joined Britain to the rest of the world, and with categories within Britain taking on meaning in terms of these divisions. Thus, in March 2003 one preacher, Abdullah el-Faisal, was convicted and imprisoned for soliciting murder as a result of his exhortations to kill Hindus and Jews. The previous December, a poll suggested that 8 per cent of the British Muslims it sampled would support terrorist acts against Britain.

Terrorism was linked in the public eye with asylum seekers, although most of the latter in no way sympathized with the goals or methods of terrorists. However, in part because some of those arrested for terrorist offences were asylum seekers, and, more generally, because there was concern about a sense of challenge from outside, the issue of asylum became a central one in 2002–3 with populist newspapers, such as the *Daily Mail* and *The Sun*, claiming that the country was being taken over or overrun. In 2001 the Conservative leader, William Hague, described Britain as becoming a foreign land to many of its inhabitants. The issue helped to exacerbate relations with other countries, especially France, that were perceived as failing to stem the flow of asylum seekers.

Immigrants themselves made multiple contributions to British society. By the 2000s one of the most important was in strengthening the labour force. This was recognized by the introduction of fast-track work permits in some industries, while the Highly Skilled Migrant Programme came into force in January 2002. Immigrant workers made a crucial contribution to the NHS at all levels. Furthermore, the increased development of 'caring' jobs, mostly low paid, provided a sphere in which immigrants featured prominently.

In 1999 the Commission on the Future of Multi-Ethnic Britain declared that 'Britishness, as much as Englishness, has systematic, largely unspoken, racial connotations', not least because it was associated with whiteness, and also called for a change in their historical treatment, specifically 'reimaging' to challenge racism. The accuracy of the report, and the very concept of 'institutional racism', were topics for debate, but the preference for socio-cultural engineering was clear. This was an aspect of a more widely contested nature of British identity. Multi-culturalism was increasingly a theme in British culture and government. This had been less the case under the Conservatives, for example, the Education Reform Act of 1988 ignored the idea, but, under Labour, multi-culturalism was pushed more actively, and intolerance was expressed towards other attitudes. This was one aspect of the authoritarianism of the Blair government.

BRITAIN AND EUROPE

Britain joined the EEC on 1 January 1973 (the treaty of accession was signed in Brussels on 22 January 1972). Membership had been pushed hard by Edward Heath, who saw it as crucial to his vision for the modernization of Britain and as a way for the country to play a convincing role on the world stage. He emphasized the economic benefits of membership, arguing that it would open up markets. In contrast, Heath said little about possible political consequences. He misleadingly claimed that there would be no lessening of national identity, and ignored prescient warnings to the contrary.

Entry into the EEC was seen by many former colonies as a rejection of their interests. Indeed, prior to entry, British trade with the Commonwealth was greater than that with Europe. Heath accepted the EEC Common Agricultural Policy, although it had little to offer Britain. Cheap food from the Commonwealth, especially New Zealand lamb, was to be excluded, in order to ensure a market for more expensive, subsidized Continental products. Entry into the EEC also led to a loss of national control over nearby fishing grounds. Combined with the exhaustion of fish stocks, this was to help destroy much of the fishing industry.

There was only limited opposition to entry into the EEC within the Conservative Party, still less the government. Membership was criticized most strongly by the left wing of the Labour Party, whose dominance forced Harold Wilson to declare that he opposed entry on the terms that Heath had negotiated. However, Labour supporters of EEC membership, led by Roy Jenkins, were willing to vote with the government, thus providing crucial parliamentary support.

EEC membership was re-examined after Labour returned to power under Wilson in February 1974, in large part in an effort to quieten critics on the Labour left. Far from displaying a principled commitment to a European cause, the divided government entered into a protracted and largely cosmetic renegotiation of Britain's terms of entry. To surmount party divisions, Wilson then launched a constitutional novelty: a referendum campaign on Britain's continued membership of the EEC. So that supporters and opponents could both campaign, the principle of collective Cabinet responsibility did not apply in the referendum.

Held on 5 June 1975, 67.2 per cent of those who voted favoured membership, the only areas showing a majority against being the Shetlands and the Western Isles (of Scotland). The available evidence suggests that public opinion was very volatile on the EEC, implying a lack of interest and/or understanding, and that the voters tended to follow the advice of the Party leaderships, all of which supported continued membership. The opposition was stigmatized as extreme, although it was from across the political spectrum, from Enoch Powell on the nationalist Right to Tony Benn on the Socialist Left. Benn presented the EEC as an undemocratic 'capitalist club', and told the Cabinet that 'on the EEC Commission, unlike the Council of Ministers, there is no British veto at all. You don't elect these people, they are Commissioners, and they are not accountable'. Benn also presented the EEC as incompatible with a truly Socialist Britain, not least by ending the possibility for national economic management. He argued that economic problems required the retention by the British government of power to introduce import surcharges, devalue the pound and control capital movements, all of which would be threatened or lost if sovereignty was pooled within the EEC.

Benn saw the size of the opposition vote as 'some achievement considering we had absolutely no real organisation, no newspapers, nothing'. This was scant consolation. The referendum result was decisive. Britain stayed in. As a consequence, relations with the EEC were not to become as divisive a political issue again, until they emerged in the late 1980s as the focus for the split within the Thatcher government. There was no real controversy in 1979 when, fearful of the deflationary consequences of tying sterling to a strong Deutschmark, the Callaghan government decided not to join the Exchange Rate Mechanism (ERM), the only one of the then nine EEC states not to do so. Other issues took centre-stage: the economy, union relations, and Scottish and Welsh devolution.

FOREIGN POLICY

Outside Europe, the Labour governments of 1974–9 took a much less assertive stance than their predecessors of 1964–70. Callaghan, nevertheless, ordered a continued naval presence in the South Atlantic in order to deter the Argentinians from action against the Falklands. Defence priorities, however, were centred on deterring a Soviet invasion of Western Europe, not on the remains of empire. Imperial fragments continued to gain independence: the Bahamas in 1973, Grenada in 1974, the Solomon Islands, Ellice Island and Dominica in 1978, and the Gilbert Islands (as part of Kiribati), St Lucia and St Vincent in 1979. The abandonment of the overseas system of bases continued when the Navy left Malta in 1979. Hong Kong was the sole colony with a substantial population not en route for independence; and this was largely due to Chinese irredentist interest in the colony, which compromised the possibility of independence, and to poor British relations with Communist China.

From the late 1960s British options had no longer seemed to be those of independence and alliance from a position of strength, but, instead, to be those of centring political interests and defence undertakings on American or European systems. Although lessened by the role of NATO, this tension was to be the theme of British power politics thereafter. Thus, when Britain acted against Iraq in 2003 it did so as an adjunct to American power and against the wishes of France and Germany; when Britain had returned to act east of Suez in 1991, however, also against Iraq, it had done so in pursuit of United Nations' goals, and in co-operation with France as well as the USA.

Thatcher sought to centre Britain's international position on alliance with the USA, not membership of the EEC, and was fortunate that she got on very well with Ronald Reagan, the American President in 1981–9. East–West tensions had revived with the Soviet intervention in Afghanistan at the close of 1979. Tensions became particularly acute in 1983, with the Soviet fear of attack during the NATO command and control exercise Able Archer 83, the Soviet shooting down of a Korean civilian airliner, and the deployment of American Pershing II rockets in West Germany. Co-operating against Communism, the relationship with Reagan was special to Thatcher for it gave her great influence on the world stage. She supported the USA over Afghanistan, Star Wars, and the deployment of Cruise missiles in Britain, and told a dinner held in Washington in 1985 to celebrate 200 years of Anglo-American diplomatic relations: 'There is a union of mind and purpose between our peoples which is remarkable and which makes our relationship truly a remarkable one. It is special. It just is, and that's that.' Reagan was willing to let Thatcher take a role that was disproportionate to the respective strength of the two countries, although she did not always take the lead. Thatcher felt that Britain was under threat from the Soviet Union and its supporters. In 1987, Britain spent 5.2 per cent of her gross national product on defence, compared with 4 per cent for France, 3.1 per cent for West Germany and 6.7 per cent for the USA.

Soviet espionage remained a source of concern. In 1982 Geoffrey Prime, formerly a Soviet agent at the Government Communications Headquarters (GCHQ) at Cheltenham, was convicted of espionage. Two years later, Michael Bettaney, a British spy, was arrested for espionage and the KGB Resident expelled, and in 1985 the defection of Oleg Gordievsky, the KGB Resident-designate, led to the expulsion of 25 Soviet intelligence officers. There was also suspicion that left-wing individuals and organizations, such as certain prominent trade unionists, especially within the NUM, and also the Campaign for Nuclear Disarmament, were fronts, often willingly so, for Communist propaganda and Soviet subversion. This led to an emphasis on counter-subversion rather than counter-terrorism, especially, in 1981–5, while Sir John Jones was Director-General of MI5.

The relationship with the USA proved divisive within Britain, as the Labour Party's move to the left led to its rejection of key aspects of foreign and defence policy. In particular, the unilateralist tendency in Labour circles appeared to threaten the ability to respond to Soviet power. From the perspective of 2003, issues such as the deployment of American Cruise missiles, and sites of protest, especially Greenham Common, seem distant memories, but at the time, in what was referred to as the 'Second Cold War', they had a capacity to energize commitment that was important to the divisive politics of the 1980s. They also contributed powerfully to its international character, and, in the eyes of critics, to a militaristic dimension to Thatcherism. There were no such issues in the 1990s.

Thatcher was critical of what she saw as a preference for economic controls and centralist planning in the EEC. She felt closer to Reagan than to European leaders. Her government was more influenced than its Continental counterparts by the emergence of neo-liberal free-market economics in the 1980s. Thatcher's own attitude towards the EEC was more bluntly put by Nicholas Ridley, a minister close to her, who was forced to resign from the Cabinet after telling the editor of *The Spectator* in July 1990 that the European Community (EC, as the EEC had become) was 'a German racket designed to take over the whole of Europe'. Thatcher's alienation became more serious as the EC developed in a more ambitious direction, and she was also unhappy about the unification of Germany in 1990, which followed the collapse of European Communism.

Furthermore, economic links with the EC were becoming closer. This was true of markets, suppliers, investment and regulation. The adoption of the Single European Act in 1986 committed Britain to remove all barriers to the creation of the Single European Market, and also altered the framework of British economic activity. The EC and the domestic market were legally joined, and it was necessary to comply with the Single European Market in order to operate in the EC and therefore in Britain.

As a member of the EC with, from the 1980s, less restrictive labour and financial conditions than elsewhere in Western Europe, Britain attracted considerable 'inward investment' from Japan, Korea, the USA and other states. In 1991, 53 per cent of all Japanese direct investment in the EC came to Britain. By April 1993 Japanese car-makers had invested £2.4 billion in Britain, transforming local economies with factories such as the new Nissan works near Sunderland, and the chairman of the rival French car-maker Peugeot called Britain a 'Japanese aircraft carrier' ready to attack Continental markets. Britain was second only to Canada in 1991 for the number of new American foreign manufacturing projects. This created many jobs, helping to ease the impact of the decline of heavy industry in Britain. Similarly, American and Japanese securities houses and investment banks used London as the base for their European operations.

Although the Cold War and eventually the EC were the foci of Thatcher's international concerns, she also had to respond to other issues. Thatcher had difficult relations with the Commonwealth, not least because of serious differences over policy towards South Africa. This had already been a problem prior to 1979 as newly independent states had developed their own views. This difference reached a highpoint with Thatcher's refusal in the 1987 and 1989 meetings of Commonwealth Heads of Government to accept the Commonwealth policy on sanctions against South Africa and the conference communiqués' resulting clause 'with the exception of Britain'. More generally, the Commonwealth did not meet British hopes that it would serve as a continuation of imperial cohesion, not least because of a reluctance to follow the British lead, which reflected scepticism about British intentions and moral authority. The creation of an equal partnership proved a goal that was incompatible with British leadership.

Imperial fragments continued to gain independence: Zimbabwe in 1980 (after the end of White rule had been followed by a resumption of British control and then elections), Antigua and British Honduras in 1981, and St Kitts-Nevis in 1983. Brunei, hitherto a protectorate, became fully independent in 1984. The Zimbabwe settlement further helped to ensure the focus of British foreign policy on the Cold War, while British concern in 1983 about the American invasion of Grenada, a Caribbean island and member of the Commonwealth that had been violently taken over by a hard-line left-wing group, did not have a major impact on Anglo-

American relations. The British government did not take a prominent role when Fiji, a member of the Commonwealth, had two coups in 1987.

That Britain was to fight a last imperial war in 1982 was unexpected. The Falklands had been under British control from 1833, but were claimed, as the Malvinas, by the Argentinians, whose ruling military junta was convinced that, because the British government was uncertain of the desirability of holding on to the colony, it would accept its seizure by the Argentinians. The decision in 1981 to withdraw the Antarctic patrol ship *Endurance* was seen as a sign of British lack of interest in the South Atlantic. On 2 April 1982 the virtually undefended islands were successfully invaded. Assured that the Navy could fulfil the task, and determined to act firmly in what was seen as a make-or-break moment for the government, Thatcher responded with an expeditionary force that included most of the Navy, while liners and container ships were leased to transport troops and supplies. American mediation attempts that would have left the Argentinians in control were rejected.

Argentinian missiles (the word Exocet became something of a metaphor in Britain) and bombs led to the loss of a number of British ships. Nevertheless, British forces successfully landed on 21 May. Although outnumbered, they advanced on the capital, Port Stanley, fighting some bitter engagements on the nearby hills and forcing the isolated, demoralized and beaten Argentinians to surrender on 14 June. American logistical and intelligence support aided the British (as did the purchase of Exocet missiles through third parties from France to prevent their sale to Argentina), but in the end it was a matter of bravely executed attacks, the careful integration of infantry with artillery support, and the ability to continue without air supremacy.

The war led, among much of the population, to an imperial afterglow that helped the Conservatives win re-election in 1983, but to many it seemed anachronistic. This was even more true of the former empire. New Zealand had offered naval support, but Britain had fought alone. After the war the Falklands were developed, at considerable expense, as a military base. Hong Kong, however, after a negotiated settlement, was turned over to China in 1997 (the year in which the lease on the mainland territories ran out). There was no attempt to hand the issue over for decision to local views. Despite concern about the authoritarian nature of Chinese rule, the desire to win the goodwill of the Chinese government and an acceptance of the dominant position of China prevailed. Relations with China had improved considerably after the death of its radical leader Mao Zedong in 1976.

Military power, however, continued to be deployed. The outbreak of the Iran–Iraq war in 1980 led to the establishment of the Armilla patrol in the Persian Gulf, which continued until responsibilities broadened in 1990 with the outbreak of the Gulf War. The British took a prominent role in this conflict, although it was very much secondary to that of the USA. Meanwhile the nuclear deterrent was maintained. Four submarines armed with Trident missiles, the replacement to Polaris, were laid down in 1986–93 and the first, HMS *Vanguard*, was commissioned in 1993.

Although Major initially spoke about his desire to place Britain 'at the heart of Europe', he resisted the concentration of decision-making within the EC at the level of supranational institutions. In the Maastricht conference of December 1991, Major obtained an opt-out clause from the single currency and from the 'Social Charter', which was held likely to increase social welfare and employment costs. His government, however, was characterized by failure over the EC: an inability either to shape it or to limit its consequences and its impact on British politics. This divided the Conservatives and also led to the formation of the Referendum Party. Opposed to the European Union, this Party failed, however, to make much of an impact in the 1997 general election, other than further sapping support for the Conservatives, although the United Kingdom Independence Party won three seats in the 1999 Euro-elections.

BLAIR AND FOREIGN POLICY

Blair took office in 1997 intent on mending relations in Europe. More sympathetic to the European ideal than his predecessors since Heath's fall in 1974, Blair was convinced that closer European integration was central to his strategy for modernization. The opt-out from the social chapter was relinquished in 1997, and this led to more regulations for employers, contributing to their accurate perception that the return of Labour led to more 'red-tape'. Attention focused on the single currency (the Euro), as what had become the European Union (EU) moved towards establishing it. In a Commons' statement on 27 October 1997, Gordon Brown stated that there was no constitutional reasons why Britain should not join the single currency, although, as short-term interest rates then were nearly 4 per cent higher in Britain than in Germany or France, he judged the economic case as not then favourable. On 23 February 1999 a government-sponsored national changeover plan to ease the introduction of the single currency was introduced. The following year William Hague launched a 'Save the Pound' campaign.

Blair felt obliged to be cautious because of the more sceptical nature of public opinion, not least the popular press, and because the economy was on a different cycle from the rest of the European Union. Britain did not join the single currency, the Euro, when it was launched, and has still to set a target date for a referendum on joining. The failure of 'Euroland' to free up capital and, in particular, labour markets as promised, and the tightness of monetary policy set by the European Central Bank helped discourage the Treasury, as did Britain's success, while fiscally independent, in achieving higher growth rates than the Euro area in 1993–8 and 2001–3. The Treasury argued that the Bank of England's freedom to set interest rates, specifically to address British fiscal circumstances, was important, not only to economic growth, but also to ensure appropriate domestic fiscal policies. The housing market was particularly responsive to interest rate movements. The five economic tests the Treasury had highlighted – how far the economy was convergent with the Euro area, whether it could take the loss of its own exchange rate, and the impact of the Euro on investment, the City and the economy as a whole – were made even more problematic as a consequence of the international economic downturn of the early 2000s, and in 2003 the Treasury decided that these tests had not yet been met. Furthermore, the increase in public expenditure under Blair's second government involved running a budget deficit that threatened to breach the EU's stability pact. In February 2002 this led the European Commission to voice its criticism publicly. It would only be possible for the government to address such concerns and meet its own spending plans by greatly increasing taxation.

The Euro had appeared to be the most serious international issue for Blair, but the crisis stemming from confrontation with Iraq in 2002–3 changed this. The robust support that Blair offered to the Americans after the terrorist attacks on 11 September 2001 dominated foreign perception of Britain. As a consequence, criticism of Blair was seen as, in some ways, essentially criticism of a resolute approach towards Iraq and/or terrorism, and, in some quarters, this was indeed the case. However, this criticism was in fact multi-faceted and of longer duration, and it was not helpful to assess current British debates on international relations simply in light of the crisis, important as that was.

Much of the domestic criticism of Blair rested on a fundamental unease about his policies, both external and domestic. In particular, there was a feeling that his desire to remould Britain risked comprom-ising long-established senses of identity. Blair and his ministers did not appear to have a clear understanding of what they meant by nation or state. This was important to their relations with other countries. Furthermore, the extent to which the constitutional experimentation seen since Labour gained power in 1997, which has so far led to the creation of assemblies in Northern Ireland, Wales and Scotland, and which may lead to regional assemblies within England, seems likely to lead to a replacement of the United Kingdom by an unstable coalition of polities, which necessarily has implications for foreign and defence policies. These will need to be 'negotiated' within the British Isles: espe-cially if competing political groupings are in power in Belfast, Cardiff, Edinburgh and London, not to mention Dublin. The Scottish and Welsh Nationalists, for example, are more neutralist and critical of the USA than the other political parties in Scotland and Wales, while Irish nationalism has marked left-wing leanings and is closer to Castro and Colombian terrorism than to mainstream international politics.

This process of negotiation within the British Isles will be even more difficult because the pretensions and prerogatives of the European Union extend far into what has until recently been regarded as domes-tic policy. It is naïve to assume that it will be possible to keep this process politically separate from that of the settlement of differences between parts of the British Isles. The ambition of the European Union has markedly extended with the adoption of the single currency.

Aside from the 'British' dimension to foreign policy, there is also the problem of excessive optimism about the possibility of moulding change. A government that came to power on the basis of welcoming change and rejecting the past is necessarily one that is optimistic about the prospect for improvement and a better future. This also has a partisan aspect, with the specific denial of attitudes and policies associated with both Conservatives and 'Old Labour'. Indeed, Blair's presentation of himself as 'New Labour' encourages the rejection of established assumptions of national interest and policy.

However, an assessment of positions in terms of 'New Labour' confuses what might at present be thus identified and the more long-term plasticity of the concept. There is a danger that Blair's views will be seen as co-terminous with – indeed the definition of – 'New Labour'. However, Blair will eventually go, probably resigning after winning the next general election, which has to be in 2006 at the latest. The long term is a sequence and sum of short terms, but commentators should try to look beyond the particular moment in order to consider how attitudes to foreign policy held among the major political groupings may change in what is a volatile international situation. Certainly, recent history suggests the need to be adaptable to rapid shifts in international circumstances.

The rejection of the past currently associated with 'New Labour' is assisted by the sense that the end of the Cold War in 1989–91 created an opportunity and a need for new assumptions. Until the Iraq crisis of 2002–3, Blair had encouraged a stronger EU foreign policy and defence identity for Britain, and had sought to develop military co-operation with France. However, even prior to the serious division over Iraq, it was, as the Kosovo crisis of 1999 showed, by no means clear that the EU was capable of fulfilling the hopes placed upon it in this sphere. It has not only failed to meet British needs for an effectively managed free-trading area, but has also proved inadequate as a body through which to advance wider interests elsewhere in Europe. For example, Britain has found its freedom in international trade negotiations, a key aspect of foreign relations, circumscribed and its interests slighted.

The EU itself suffers from disunity, a lack of military resources and an ambitious extension of interests and commitments, all of which were amply displayed in the Yugoslavian crises of the 1990s.

Europe as a whole is a region that bears little relationship to long-established British national interests. Instead, these are being reconfigured (or Europeanized) in a policy that testifies to the governmental view that Europe is the crucial international unit for Britain, and also the optimistic hope that it can be made to work as such. This Europeanization reflects an old-fashioned emphasis on propinquity (nearness) that dates from mid-twentieth-century assessments of security and economic relations. In practice this is flawed, since propinquity means far less in terms of the global economics and geopolitics of the present day. Furthermore, the emphasis on Europe is a flawed assessment of the multiple links of Britain. For centuries Britain has been closer to Boston, Kingston or New York, than to Bari, Cracow or Zagreb, and this situation has not changed. Indeed, cultural, economic and demographic developments over the last half-century, ranging from the impact of American television and American and Japanese inward investment to New Commonwealth immigration, have accentuated these links and indicated the limited usefulness of a definition of Britain in terms of Europe.

Empire certainly no longer worked as a definition of national interest. At the start of 2003 there were still imperial possessions across the oceans. Alongside islands in and near the West Indies (Anguilla, Bermuda, the Cayman Islands, Montserrat, the Turks and Caicos Islands, and the British Virgin Islands), there were possessions in the mid-Atlantic (Ascension Island, St Helena and Tristan da Cunha), in the Pacific (the Pitcairn Islands), the Indian Ocean (the British Indian Ocean Territory, especially Diego Garcia, with its airbase), and in and close to Antarctica (the British Antarctic Territory, South Georgia, the South Orkney, South Sandwich and South Shetland Islands, and the Falklands). The British bases in Cyprus were also sovereign territories.

Some of the territories were unoccupied, but in others there was no support for independence. Bermuda voted against it in 1995. The determination shown in a referendum in 2002 organized by the inhabitants of Gibraltar, in defiance of the British government, to remain British rather than be party to any agreement between the governments of Britain and Spain to introduce a measure of Spanish control, struck a resonance in British domestic opinion. Nevertheless, in Britain, the empire was no longer seen as a community. Nor was there much interest in the assets, strategic and economic, that it offered. Gibraltar still has importance as a military base, and there was interest in the resources of the Falklands and surrounding seas, but there was scant commitment to the other territories.

British foreign policy under Blair has been shot through with an optimism and a universalism that is problematic. The latter rests in large part on the attempt to make human rights a central feature in policy, at once replacing the moral imperative of resisting Soviet imperialism, as well as explaining and justifying power projection. Blair told the Labour Party conference in 2001 that he wanted to help 'those living in want and squalor' across the world.

The Blair government's assessment of British relations with the EU rests on the misleading tendency of arguing that their policy is the only one that can work. In 2002 Blair told the Labour Party conference, 'The euro is not just about our economy, but our destiny. We should only join the euro if the economic tests are met. That is clear. But if the tests are passed we go for it'. In practice, however, interdependability with the EU did not, and does not, dictate the contours and consequences of the relationship and there is no such inevitability. Choices on policy existed, and exist, but that has long been denied by politicians and polemicists keen to advocate a particular point of view: the deterministic polemics of Euro-enthusiasm.

Blair – the youthful Mr Toad of British politics, with his faddish enthusiasms for novelty and his determination to ignore an ancestral heritage – clearly felt that he could square the circle, or rather circles. As a parallel to the attempt by his first Foreign Secretary, Robin Cook, to introduce an ethical slant to foreign policy, Blair intended to reconcile traditional assumptions with new identities and to keep different alignments and commitments – especially NATO and the EU, the USA and the (European) Continent – in concert and, indeed, mutually supportive.

The attempt was likely to end in failure even before the Iraq crisis of 2003. Certainly the EU did not fulfil boasts of providing an effective international force. In the Balkans, for example, Britain and France found themselves bearing most of the European military burden in the Bosnia and Kosovo crises of the 1990s. Furthermore, the reduction in military expenditure by other European states suggests that future crises will find Britain bearing a disproportionate share, and clearly troubles the USA.

In addition, the history of Britain's relations within the EU in the 1990s and 2000s does not suggest that bearing a heavy military burden will yield benefits in other fields. This failure can ironically be seen as part of a post-1945 trend in which successive British governments have exaggerated the likely benefit that would flow from high military expenditure. In the case of New Labour, seeing the benefit in European terms does not lessen the error. Under Blair, the percentage of national income spent on defence (i.e. the military) in the early 2000s was well below the figure for the 1980s, but it was a percentage of a larger income, and was greater than that spent by Germany, Italy and Spain.

Until the Iraq crisis, the Blair government's support for greater European integration and for a European identity for Britain had appeared to lessen Britain's ability to retain practices and politics of self-reliance, of national accountability, and of reacting to developments on their merits and with reference to the contingencies of the moment. This was particularly troubling given the volatility of the international system. In the event, in the circumstances of the Iraq crisis, Blair chose to be a firm ally of the USA rather than to maintain the thrust of his earlier policy.

More generally, Blair falls squarely into the Whiggish tradition of interventionism and the creation of systems to solve problems and prevent their recurrence, and is apt to underrate the pragmatic and prudential approach to foreign commitments. There is, however, no clear-cut agreement over these issues and, at the time of writing, the uncertainty about international developments underlines the room for disagreement, which is an important aspect of recent British history.

The international crisis also led to a new focus on the potential political consequences of immigrants who were willing to aid terrorism. The government responded by changes to the law that critics saw as illiberal. Thus the Anti-Terrorism, Crime and Security Act, passed in December

2001 in the aftermath of the September 11 attacks in the USA, gave the government power to have those suspected of terrorism locked up without trial if they were not British; a major breach in the principle that everyone should be treated equally under the law, and one that was criticized in the European Union's annual report on human rights issued in January 2003; that report, however, failed to address adequately the challenge posed by terrorism. Legislation to withdraw citizenship from those with dual nationality was also a new departure.

The crisis led the government to take a more critical line towards the European Convention on Human Rights. In January 2003 Blair, characteristically mentioning a policy prospect on a television programme, in this case *Breakfast with Frost*, suggested that, in his quest to restrict the number of asylum seekers, it might be necessary to look at British obligations under the Convention.

The government has also adopted practices that seem necessary in a war against terrorism but are still viewed with concern, for example the more extensive use of tribunals meeting in secret, and with evidence that can be kept secret, and with only a limited right of appeal. The supposition of innocence until proved guilty has been overthrown, while the central role is taken by politicians and officials, not judges. The government, however, took great pains to stress the short-term nature of these regulations, many of which require renewal by Parliament, and all of which are subject to independent review. The crisis also led to a marked expansion in expenditure on the security services, which had already increased in real terms in the late 1990s. One testimony to the character of the British state was provided by the very expensive new headquarters of the security services: Thames House (the Security Service, MI5) and Vauxhall Cross (Secret Intelligence Service, MI6) in London, and Benhall, near Cheltenham (the government's communication headquarters focusing on signals intelligence, GCHQ).

Chapter 8

British Questions

Re-mapping Britain was one consequence of Blair's policies. Increasingly, policy was set with reference to the European Union, not least because of the role of European law, and the value of presenting Britain as a political unit independent of the Continent was questionable. In some respects this was both a continuation and culmination of the policies of Edward Heath. As Prime Minister in 1970–74, he had pushed through change in what he saw as an attempt to modernize Britain: modernization was a buzz word in politics long before Blair began to use it. The decimalization of the currency in 1971 discarded centuries of usage and contributed to inflation.

The following year, the Local Government Act altered historic territorial boundaries, greatly challenging senses of local identity. The Act was based on the Royal Commission into Local Government in England under Lord Redcliffe-Maud, which had been established by the Labour government in 1966 and had reported in 1969. Coming into force on 1 April 1974, the new Act redrew the map, in order, it was hoped, to create a more efficient system that would overcome earlier unitary divisions. The recommendations of the Royal Commission were not implemented in full. The top tier of Provincial Councils was not established, and the process was to be resumed under the Labour government elected in 1997. There were still major changes in 1974. New counties were created, including Avon, Cleveland and Humberside, while others, such as Rutland, were destroyed. There were also mergers, such as Huntingdonshire and Cambridgeshire, and Herefordshire and Worcestershire, major changes in the boundaries between counties, for example Berkshire and Oxfordshire, and a reorganization of the Yorkshire Ridings.

As instances of the extent of change, in the North-West, Westmorland, Cumberland and the Furness region of Lancashire were merged into Cumbria. Lancashire also lost Warrington, Widnes and part of Whiston to Cheshire, although it gained Barnoldswick, Bowland, Earby and part of Skipton from Yorkshire. In the North-East, County Durham lost the county boroughs of Gateshead, South Shields and Sunderland, to the new county of Tyne and Wear, while the southeast part of the county became part of Cleveland, Durham losing a total of 295,000 people (36 per cent of its pre-1974 population). In turn, the county borough of Darlington became part of the county and Startforth rural district was transferred from the North Riding of Yorkshire. In the Welsh Marches, Worcestershire was absorbed into the new county of Hereford and Worcester, but lost Halesowen, Stourbridge and Warley to the new West Midlands metropolitan county.

In addition, counties were divided into new administrative districts, which were created by amalgamating the pre-1974 urban and district areas, and redrawing boundaries. Thus, in County Durham, new regions, such as Derwentside and Teesdale, were created. There was also extensive reorganization in Scotland and Wales, including the establishment of a tier of regional government. All this was pushed through in the name of rationality. New units were generally bigger and were supposed to be the best option for the provision of services, such as education or the fire service. In practice, in this classic example of government tinkering and failing to solve many of the apparent problems that were to be solved, scant consideration was given to local views, or to the value of traditional identities in providing a sense of place and belonging. Instead, there were further tinkering and adjustments.

Nationalist activism in Scotland and Wales in the 1960s had led the Labour government to establish a Royal Commission on the constitution in 1969. This produced the Kilbrandon Report four years later. Concerned about nationalist gains in the 1974 elections, the Callaghan government, with its vulnerable parliamentary situation, sought to win the backing of Plaid Cymru (the Welsh nationalist party) and the Scottish National Party (SNP). Their support had greatly increased. In 1970 the SNP gained 11 per cent of the Scottish votes, the first time a fourth party had achieved a significant share of the vote in mainland UK. In February 1974 the SNP won seven parliamentary seats, while at the October election it took eleven seats, and was second in 42 more, with 30 per cent of the Scottish vote. The discovery of North Sea oil appeared to make Scottish independence credible: in 1973 the SNP launched an 'It's Scotland's Oil' campaign. The Conservative Party began a long-term decline in Scotland from the late 1960s, a decline that both hit the Unionism it represented and was reflected by its decline. Working-class Scottish Conservatism/Unionism was particularly badly hit. In Wales, in October 1974, Plaid Cymru, which had not won any seats in the 1970 election, won three.

In response to the nationalist advance, the Labour government published the White Paper *Democracy and Devolution* in October 1974 and introduced a Scotland and Wales Bill in 1976, which proposed for each an assembly with control over health, social services, education, development and local government, but with no taxation powers and with the Westminster Parliament retaining the veto. The Bill met opposition from nationalists who felt that it did not go far enough, from the Conservatives who regarded devolution as a threat to Britain and as a way to weaken the government, and from some Labour politicians, such as Neil Kinnock and Leo Abse. They focused on the consequences of dividing Labour's strength and, for Wales, on the danger of discrimination against the non-Welsh speakers of South Wales. There was also concern about the unattractive consequences of regional dominance within an autonomous Wales. In Scotland there were similar regional tensions, especially in Orkney, Shetland, the

South-West, the North-East and the Borders, which feared dominance by Scotland's Central Belt: in each of these regions the majority of those voting in 1979 were to be against devolution.

In order to secure the passage of the legislation, the government had to concede new Bills that included provisions for referenda. Separate Bills for Scotland and Wales passed in the spring of 1978, but the referenda, held on 1 March 1979, were a different matter. As the result of an amendment introduced by George Cunningham, they required the support of 40 per cent of the electorate, not simply the majority of votes cast. This was not obtained in Scotland since, although the majority of votes cast there were favourable to devolution (52 per cent), only 64 per cent of the electorate voted. The Welsh referendum found only 11.8 per cent of the electorate in favour of devolution, with 46.5 per cent voting against and 41.7 per cent not bothering to vote. Even in Gwynedd and Dyfed, the strongholds of the Welsh language, the overwhelming majority of those who voted did so against devolution, in the former case because they did not want to be run from distant Cardiff. The unpopularity of the Labour government of Callaghan (who himself sat for Cardiff South-East) in its last months sapped support for devolution.

THATCHER AND THE BRITISH QUESTION

After the failure of devolution in 1979, the nationalist issue interacted with the generally hostile response to the Conservative governments in 1979–97, although the 1981 riots in England were not matched in Scotland and Wales. Election results in Scotland during the Conservative years were very different from the Conservative triumphs in England, and this provided the nationalists with ammunition, although Scottish electors were also capable of contributing to British politics as, for example, when Roy Jenkins helped establish the Social Democrats by winning Glasgow Hillhead in a by-election in March 1982.

The Conservative Party's historic claim to be the Unionist Party, for long its official title, was fatally undermined during the Thatcher years, as the Parliamentary Party became predominantly representative of the more affluent parts of southern England. In 1979, because the SNP lost badly (including nine of its seats), the Conservative percentage of the Scottish vote rose by 6 per cent. However, Thatcher was to be very unpopular in Scotland, and in 1983 there was an anti-Tory swing. The link between the Conservatives and working-class Protestant culture declined markedly: there were no Tory seats in Glasgow after 1982; whereas Labour's links with Irish Catholic Glasgow-Celtic nationalism were not weakened. Hit by the negative response to proposals for the Poll Tax, the Conservatives won only 10 of Scotland's 72 parliamentary seats in 1987 (they had held 21 before the election); and only 11 in 1992.

The Poll Tax was particularly unpopular in Scotland because of the relatively high rate of council housing and because it was introduced a year early, leading to the sense that Scotland was a guinea-pig. This provided the SNP with a significant boon. It ran a non-payment campaign, embarrassing Labour local authorities that were ready to collect the tax, and took Govan from Labour in a by-election in November 1988. Labour decided, however, not to promote civil disobedience and refused to campaign for non-payment. Labour was in a difficult position since it sought to act as an effective British opposition party without being outflanked in Scotland by the nationalists.

The Poll Tax helped to drive forward the discussion about a new constitutional settlement for Scotland. The Claim of Right of 1988 stated that 'the Union has always been, and remains, a threat to the survival of a distinctive culture in Scotland'. Instead, it saw sovereignty as resting in the people of Scotland. This led to pressure for a Scottish Constitutional Convention designed to produce plans for a Scottish Parliament. Supported by Labour and the Liberal Democrats, the Convention was rejected by the Conservatives, who supported the Union in its current form, and who vigorously defended it, with some success, in the 1992 election. Labour had only embraced the idea of a Constitutional Convention after the SNP won Govan. This was an instance of the role of the SNP in driving Labour policy, specifically into a stronger commitment to Home Rule. The SNP response to the Convention was to propose independence, and to withdraw from it before it was launched in November 1990. The SNP had little truck with a Convention that seemed only to offer a Labour dominance (albeit with Liberal support), and with a timetable dependent on Labour victory in a general election.

The Conservative victory at the national level in the 1992 election thwarted this aspiration in the short term. The Conservative government increased the role of the Scottish Grand Committee, and in 1996 returned the Stone of Scone to Scotland, but Scottish political aspirations were not assuaged.

Scotland avoided the lawlessness seen in Wales, where the failure of devolution in 1979 and the unpopularity of the Thatcher government led to an upsurge in terrorism. Arson attacks on houses bought by outsiders and on estate agencies were met with a firm response from the security services. They were fearful of parallels to the violent situation in Northern Ireland, and benefited from support from the national government. In 1980–82 there were widespread arrests, as activists were subject to Special Branch surveillance. The arrests led to controversial court cases, and to disquiet about police tactics. Yet the militants were resorting to a terrorism that threatened a measure of destabilization.

In Wales, unlike Scotland, there was no major swing against the Conservatives until the 1997 election, although, even at their height, the Conservatives in no way challenged the position of Labour. Furthermore, Liberalism was powerful in Wales. Some Liberals there, such as Emlyn Hooson, MP for Ceredigion in the 1970s and '80s, were further to the right of the Conservatives, but, thanks to the Liberals and Plaid Cymru, anti-Conservatism was entrenched even in rural Wales. Nevertheless, the Conservatives won eleven seats in Wales in 1979 on a swing to them of 4.8 per cent, and fourteen in 1983, in part thanks to the establishment of the Welsh-language television station. Although the number of Conservative seats fell to eight in 1987 and six in 1992, their share of the Welsh vote – 29.6 per cent in 1987 and 28.6 per cent in 1992 – was greater than that of Plaid Cymru. There was no debacle in Wales comparable to the introduction of the Poll Tax in Scotland, and the fusion of anti-English and anti-Conservative sentiment that was so bitter in Scotland was less so in Wales.

That the reaction against the Conservatives came later in Wales owed much to policies and personalities. Thatcher appointed 'One-Nation' Tories as Secretary of State for Wales: Nicholas Edwards (1979–87) and Peter Walker (1987–90). Throughout the Thatcher years Wales was a place apart, enjoying considerable public investment and public–private partnership. So keen was Thatcher to keep Walker in the Cabinet in 1987, that she agreed to let him run Wales his way. Walker would always support the general Thatcherite line in Cabinet, but then add that Wales was a special case; this was bearable since the resulting costs were not large. Walker, who did not read Welsh, was using Wales as a demonstration of one-nation Toryism, not in order to further Welsh nationalism.

BLAIR AND DEVOLUTION

It was Labour, not the nationalists, that was to be instrumental in changing the general situation. In the 1997 general election the Conservatives lost all their Scottish (for the first time) and Welsh seats: the collapse of their position was structural, not the result simply of tactical voting. The SNP won 22 per cent of the vote in Scotland. In Wales, Labour won 54.7 per cent of the vote and 34 seats, whereas the Conservatives, who polled 19.6 per cent, gained no seats for the first time since 1906. Plaid Cymru won the fourth largest percentage of votes, with 9.9 per cent. Although this was enough to gain four seats, owing to the regional prominence of its support, Plaid Cymru was still of little relevance in many constituencies, a major challenge to its description as a Welsh National Party. In the election the general unpopularity of the Conservative government interacted with a specific sense of grievance in Wales. The appointment of English Secretaries of State – John Redwood (1993–5) and William Hague (1995–7) – did not help. Nor did the transfer of powers from local authorities and locally nominated bodies to quangos appointed by the central government and heavily Conservative in composition. With the appointment of Redwood, an ardent Thatcherite who attempted to bring Wales into line with the rest of the United Kingdom, John Major brought the tradition of regarding Wales as a special case to an end. Redwood's preference for free-market solutions and limited government involvement undermined the credibility of the Conservative Party in Wales.

The Labour government elected in 1997 had such a powerful position in Parliament that it had no need to fear nationalist moves there, but Labour had decided to support devolution as a means to assuage nationalist sentiment. Devolution also sat easily with 'New' Labour's drive to create what it presented as a new Britain with modernized institutions, and with its claim to replace what were seen as the over-centralized character of the British constitution and government. The Scottish Parliament and the Welsh Assembly were presented as legislative and executive bodies designed to match and control the developing pace of administrative devolution. In Scotland, the vote for the creation of a parliament was 74 per cent on a turnout of 60 per cent. A separate vote on the same day gave the parliament the ability to vary the basic rate of income tax by up to 3 per cent.

Nevertheless, the very narrow majority for a Welsh assembly in the 1997 referendum, despite backing from Labour, Liberal Democrats and Plaid Cymru, suggests that the Welsh are far more likely than the Scots to identify with a British future. Furthermore, just under 50 per cent of the electorate abstained in the Welsh referendum.

The 1999 elections for the Scottish Parliament and Welsh Assembly left Labour as the largest party in both, but without a majority in either. This meant a Labour-Lib Dem Coalition executive in Scotland and a minority Labour executive in Wales, with the nationalists as the official opposition party in both. In Wales, Labour won 28 of the 60 seats, Plaid Cymru 17, the Conservatives 9, and the Liberal Democrats 6. In Scotland, Labour won 56 of the 129 Scottish seats, the SNP, despite predictions at one stage that they might win, 35, the Conservatives 18, and the Liberal Democrats 17. In Scotland, the SNP came first in 7 and second in 54 of the 73 constituencies; the other 56 seats were regional top-up seats calculated with reference to the proportion of votes cast allowing for representation among the constituency MPs. The Conservatives remained weak. Winning one Scottish seat from the SNP in the 2001 general election, the only seat that changed hands in Scotland, made no difference.

The 2003 local election results represented serious defeats for both the SNP and Plaid Cymru. The SNP's percentage of the vote fell 6.4 from the 1999 results to 20.9, and it lost eight seats. Plaid fell 10.8 per cent to 19.7 per cent, and lost five seats. Labour remained the leading party in both Scotland and Wales respectively, although with different results: down 4.3 per cent to 29.3 in Scotland, where they lost six seats, and up

1.2 per cent to 36.6 in Wales, where they won two seats. The striking difference was the rise of the Greens, who won 6.9 per cent of the Scottish vote and seven seats, and of the radical Scottish Socialist Party, which gained 6.7 per cent of the vote and six seats. The turnout indicated limited public interest: it fell 8.2 per cent from 1999 figures to 38.2 per cent in Wales and 8.8 per cent to 49.4 per cent in Scotland.

Labour's strategy was to use the Scottish Assembly to undercut the SNP, while at the same time using Scotland to support its position in Westminster, where Scottish constituencies are heavily over-represented. This posed the question of equity in representation within the UK. As a result, it was decided to cut the number of Scottish MPs from 72 to 57 at the election after the 2001 one. The maintenance of the 'Barnett Formula', under which the allocation of national funds leads to per capita public expenditure in Scotland that is 23 per cent higher than in England, is also an issue. The difference was readily apparent in numbers of doctors. Part of the money was spent by the Scottish Assembly on themselves and their incredibly expensive building, as well as on an expansion of public-sector jobs. Nothing was done to address Scotland's relative lack of economic competitiveness. In 2000, Scotland contributed 8.3 per cent of the UK's GDP, compared to 85.3 per cent for England, 4.1 for Wales and 2.3 for Northern Ireland.

NORTHERN IRELAND

Following sectarian tension that led to fighting in 1968 and a breakdown in law and order in 1969, troops were deployed in Northern Ireland in August 1969. Their very presence became an issue, however, and 1971 saw the first major offensive by the Provisional Irish Republican Army (IRA), which had been founded in 1970. The Catholic population and the army increasingly saw each other as enemies. The British government made a determined attempt to re-impose control, increasing the number of troops to 20,000 in 1972, and forcibly reopening IRA 'no-go' areas for military and police patrols.

The continued intractability of the situation led to the imposition of 'direct rule' from London: the Unionist regional government and the

Stormont Assembly were suspended in March 1972. The Heath government wanted to establish the conditions under which Northern Ireland could become self-governing again, but on a different basis than before: this time there would be a genuine cross-community government in Northern Ireland. The government sought, with the Sunningdale Agreement of 1973 and the creation of a non-sectarian power-sharing Executive, which took office in 1974, to negotiate a settlement, but they did not command sufficient cross-community support, and the Protestant Ulster Workers' strike of May 1974 led to the resumption of direct rule that spring.

In large part in order to limit cross-border support for the IRA, the Thatcher government also sought to give the Northern Ireland problem an Irish dimension. The government of the Republic of Ireland was brought into the equation through the Anglo-Irish Agreement of November 1985, which gave the Irish government a formal role in the affairs of Northern Ireland through an Anglo-Irish Secretariat and an Inter-Governmental Conference. The Unionists responded with fury, regarding such steps as the prelude to a British sell-out.

Despite greater Conservative sympathy for the Unionists, Conservative and Labour governments essentially followed a bi-partisan policy. There were traditional Labour sympathies for the nationalist cause, but this bi-partisanship represented a more serious abandonment of tradition for the Conservatives. In one respect, it was an aspect of the 'modernization' that Heath sought, combined with a desire on the part of central government to make the decisions, that clashed with Unionist support for devolved government in Northern Ireland.

IRA terrorism on the British mainland began in 1973. It included a bomb attack on the Conservative Party conference at Brighton in 1984 and a mortar attack on the Cabinet in 1991, and led to the deaths of three Conservative MPs, including Airey Neave, a close ally of Margaret Thatcher. IRA terrorism also affected aspects of the political culture. The Birmingham pub bombings of 1974 led to the limitations of the civil rights of suspected terrorists in the Prevention of Terrorism Act.

By September 1992, 3,000 people had died in the 'Troubles', many as a result of terrorism by the IRA, although with an increasing number killed by Protestant paramilitary groups, such as the Ulster Volunteer

Force and the Ulster Freedom Fighters, who were determined that Northern Ireland should remain part of the United Kingdom. The bloody disintegration of Yugoslavia, and the development of 'ethnic cleansing' there, led to new fears about the future of Northern Ireland.

In 1993 new talks between the British and Irish governments produced the Downing Street Declaration, in which John Major and Albert Reynolds, the two Prime Ministers, agreed to a shared sovereignty that would guarantee the rights of nationalists, while Unionists were assured that they would not be forced into a united Ireland. Sinn Féin was to be allowed to enter the talks if the IRA ended their violence.

A paramilitary ceasefire followed in 1994, and negotiations began between government officials and Sinn Féin. The cease-fire was followed by inward investment and a rise in house prices, but it broke down on 9 February 1996 when there was a devastating IRA bomb attack on Canary Wharf in London, the symbol of Thatcherite enterprise. Four months later, Manchester's shopping centre was bombed. The IRA was unwilling to accept the decommissioning of its arms, which was then regarded as a condition for Sinn Féin to enter all-party talks. Major devoted much effort to the negotiations, but his efforts foundered on the intransigence of the IRA and on his government's increasing dependence on Ulster Unionist support in the House of Commons.

The peace process was carried forward by Blair after he won power. In July 1997 the IRA declared a resumption of the 1994 ceasefire. Blair was assisted by American pressure on Sinn Féin and, in 1998, the Good Friday (10 April) Agreement laid the basis for the resumption of provincial self-government. After it was endorsed by 71 per cent of those who voted in a referendum on 23 May 1998, an Assembly and a Northern Ireland Executive were both created. Power in the Executive, which met for the first time in December 1999, was shared by Unionists and Nationalists. The Agreement allowed Sinn Féin to enter the Executive but required the IRA to finish 'decommissioning' its weapons by May 2000. Disputes over the lack of progress in decommissioning IRA weapons proved a bar to further stabilization and undermined the Executive, with a breakdown both in the Assembly's cohesion and in the political process. The fundamental flaw with the Agreement – that the Nationalists regarded it as a stage towards further gains, while many of the Unionists found it difficult to accept even the Agreement – undermined it. In 2002 the Unionists withdrew from the Executive and direct rule was re-imposed.

ENGLAND

Regional assemblies within England returned as an issue in the late 1990s: they were advocated by New Labour and the EU, and were seen as a counterpart to the Scottish, Welsh and Northern Irish assemblies. The alternative, a body for England as a whole, met no favour from Labour. Instead, in July 1999, it was the Conservative leader, William Hague, who suggested that, when English matters came up for debate in the Commons, they should be debated only by English MPs. He did not press on to advocate English autonomy, but his was an image of England very different to that of regional assemblies. Devolution elsewhere highlighted the position of England, although the pace of change was slower, in large part because there was no nationalist pressure to assuage or counter. Instead, after legislation for Scotland and Wales, the constitutional focus for the Blair government moved on to the House of Lords.

In 1994 the Conservative government had moved towards administrative, but not political, devolution with the establishment of ten 'integrated regional offices' in England. They were created by combining existing regional offices of the Departments of the Environment, Transport, Trade and Industry, and Employment, and appointing a single director. The offices were designated as the single contact point between the central government and the localities, but they were not based on co-operation with local government. In 1999, under Labour, in contrast, a new system began operation when eight Regional Development Agencies (RDA) started work, under instructions to prepare an economic strategy for each region. The agencies were less exclusively under central government control. They were under a statutory duty to consult Regional Chambers, non-elected bodies, of whom 70 per cent were representatives from all the local authorities in the region.

The Conservatives' allegation that the RDAS were bureaucracies that did not create many productive jobs was a fair charge, but, politically, they met Labour's wish to be seen to be doing something new. This process was taken further in April 1999 when, following the Scottish model, the North-East Constitutional Convention first met, charged with drawing up a blueprint for a directly elected English regional assembly. In January 2003 the Regional Assemblies (Preparations) Bill passed the Commons. It established the basis for referenda to determine regional support for such assemblies, although the regions proposed were often of limited cohesion and commonality.

Alongside these developments came a greater consciousness of Englishness. The survey of British Social Attitudes in 1999, produced by the National Centre for Social Research, indicated that the number who saw themselves as English, not British, more than doubled in 1997–9. An English identity expressed through a separate assembly and executive might be in the interests of the English, a term understood to mean the inhabitants of England, not some ethnic group. It might lessen the divisions that would stem from regional governments and assemblies, both the difficulties that might derive from the creation of such bodies and their subsequent rivalries over policy and funding. Furthermore, it would provide a representation that could compete with those of Scotland and Wales in order to give due weight to English interests within both Britain and the European Union.

The regional assemblies proposed by Labour reflect a very different emphasis. This links local politics to a sense that the very wide variations within England reflect regional identities. These identities, and the comparable ones in other parts of the United Kingdom, are indeed more important to the history of recent decades than is generally allowed in broad-brush accounts. For example, the tension between the attitudes and interests that were most strongly represented in London and the South-East and those that focused in 'the North' was important to the dynamics of the period. It challenged and, at times, undercut attempts to suggest that there was a consensus. The tension also provided much of the emotional dynamo behind class politics: a different sense of 'place', as well as of class attitude, was at issue.

More than image and perception are involved. There are also important differences between areas. And there may well be a resurgence of regional identity, and even Englishness, as the counterpart to an assertive Welshness and Scottishness. Football loyalties can be seen as an aspect of this. People, however, do not identify with government-defined regions or development agencies, any more than they did with areas and bodies created in the early 1970s by local government reform, such as Humberside and Avon. John Major's wish to privatize British Rail on a regional basis in order to recreate the world of pre-nationalization companies such as LNER and GWR did not win much popular support. However, people do identify with old counties, and, in addition, the North/South divide still represents a difference and a division. The provision for elected mayors was better placed than projected regions to harness traditional loyalties, although the elections for them held in 2002 did not suggest large-scale public interest. The earlier establishment of an elected Mayor and Assembly for London was more successful. It certainly aroused voter interest in a way that most local government elections did not. Those in 2000 drew only a 28 per cent turnout.

Economic developments accentuated divides. Greater regional specialization exacerbated regional differences. Management, research and development jobs were increasingly separate from production tasks: the former concentrated in south-east England, in areas such as the M4 corridor west of London, near Cambridge and, to a lesser extent, in 'new towns' in southern England, such as Milton Keynes and Stevenage. Furthermore, innovation-driven industries, such as electronics, which grew markedly in the period, were located in these areas. The Conservatives, and the 'Establishment' in general, became more focused on London, the South-East, and the world of money and services there, largely to the detriment of traditional interests that they had also represented. The South-East also paid a disproportionately high percentage of taxation, and thus benefited particularly from Thatcher's major cuts in income tax. The tower office blocks of Canary Wharf in London's former docklands, developed by the London Docklands Development Corporation created by the Conservative government in 1981, were a symbol of this new economy. By 2003

Canary Wharf contained 13.1 million square feet of office space. This process continued under Blair, with the South-East being responsible for a growing share of GDP. At the same time London faced the major social burden of coping with half the net international immigration affecting the United Kingdom. This pushed its population up.

Employment levels and wage rates varied greatly across the country. Unemployment was highest in traditional mining and industrial areas, and they also had the highest expenditure per head on income support and the highest percentage of households with a low weekly income. In 1994 the average weekly earnings of a working man was £419.40 in south-east England, £327.80 in northern England and £319.20 in Northern Ireland. Regional economic differences encouraged migration, leading people, especially young adults, to move to the south of England, although this was hindered by inflexible public housing policies and a restricted low-cost private rental sector. Nevertheless, variations in property prices provided an indication of a more general divergence in prosperity and economic fortune. In 2003 the government responded to these variations with proposals for 'Sustainable Communities' – new housing in the south of England and regeneration in the north. These were castigated by the Conservative spokesman David Davis as proposals to 'concrete the south and bulldoze the north'. Attitudes towards development also reflected this divergence: they were far more welcome in areas of economic difficulty, particularly high unemployment, such as north-east England.

Regional disparities were also marked at the more local level, and this provided much of the detailed fabric of social geography and collective experience. Crude regional indices concealed striking variations. Thus, in Scotland, the decline of heavy industry in Strathclyde and the loss of population from Glasgow and Dundee took place alongside a major growth in financial services that centred on Edinburgh but was not restricted to it. In 1992, 11 per cent of Scotland's labour force was employed in financial services. In south-east England there was much poverty, not only in London, but also along the Thames estuary, in the Medway towns, especially Chatham, in Brighton and other coast towns such as Hastings and Ramsgate, and in the new town of Crawley. In the South-West the unemployment and poverty of much of Cornwall, hit badly by successive crises in tin-mining, fishing and upland farming, was very different to the situation in east Devon and west Dorset. The rundown of the military after the end of the Cold War also hit parts of the South-West hard. In south Devon, Dartmouth and Totnes were far more prosperous than Paignton. In 1987 rates of unemployment in the Newcastle wards ranged from 8.9 per cent in Westerhope to 36 per cent in West City.

Political differences arose in large part from this local geography. Thus, the Conservatives in 1979 and 1983 benefited from social changes in South Wales, not least the growth of a white-collar workforce living in the Cardiff urban region and on the south coast, for whom the traditional loyalties of the Valleys had scant interest. Cornwall in 1997 returned ten Liberal Democrat, one Labour and no Conservative MPs. In contrast, both Labour and the Conservatives were stronger in neighbouring Devon.

These differences were also reflected in industrial militancy. Thus, the particular characteristics of South Wales industrial culture encouraged high rates of militancy among miners. This showed in the area strike ballots of December 1971, February 1974, November 1979, January and October 1982 and March 1983, in each of which the vote for a strike was above the national average, most markedly on the last occasion (68 per cent to 39 per cent). In 1984 there was no ballot before supporting the coal strike: traditions of industrial militancy and Socialism interacted with strong concerns about pit closures and unemployment. The situation in the north-east Wales coalfield was very different. Only 32 per cent voted for a strike in the area strike ballot in 1984; work continued during the dispute at Point of Ayr; and there was an important return to work at the Bersham Pit in August 1984. Pits where work continued still closed, however, Point of Ayr in 1996.

Local contrasts deepened in the 1980s, in part owing to shifts in housing, especially the skewed pattern of council-house sales. The better housing in the wealthier areas sold, while the public sector increasingly became 'sink housing', rented by those who suffered relative deprivation. Thus, in Newcastle there were above-average sales of council houses in the western and northern estates, and below-average sales of those along the river and in the east. Other cities had similar trends.

Local identities are often only imperfectly described in their regional counterparts, and regional, in turn, in the national. Thus, the overlapping senses of collective self-awareness that people have do not always readily correspond. The process is easiest in the South-East, where regional identity plays only a minor role. This is linked to its economic dynamism and to the role of national economic and commercial policies, trends and products, as well as national education, leisure and broadcasting policies, practices and institutions, all of which are particularly effective in the South-East.

NATIONAL IDENTITY

At the national level, attempts were made in the 1990s, closely linked to 'New Labour', to 'repackage' national identity in a modernizing fashion, with soundbites such as 'A Young Country'. Attempting to answer what was said to be the need for a new identity for a post-industrial age, these terms sought to suggest that modish urban life, or, more generally, a supposed set of modish national values, could provide identity. This has not elicited much popular support, and in 2001–2 was rejected by both the government and the British Tourist Authority (BTA). Tessa Jowell, Secretary of State for Culture, Media and Sport, stated in November 2001, 'You can't distil our national character to a liking for designer water or retro lamps', while the BTA shifted to heritage in order to market Britain.

The impact of the interlocked cultures of sport, television and celebrities has been more important than rebranding in influencing roles and identities. Thus, the Race Relations Acts were probably less important in countering often vicious racialism than the ability of many from immigrant backgrounds to take advantage of economic growth, and also the success of role models in a series of high-profile activities, such as athletics, football and television.

These interlocked cultures are the counterpart to the social trends of democratization and the cult of youth. They lead to a notion of community that is hedonistic and individualistic, and, to critics, it is unclear that they offer much in the way of an effective collective response to domestic or external challenges. This may be hedonism and individualism by the standards of the 1950s, but, nevertheless, both are affected, if not constrained, by collectivist assumptions and pressures. Thus, in 2003, Blair was criticized by some union leaders for distancing himself by his lifestyle from ordinary people.

The role of the state in wide parts of national life and the scope of judicial intervention were such that collective pressures were expressed through government. The attack on fox-hunting is an instance of individualism being constrained by collective pressure, with legislation used to criminalize a hitherto legal activity. In 2002 Parliament debated a contentious bill to allow unmarried couples, including homosexuals, to adopt children, rather than the matter being left to individuals. Collectivity was fostered in another respect by the use of guidelines and standards to monitor institutions. In education there were both more tests for pupils and more accountability for schools. The values propagated by the BBC were also seen by critics as a bias, if not an ideology, that distorted, if not constrained.

Yet, to its supporters, the BBC was an aspect of national identity, an institution that reached all, like the NHS. This helped make it difficult to challenge some public services, as the Conservatives acknowledged in government when they did not privatize the BBC or the Royal Mail, or dismantle the NHS, which is Western Europe's biggest employer. Conversely, Labour's advocacy of public service provided it with a form of patriotism that helped to exploit, or at least benefit from, a taproot of identity, or, looked at differently, drew on the extent of dependency on the state and the widespread reluctance to make necessary individual provision for the future.

Once returned to power in 1997, Labour talked of reforming the public services, but the emphasis was on their retention. Indeed, in July 2002 an increase of expenditure on the public services of £61 billion over the next three years was announced. The NHS budget had already risen by a third since 1998, while, over government as a whole, spending in real terms was 22 per cent higher in 2002–3 than in 1998–9. Despite this, the link between Labour and the public sector was weaker than during the 1974–9 Labour governments, not only because the Blair government kept the unions at a distance, but also because the unions were less powerful in the public sector. In 2001 only 59 per cent of public-sector workers were members of unions, although this was a far larger percentage than their private-sector counterparts, who had a rate of less than 20 per cent.

The issue of identity and community can be related to the collapse of cultural continuity that occurred with the social revolution of the 1960s. The consequences of this collapse help to define recent decades. They also make it difficult to address the issue of national identity. Thus, the destruction or weakening in the 1980s and '90s of traditional and, till then, vital benchmarks of either British or English identity – Parliamentary sovereignty, national independence, the Union between England and Scotland, the monarchy, the Common Law, the Church of England – was not followed by the creation of any viable alternatives.

The most successful, Scottish nationalism, was indeed part of the problem, since it helped to undermine notions of Britishness. A poll in 2000 revealed that 84 per cent of Scots sampled would describe themselves as Scottish rather than British. In 2002 the *Daily Record*, the most successful Scottish tabloid, urged Scots to support England's opponents in the World Cup, and they did so. The bullying of English children in Scottish schools and the beating up of English students on Scottish streets became more common. Alongside collective pressures on British identity, there are signs that devolution will lead to a variety in government policies that might be further accentuated by regional assemblies within England. Thus, in Scotland after devolution the personal care costs of old people were paid by the Scottish Executive and there were no university fees, while the situation in both respects was the opposite in England. In early 2003 there were tensions between the Executive and the government in London over the response to the firemen's strike and over the British negotiating position on European fisheries policy.

At the same time, there are important parallels between Scotland and England. For example, in both there are similar social and geographical shifts, including a move to the countryside and the erosion of its rural character as a result of commuting. Furthermore, both were brutally subject to the impact of economic competition, international capital flows and technological change. This was true even of the most remote areas, a theme taken up in the film *Local Hero* (1983), which depicted the impact of the international demand for oil on a remote corner of Scotland.

Weakness in British identity made it difficult to adjust to the growing pretensions of the European Union and to respond to the changes stemming from the incorporation of the European Convention on Human Rights with the Human Rights Act of 1998. Another aspect of the change in identity, which indicates the range of the process, is the increasing marginalization of Received Pronunciation in favour of demotic regional accents such as Estuary English.

Television played a central role in a society increasingly dominated by visual images. As an instance of changing images of greatness and identity, the list of one hundred Great Britons produced by popular choice for the BBC in 2002 was singularly short of imperial heroes. Martial figures as a whole were in short supply: only Nelson and Cromwell made the last ten, and if the winner, Churchill, can be seen as the greatest as well as the last of the imperial heroes, he was presented, as were Nelson and Elizabeth I, as defenders of an endangered country/people/culture, rather than as an exponent of empire. Elizabeth I herself gained far fewer votes than Diana, Princess of Wales. The mural on the New Palace Theatre in Plymouth's Union Street showing the defeat of the Spanish Armada in 588 now looks out on a world for which such events are largely drained of meaning and resonance.

Chapter 9

Conclusions

The value of Kilburn depended on not knowing particularities,
because it changed to the eye and the brain according to yourself,
your mood and the day.

Metroland, novel by Julian Barnes (1980)

UNCERTAINTIES

Uncertainty is the dominant theme in the early 2000s, an uncertainty
underlined by the combination of troubling individual and problematic collective experiences. In the former case, the major fall in the
stock market, which fell below 4,000 in July 2002, threatened pensions
as well as individual stock holdings, and the crisis in pension provision
led to a profound sense of uncertainty about the future. In the latter
case, economic problems combined with a number of difficult social
issues, and the sense of a less benign world, were driven home by the
terrorist attacks in New York and Washington on 11 September 2001
and by the international crisis over Iraq. The 'peace dividend' that
followed the collapse of the Soviet Union proved all too brief.

A country being warned by its leaders to prepare for terrorist attack,
and being told by its popular press that it was being swamped by
asylum-seekers, was not one where optimism was readily apparent. The
goal for the Home Office outlined in the Public Service Agreement
issued in 2000 was 'to build a safe, just and tolerant society, in which the

217

rights and responsibilities of individuals, families and communities are properly balanced, and the protection and security of the public are maintained'. By 2003 the precariousness of the latter objective far overshadowed the nebulous character of the former.

Public uncertainty, however, was more wide-ranging in its scope. The breakdown of the corporatist stage of British history that had prevailed from the 1930s to the 1980s made, and makes, it less easy not only to focus on fixed interests and clear identities, but also to adopt a readily accepted standpoint for discussion. Thus assumptions about state policy, let alone economic management, are affected by views about the desirability of public ownership. More generally, the atomization, or individualism, of British culture made it difficult to make judgements.

There is also a tendency to see policy as coherent and planned when it is often, in large part, a response to circumstances. Thus, it is unclear how far there is a Blair project comparable to what was referred to in the 1980s as the Thatcher project. Blairite views can be seen as a programme for modernization combining constitutional remodelling, economic policies seeking to reconcile free-market doctrines with increasingly pronounced Keynesian elements, and social policies combining authoritarianism with liberal features. Yet, it is also possible to point to an era of pragmatic, incremental change responding to the shifting and temporary clustering and dispersal of interests in British society.

This process could also be seen in the British response to the international situation, which became far more volatile with the end of the Cold War. Alongside the appearance of a planned response and a coherent set of policies, there was considerable improvization, particularly, in the 1990s, in Balkan policy and, in 2001-3, in responding to American moves. Thus Blair's attempt to help influence the latter was necessarily dependent, in part, on the struggles for primacy in Washington.

In terms of the reconfiguration of interests and identities within Britain, it is possible to look at changes in terms of policy, a top-down view, or to search for a different approach that would place a greater focus on the extent to which developments were not under the control of government. In the former case, the emphasis is on the impact of a particular series of beliefs, especially Europeanization, constitutional remodelling within the UK, and an acceptance of Scottish, Welsh and Northern Irish separatism, on the continual process of change. This has brought in a degree of remoulding of identities that has been unprecedented since the Protestant Reformation of the sixteenth century, although that reflects the exceptionalism of British history, for such a remoulding, or, at the very least, a sustained period of political and constitutional change, affected France, Germany, Japan and Russia in the earlier twentieth century.

The sovereignty and the cohesion of the United Kingdom are being recast (or is it destroyed?) in the name of modernity, with the argument that cohesion could be enhanced by devolution and that there would be greater divisions without it. Some aspects of this modernization are surprising. Thus, in 2001 Blair advocated more state funds for schools controlled by 'faith-based organizations', although the very divisiveness that this had caused in Northern Ireland was an important aspect of community tensions, and there was a threat that this would be reproduced in British cities. Long-term tensions came to a head in 2001 with serious riots in Burnley, Oldham and Bradford that were partly blamed on the separation between communities. Looking to the future, the differing ability of particular ethnic groups to achieve educational and employment standards, and to attain average rates of prosperity, threatened to combine with cultural alienation in order to challenge social cohesion.

Conversely, there were signs of a more successful bridging of ethnic divides than in most of Europe. These included relatively high rates of sexual relations and marriage across such divides. At the same time, racial abuse was all too common. Much of it was of the type described by Reginald Hill in his novel *Deadheads* (1983):

Cadet Shaheed Singh was the city's first Asian police recruit, who had brought out all that was colonial in Dalziel. The boy came from a Kenyan Asian family, and had been born and bred in Yorkshire, but neither bit of information affected Dalziel's comments, which were at best geographically inaccurate, at worst criminally racist. 'Well, it'll make a change from rickshaws for the lad'.

The recasting of the United Kingdom is in accord with the intellectually fashionable notion that communities are imagined and traditions created, with the obvious corollary that their validity and value are limited. However, to claim that traditions can be and are moulded, even created, is not the same as suggesting that they are without value. Nor is it the case that this process of moulding and creation necessarily justifies the replacement of existing practices and ideas that give people a sense of continuity, identity and values.

The latter response was most strongly held by communities that felt threatened by change, such as those focused on heavy industry and mining, because they were heavily buffeted, especially in the 1980s, and, again, by the rural community in the early 2000s. In each case there was the sense of a malign metropolitan political culture directing damaging government policies. The landscape was also changed by international economic pressures as mediated and sometimes accentuated by government. Thus, 'set aside' fields were neglected and taken over by weeds, while industrial plant that had dominated communities was destroyed, whether at Consett or at Ravenscraig, where the steelworks, closed in 1992, were blown up in 1996, leaving a polluted environment.

The rise of popular interest in the industrial heritage is instructive as an indication of changing identities. Some of the past grime and slag heaps became parts of the national heritage, as with the Beamish Open-Air Museum and the Ironbridge Gorge Museum. The Earth Centre was opened outside Doncaster on the site of a former colliery, while the Magna Centre, an industrial heritage museum in Rotherham, won the Stirling Prize for architecture in 2001.

CONTINGENCIES

It is also appropriate to focus on the impact of the contingent. The striking coal miners might have succeeded against Heath in 1974, but failed against Thatcher a decade later. Had there been no means of exploiting natural gas or oil in the North Sea, its absence would have put great pressure on Thatcherite public finances, making it harder to cut taxes and thus expand the private sector. It is instructive to contrast Britain with the majority of European states, which lacked this resource. Alternatively, earlier exploitation of the oil might have weakened the position of the coal industry (as well as removing the need to invest in nuclear power) and, also, possibly saved the reputation of the Wilson government by permitting it to avoid devaluation in 1967 or, even, enabled Heath to see off the miners' strikes. The ability of the Thatcher government in early 1985 to claim that, thanks to the state of electricity supplies, there would be no power cuts, helped to speed the demise of the miners' strike. By calling the election in 1978, Callaghan might have thwarted Thatcher, while the Argentinian military, by not invading the Falklands in 1982, might have denied Thatcher the opportunity to regain the domestic political initiative. She might have been killed by the IRA, either at Brighton in 1984 or elsewhere. By failing to replace Thatcher in 1990, the Conservatives might have helped Labour to victory two years later, and left them to bear the burden of the 1990s recession and the Maastricht debate, helping the Conservatives to return to power in 1997, if not earlier. By refusing to support the USA in war with Iraq in 2003, Blair would have faced a very different international situation, and this would have affected the domestic political debate about relations within Europe.

The sum of these 'what ifs' is that these processes are fragile and largely involve luck and circumstances. They also point out how much events hang on circumstances. For example, the militancy of the petrol dispute in 2000 owed much to the extent to which farmers had been badly and recently affected by events. A number of the leaders were hauliers with farms who seemed doubly hit.

The electoral system could also have been changed, as the parties of the centre – Liberals, Social Democrats and, later, Liberal Democrats – demanded, producing the 'realignment of British politics' pressed for in the SDP's founding Limehouse Declaration in 1981. Labour's failure in the Euro-elections in 1999, the first national election in Britain under a system of proportional representation, led the Labour government to abandon its commitment to holding a referendum on proportional representation before the next general election. Had such a system been introduced then, or earlier, it is likely that all governments would have been coalitions, and probable, therefore, that centrist tendencies would have been dominant. This would have dramatically changed the history of the individual political parties and the political history of the country itself.

The wider impact of such a 'high political' change is less clear. There might have been, as is normal with PR systems, a fragmentation of political parties as well as an entry into mainstream politics of hitherto marginal groups, which would have given political extremists, such as the British National Party, and ethnic groups a particular voice. The impact of PR, or, for that matter, the existing electoral system, on social and economic developments is less clear.

Such counterfactuals are not idle speculation. At any one moment, various developments seemed possible to people in the past, and the sole guarantee was that what was going to happen was not known. We need a powerful leap of the imagination to recover the uncertainty of the past and to make judgements accordingly, especially sometimes when we are discussing the recent past.

Contingency can also be extended to aspects of history that are not usually tackled through the 'what if' approach. It is possible to consider different developments in public culture, for example arising from policies towards media regulation. In the case of the environment and transport, the consequences of more stringent restrictions on building on greenfield sites and of heavier fuel prices invite consideration. This is not idle. Such options play a major role in economic modelling and social planning.

Contingency also plays a role in international comparisons, not least in those that affect national attitudes towards relative success or influence government policies. There are also a number of pressures that encourage conformity in policy with the situation abroad, in particular interest rate policies. Britain's relative economic decline increased its dependence on international developments, both interest rate policies and the inward flow of investment capital. Thatcher's appreciation of this helped to underline her general opposition to domestic and European fiscal and economic regulation, and, to a considerable extent, this was sustained under Blair. Both sponsored policies and drew on attitudes very different from what they had been under the corporatists prior to Thatcher, particularly, but not only, under Labour.

CHANGE

'Culture' and 'environment' do not exist in isolation. They are shaped as issues by society. Since the 1960s there have been important changes in social aspirations. Notions and practices of personal responsibility have altered in a more atomized and individualistic society. Ideas of social order have changed. Furthermore, as elsewhere in Europe, it is not just that Britain no longer has an empire, but also that the attitudes that gave rise to one have gone. The varied responses to the Falklands War of 1982 were more generally indicative of changing values. The war was followed by a national commemoration service in St Paul's Cathedral in which the clergy also prayed for the defeated Argentinians. Thatcher's earlier call during the war to 'Rejoice' when South Georgia was recaptured did not strike a universal chord, and was heavily criticized in some quarters, as was *The Sun's* headline 'Gotcha' when the Argentinian flagship, the *General Belgrano*, was torpedoed with heavy loss of life.

Changing attitudes and aspirations on the part of many of those who had voted the Conservatives into power in 1979–97 played a major role in the death of Tory Britain. In part, these changes were themselves expressed through the policies of the Conservative governments, especially with the emphasis on economic individualism. Initially Thatcher, at least for her supporters, successfully reconciled the widespread desire for cultural stability and the quest to restore incentives, although the social stability of communities affected by serious economic problems was hard hit. By the late 1980s, however, and then again from late 1992, the Conservative achievement appeared to unravel.

In some respects, such comments underrate the factor of contingency already referred to and also the limitations of government discussed earlier in this work. It was beyond the ability of politicians to ensure cultural and social stability. However, because they were generally unwilling to draw attention to such limitations, politicians suffered the criticism that arose from the disappointed expectations of the public. As the latter increasingly saw themselves as consumers of public services with well-deserved rights, so the governmental process was increasingly managerial. Partly as a result, politics lost the ability to inspire, as was seen through disillusionment with Labour in the early 2000s and low electoral turnouts, including the 2001 general election and in local and European elections in the 1990s and 2000s, for example the 2003 local elections.

The failure of Thatcher to alter public expectations about state provision and the extent to which, despite Blair's soundbites about novelty, Labour extended social welfare, so leading to talk of a dependency culture (although it could not tackle lawlessness, or greatly improve the NHS), ensured that the limitations of government were made readily apparent. At the same time, the often negative popular response to governmental injunctions and policies led to an authoritarianism directed against those who did not co-operate; the 'wreckers' in Blair's overblown phrase. This sat uneasily with talk of a liberal, free-thinking society. Prudential reasons could be advanced why handgun ownership or fox-hunting with hounds should be prohibited, or why jury trials for complex cases such as fraud were inadvisable, or why, as David Blunkett proposed, it was necessary to have identity cards; to critics, however, this amounted to an attack on civil liberties.

This was further seen with the rise of environmental 'protectors' – for birds, bats, wild flowers, trees and buildings – and other regulators; unelected officials with considerable powers. The net effect was a resort to greater regulation as an automatic response to apparent problems; or, looked at differently, the state was becoming the arm of certain fashionable aspirations. Since this authority was constrained by the rule of law, and the British legal system now had to accord with an external convention on human rights, it would be wrong to refer to this process as tyranny, but it contributed to a lack of support for government, if not an alienation from it, that was far from restricted to those who might be categorized as criminous or marginal. Thus, public policies abetted the process of governmental failure that marked both Conservative and Labour ministries. If social and cultural changes put paid to the traditional bases of Tory Britain, leaving Blair to triumph on the wreck, Labour itself is vulnerable to the same shifts in assumptions and attitudes.

Attitudes change. In the widest sense, that is our culture. In the 1960s and '70s it was possible to aspire to the status quo – now that is almost impossible. Change is also the badge of the Conservatives, who no longer want to conserve. So society has to get used to constant change in schools, public services generally, products and services, and therefore our expectation is that only change is certain. This fuels uncertainty. At the start of both century and millennium, the British were more prosperous than ever before, but polls indicated that they were not content: happiness has not risen with prosperity. Whether they would have been content under other circumstances is unclear and unlikely. An essentially secular and individualistic society in an economic system without certainty, and with traditional family, gender and other practices and assumptions under great strain, was not one in which it was easy to feel secure. But then such security has generally been fragile. This is not a triumphalist note for the Conclusions; but triumphalism is out of place, itself a comment on current attitudes.

Selected Further Reading

Useful political memoirs include Denis Healey, *Time of My Life* (London, 1989), Roy Jenkins, *A Life at the Centre* (London, 1991), Margaret Thatcher, *The Downing Street Years* (London, 1993), and Roy Hattersley, *Fifty Years On: A Prejudiced History of Britain since the War* (London, 1997). Those who enjoy politicians' speeches and articles can turn to *New Britain: My Vision of a Young Country* (London, 1996) by Tony Blair.

Valuable introductory works providing background include David Childs, *Britain since 1939* (2nd edn, London, 2002), Peter Clarke, *Hope and Glory: Britain, 1900–1990* (London, 1996) and Martin Pugh, *Britain: A Concise History, 1789–1998* (London, 1999).

MORE SPECIALIZED WORKS

P. Anderson and N. Mann, *Safety First: The Making of New Labour* (London, 1997)

Alan Booth, *British Economic Development since 1945* (Manchester, 1995)

D. G. Boyce, *The Irish Question and British Politics* (2nd edn, London, 1996)

Sue Bruley, *Women in Britain since 1900* (London, 1999)

J. Campbell, *Edward Heath* (London, 1993)

John Charmley, *A History of Conservative Politics, 1900–1996* (London, 1996)

R. Church, *The Rise and Decline of the British Motor Industry* (London, 1994)

Peter Clarke and Clive Trebilcock, eds, *Understanding Decline: Perceptions and Realities of British Economic Performance* (Cambridge, 1997)

Richard Cooper and Nicholas Woodward, *Britain in the 1970s: The Troubled Economy* (London, 1996)

Ivor Crewe and Anthony King, *SDP: The Birth, Life and Death of the Social Democratic Party* (Oxford, 1996)

Grace Davie, *Religion in Britain since 1945* (Oxford, 1994)

T. M. Devine and R. J. Finlay, eds, *Scotland in the Twentieth Century* (London, 1996)

Daniel Dorling, *A New Social Atlas of Britain* (London, 1995)

S. Driver and L. Martell, *New Labour: Politics after Thatcherism* (Cambridge, 1998)

M. Durham, *Sex and Politics: The Family and Morality in the Thatcher Years* (London, 1991).

M. Foley, *The Rise of the British Presidency* (Manchester, 1998)

David Gladstone, *The Twentieth-century Welfare State* (London, 1999)

Harry Goulbourne, *Race Relations in Britain since 1945* (London, 1998)

T. R. Gourvish and A. O'Day, eds, *Britain since 1945* (London, 1991)

Sean Greenwood, *Britain and the Cold War* (London, 1995)

Robert Hewison, *Culture and Consensus: England, Art and Politics since 1940* (London, 1995)

Richard Holt, *Sport and the British: A Modern History* (Oxford, 1989)

I.G.C. Hutchison, *Scottish Politics in the Twentieth Century* (London, 1998)

Will Hutton, *The State We're In* (London, 1995)

Christopher Johnson, *The Economy under Mrs Thatcher* (London, 1991)

T. Jones, *Remaking the Labour Party: From Gaitskell to Blair* (London, 1996)

D. Kavanagh and A. Seldon, eds, *The Major Effect* (London, 1994)

James Loughlin, *The Ulster Question since 1945* (London, 1998)

Rodney Lowe, *The Welfare State in Britain since 1945* (2nd edn, London, 1998)

A. McSmith, *Faces of Labour: The Inside Story* (London, 1996)

John Martin, *The Development of Modern Agriculture: British Farming since 1931* (London, 1999)

Arthur Marwick, *British Society since 1945* (3rd edn, London, 1996)

Roger Middleton, *The British Economy since 1945* (London, 1999)

Kenneth Morgan, *Labour People, Leaders and Lieutenants: Hardie to Kinnock* (Oxford, 1989)

Ralph Negrine, *Television and the Press since 1945* (Manchester, 1998)

Ben Pimlott, *Harold Wilson* (London, 1992)

Dominic Shellard, *British Theatre since the War* (New Haven, 1999)

I. G. Simmons, *An Environmental History of Twentieth-Century Britain* (London, 2002)

N. L. Tranter, *British Population in the Twentieth Century* (London, 1995)

John Young, *Britain and European Unity, 1945–1999* (London, 2000)

Ken Young and Rao Nirmala, *Local Government since 1945* (Oxford, 1997)

Index